Praise for

IN MY OWN FOOTSTEPS

"This book will intrigue, entertain and challenge students, other actors and their audiences." —Ian McKellen

"This is a remarkably detailed and evocative memoir, finely written by a fine actor." —Richard Eyre

"Waiting in the wings with Michael Pennington for the curtain to go up on *Fanny and Alexander* at the Old Vic I realised here is an actor who carries Shakespeare in his heart and a twinkle in his eye. It was clear to me that his craft and practice was still evolving even after fifty years in the business. It is a rare opportunity to be able to peek behind the curtain of a practitioner at work. This book shines a light on one of our best." —Lolita Chakrabarti

"Michael Pennington is a great actor and a great writer about actors and acting; his books have all the wit, wisdom and passion that characterise his performances. This is a page-turning artistic journey written with honesty, heart and humour by a master of his craft."
—Kenneth Branagh

"That great Shakespearian Michael Pennington, having written so eloquently about his craft, now turns a brilliant forensic analysis on his own life. As Peter Quince might have said in *A Midsummer Night's Dream*:
'The actor is at hand, and by his show,
You shall know all that you are like to know.'"
—Gregory Doran, Artistic Director, RSC.

"This great performer casts such insightful flies that the book could be re-titled *The Compleat Actor*, for that's what he is."
—Janet Suzman

"Michael Pennington is irresistibly readable." —Peter Brook

In My Own Footsteps

A Memoir

Michael Pennington

First published in Great Britain in 2021 by Michael Pennington Books

Copyright © Michael Pennington 2021

Michael Pennington has asserted his right under the Copyright, Designs and Patents Act 1988 to be identified as the author of this work.

All rights reserved. No part of this publication may be reproduced, stored in a retrieval system or transmitted, in any form or by any means, without the publisher's prior permission in writing.

This book is sold subject to the condition that it shall not, by way of trade or otherwise, be lent, resold, hired out or otherwise circulated without the publisher's prior consent in any form of binding or cover other than that in which it is published and without a similar condition, including this condition, being imposed on the subsequent purchaser.

Every reasonable effort has been made to trace copyright holders of material reproduced in this book, but if any have been inadvertently overlooked the publishers would be glad to hear from them.

An earlier version of the obituary of Harold Pinter was published in the *Independent*.

Bob Dylan, 'My Back Pages' lyrics © and by kind permission of Universal Music Publishing Group.

All images, unless otherwise identified, are from the personal collection of Michael Pennington or from open sources.

Edited, designed and produced by Tandem Publishing
http://tandempublishing.yolasite.com/

ISBN: 978-1-5272-9077-8

10 9 8 7 6 5 4 3 2 1

A CIP catalogue record for this book is available from the British Library.

Printed and bound in Great Britain by CPI Group (UK) Ltd, Croydon CR0 4YY.

Also by Michael Pennington

Rossya: A Journey Through Siberia

The English Shakespeare Company: The Story of the Wars of the Roses
(with Michael Bogdanov)

*Users Guides to Hamlet / Twelfth Night /
A Midsummer Night's Dream*

Pocket Guide to Ibsen / Chekhov / Strindberg (with Stephen Unwin)

Sweet William: Twenty Thousand Hours with Shakespeare

Chekhov's Three Sisters from Page to Stage

Let me Play the Lion Too: How to Be an Actor

King Lear in Brooklyn

Are You There, Crocodile? Inventing Anton Chekhov

CONTENTS

Author's Note ix
Preface xiii
Introduction 1

1. We Can Hardly Take Care of Ourselves… 1969–1971   9
2. The Making of Michael 1955–1964   31
3. A Tour of Mount Rushmore   57
4. Stratford 1964–1965   67
5. An Unvicious Circle 1966–1973   83
6. Breakfast in Bucharest   109
7. RSC 1973–1981   115
8. The Freedom of the City   149
9. "On, On"   155
10. The Dear Romanian: Ion Caramitru   165
11. Vile Jellies   177
12. Running the RSC   189
13. Eduardo and Antonio   213
14. Conclusion – A Rhapsody in Blue Suits   243

Acknowledgements   277

Appendices
Harold Pinter by Michael Pennington   279
Shrap by Richard Eyre   291

Index   293

As King Lear, UK National Tour, 2016.

AUTHOR'S NOTE

I share my identity with another performer of the same name, who, because he must have joined Equity much later than I did, accepted their regulation obliging him to change it (those were the days when Equity had real teeth); this he did, from Michael Pennington to Johnny Vegas. I was delighted to begin seeing reviews of a rather portly Johnny headed "Michael Pennington – larger than life again". When asked about this, Johnny says he wanted to change the situation whereby every time he did his act he was "always cheered as Johnny Vegas, but Michael Pennington has never had a round of applause in his life…" Errrrm…

Actually I'm proud of the connection: Vegas is a sweet fellow and brilliant performer whom I once invited to play Bottom in a production of *A Midsummer Night's Dream* I was going to direct in Regent's Park; but after considerable thought he demurred. I was entertained by this, because there is a tangible tradition for comedians to play Bottom: the first time I saw the play it was Frankie Howerd, in 1957 at the Old Vic. I remember the press rose up in arms at his casting; but the audiences loved him, myself included.

It has always seemed to me that a successful actor's life was a sort of road trip that leads back to where he or she started, but then subtly changed: ambition is satisfied but then bluntly disappointed, enjoyed rather than regretted. Why is it that most of us often tick off in our diaries the remaining number of performances of a show we're in but also dread finishing it and saying goodbye to colleagues we've come to love and depend on? Meanwhile why do we in general want the show to be the same each night we do it, but also totally fresh, re-thought, reinterpreted, quite differently inflected from the previous night, as if we were jazz musicians, respected by young players for having re-thought every moment off the cuff, in the very act of playing it?

The classical actor is like a marathon runner who re-enters the stadium after several hours of sweaty work, identical and repetitive ad nauseam but shot through with occasional inspirations. He or she then has to do the track two or three times round without collapsing and with the runners-up following ever closer behind.

The philosopher George Santayana said that those who can't remember the past are condemned to repeat it. We continuously forget and as continuously recover. Or to put it another way: in 'The Long and Winding Road' Paul McCartney and John Lennon sing beautifully that all routes lead to home. In 'My Back Pages' Bob Dylan likewise admits he felt more mature when he was young and has become more youthful with age. A bit later in this book I reference Hegel and Marx as two great minds who believed that all historical events come round at least twice, but in different keys: one perhaps to tragic effect, the other to that of mockery. We spend half our lives muttering to ourselves, it implies, rehearsing a quarrel, refreshing our memory for the lines or struggling to skateboard a wave with ease and without the banality of drowning. One day Odysseus left Ithaca, hastened to fight the Trojan War for ten years, and then took a dawdling further ten years to come home. When I played King Lear in New York in 2014, it was the beginning of a significant loop in my working life – from doing a play that couldn't be more English but now had to sound American; then returning to construct a new production of the same play to tour all over the UK – in a figure of eight, rather than a single explicable loop. Like Puck, I put a girdle round the world in forty minutes every day, following my own all too conspicuous footfall.

In My Own Footsteps is my twelfth published book in twenty-five years. I owe impassioned thanks to Prue Skene, my dear partner, to my grandchildren Louis and Evie and their father Mark Pennington; to John Shrapnel for a lifetime of pugnacious friendship, and to

Michael Bogdanov, not only for our long working partnership but for his translation/adaptation of the *Rubaiyat of Omar Khayyam* – which he allowed me to read in his extended radio interview *With Great Pleasure*, or I'd never have known of it, let alone been able to use it confidently in this book. The sixty years I've spent with three or more of these companions has given me the satisfaction of continually returning to where I started, except that my trajectory has not been through a simple circle but more a progressive pattern from which I've exited significantly further down my designated track, and possibly wiser. I have, in very fact, for over half a century travelled forwards into new territory within my own footsteps.

My delighted thanks also to my new friends Sam and Alice Carter, who seemed to spring out of nowhere patiently to nurse my work as editor and designer of this book. To all the photographers who have recorded me and don't mind it being known; and for the permissions-to-print I've happily accepted from interested writers likewise – let alone Homer and Shakespeare, neither of whom had a leg to stand on.

Michael Pennington
London, 2021

In 1970.

PREFACE

What would you think of a man who finds himself lost in a huge city which could be Bath or some old university town in Holland or Sweden – Utrecht or Uppsala, say – desperate to get his bearings so that he can be at the theatre for his matinée performance at 2.30pm and it is already 2.15? And what if he keeps meeting his colleagues in the street and they greet him cheerily, but he just can't bring himself to admit to them that he is lost or to ask whether there is indeed a matinée today or not. He'd rather look for an old-fashioned phone box and ring the theatre and ask them – has to in fact, as he's left his mobile … somewhere…?

Consumed with panic he wakes with a yelp.

And what would you call a nine-year-old boy who was once so enraged by an argument in the kitchen with his mother while she was slicing bread that he deemed she was waving her knife too near him (which she wasn't), and since it was that time of day and he was used to being bathed by her, he went and angrily ran his bath, detouring only to get some scarlet lipstick from her dressing-table; he then took advantage of the fact that the door to the bathroom was directly behind the occupant of the bath itself by turning his back on his mother as she came in and would see the hastily applied lipstick wound on his left arm? As she then came round to his left side and properly saw the supposed injury, he was still looking away in his sulk, until her warm Scots chuckle filled the room, shaming and forgiving him at the same time.

And this is the same boy who will try much the same trick a

generation later, when his own son is about the same age, by painting on him a black eye with Leichner's theatrical greasepaint, causing his mother – now the boy's grandmother – to rush him up to the same bathroom in her anxiety, where she is taken aback to find that the black eye comes off in a trice when she takes a cotton-wool ball and applies her cold cream make-up remover to the supposed wound.

The same trickster has grown up to be the kind of man who looks behind the reredos of any great cathedral he visits to see if it is propped up by stage-braces, like some elaborate stage set. When I look in the mirror I see an entertainer: unsure all his lifetime whether he is an ensemble company man defined by his team of fellows, or a soloist on whom everything depends and who has only himself to thank or blame. He may not seem to be someone whose confessional autobiography, written at age seventy-seven, you would want to buy; but on the other hand you might well take a look at a satisfied man's free-associating memoir in which he insists it is still only work in progress, not yet the end.

***

I'm writing in the spring and summer of 2020, as the Coronavirus threatens us all. Shakespeare would have understood: his Company were always having to pack their bags and start touring while the Plague struck London – how many times? It seems that then the dramatist would retire to his study somewhere and fashion poetry, often sonnets, which he dedicated ostensibly to his Dark Lady of the Sonnets (Lucy Negro? Emilia Lanier? Mary Fitton? John Florio's wedded wife?) – or, more likely, were addressed to his gorgeously rich young patron the Earl of Southampton. If the plans formed by Boris Johnson and his apology for a Cabinet in our time of Plague to prevent us going to the theatre exclude giving any compensation for the loss of the panache, vision and charm it offers, then it serves us right for voting for him, as in 2019 we as a nation did, rather than laughing at his mendacious inadequacy on just about every front.

None of Shakespeare's favoured poetic compensations seem quite to fit our current crisis: and I for one was never good at bitter rhyming. However, our playhouses continue closed, the self-employed waiting for some succour from an unsympathetic government, who initially looked to soften their Stalinist blows by asserting that No, they were not so much closing the theatres themselves but "inviting" them to do it "voluntarily" (which would have been a remarkable form of *hara-kiri*).

All this has coincided with my own completion of a sort of largely Shakespearean odyssey, accidentally but enthusiastically undertaken for the last sixty-odd years, by playing Prospero in *The Tempest*, probably the last major Shakespeare I'll do. I learned the part between October 2019 and late January 2020; I battled with it in restaurants in Amsterdam, I learned it again sitting in the cathedral in Antwerp, I studied it between autographs at a *Star Wars* Convention in Utrecht, mindful the while that in this same brief time before rehearsals I had to do my fairly complex VAT return and Schedule D Accounts for the Year (as always accompanied by a lively exchange of views with my accountants); then rehearsed it for a month without taking even a glass of wine, which very much went against the grain/grape, but seemed to make the process easier since Prospero is a hell of a learn, sometimes as difficult in its way as another, otherwise completely different, challenge: Lucky's monologue in *Waiting for Godot*. I have many times observed that the first scene with Miranda, followed by interviews with Ariel, Caliban and Ferdinand, are particularly tough since they are all essentially repetitive expositions and take about half an hour to play while Prospero demands attention to be paid to people we haven't met, speaks of a life we've little evidence for, and attributes crimes committed against him to suspects who are hard to assess, being as yet invisible.

Preparing to collaborate with a jewel of a Company in the New Year at the marvellously intimate Jermyn Street Theatre off Piccadilly Circus, I murmured the part on buses and at home and in the park, tormenting my dear partner Prue Skene, who had plenty of work of her own and wouldn't have minded a holiday; and when she wasn't free to hear my lines, I used the old sliding envelope trick on myself, whereby the said obstruction allows you to see the current line in the script, which you already know, but masks the next one, which you don't. What I didn't realise at the time was that Miranda was going to be Kirsty Bushell, who would have at her fingers' ends an infinity of shades of feeling and attitude as the attentive Miranda, allowing me to develop the same. And though I don't normally study another actor's performance in a classic role when I'm about to embark on it myself (though I sometimes do afterwards, in order not to be mean-spirited in my own eyes), this time I looked at Helen Mirren's Prospera in Julie Taymor's 2010 film and also John Gielgud in Peter Greenaway's *Prospero's Books*, an astonishing enterprise in which I could yet again feel the pleasure of his vocal control, though I didn't want to court any comparison and was looking forward to playing the part with a cinematic intimacy and human variety on a stage watched by seventy-five people only. I also wasn't about to do it, as he did, with a supporting cast of several hundred extras who were without exception completely naked. Mirren, however, was very good indeed and I shouldn't compare Taymor's film with anyone else's because hers had the advantage of some remarkable and uniquely convincing exterior locations that seemed entirely in tune with Shakespeare's intentions.

I'm glad to say we succeeded in our aim; the show successfully completed six performances of its planned sixty-odd and gained excellent notices and full houses before falling victim to the fate of all our other playhouses at the hands of Boris Johnson (once a potential author of a book on Shakespeare, if you can believe that). So what do I do with my time now, as we wait for the retreat of the Plague so that, among other things, we have the chance to revive the show in the autumn or next spring? Perhaps what Prospero does to Alonso and his retinue in the play – offer a momentary shelter in his cell:

> Where you shall take your rest
> For this one night, which part of it I'll waste

Michael Pennington

> With such discourse as, I not doubt, shall make it
> Go quick away – the story of my life…

He might have added: it will be a patched-up story of an unfinished life, not told in a strict sequence but depending on a series of adventitious cues which form a perfect circle, and I hope an entertaining one.

*Middlesex v. Sussex at Lord's, 18th May 1948.
Third day: Jack Robertson (Middlesex) dispatches a delivery
from P.A. Carey.*

INTRODUCTION

My grandson Louis was always a keen cricketer, but although he had everything else he'd never got quite the right bat till now; today, on his eighth birthday, this handicap is being remedied by the gift from his father of a Gray Nicolls Shockwave. At last his look is complete.

When I was eight I had the same problem, but with me it was the gloves: try as I might, I just couldn't find the design I felt I needed. Even now I sometimes dream not so much of finding myself onstage, forgetful of what play it is I'm in, as of having the wrong kind of gloves on as I go in to bat. Or no gloves at all.

It happens that at that moment, in 1951, a quiet revolution was going on in the batting world. A new kind of sausage-fingered glove was appearing, of which you can still see inherited traces on the velcro-ed hands and foam-enclosed thumbs of Ben Stokes and Joe Root in these days of Gunn & Moore, Slazenger and Kookaburra. They were most commonly white, with black flashing on the finger joints, and were held together by elastic straps wound a couple of times around the wrists. Compared to the earlier green or black rubber-spiked semi-leathered gloves – which gave, it must be said, minimal protection to the back of the hand and the fingers but maximum grip on the bat as long as you didn't let your little finger get crushed against its handle – these elasticated saveloys seemed to me the height of vulgarity, and I suspected that my own nonpareil among batsmen, my inspiration and guiding light, object of fascination and the measure of all taste and gracefulness, would agree.

For I loved Jack Robertson, Middlesex's opening bat in the immediate pre- and post-war years, relatively unsung in *Wisden* but widely admired by diehards like me. Robertson J. D., I should say; let's not forget that in the England of that time there was a subtle distinction in the composition of each team between the amateur Gentlemen with their private incomes and the professional Players, who were generally working-class and dependent on a wage. This discrimination led among other things to the Gentlemen's initials being proudly printed on the scorecard ahead of their surnames, and the Players' grudgingly after. And perhaps Robertson's finest hour was not on the pitch at all but the moment in 1946 when the MCC, getting an untypical whiff of post-war socialism, decreed at last that all players, whatever their circumstances off the pitch, were now to be known simply as Cricketers, and would hereafter make their entrances all together onto the field at Lord's from the grand central door of the pavilion rather than – in the case of the professional Players, believe it or not – from a discreet little side-gate, fighting their way through the paying plebs. The scorecard convention remained; but Robertson and Sid Brown of Middlesex became the first paid servants of the game to stride properly out to bat at Lord's from upstage centre and down the pavilion steps to take on the suicidally noble task of blunting the opposition's most violent aggressors, the pace men – without any of the benefits of helmets, thigh pads and all the rest of the body's site-specific later equipment.

Robertson deserved his reward, and not only for service to his club: he had been a Royal Army Service Corps driver during the Dunkirk evacuation and a Captain in the Duke of Wellington's Regiment. He was also responsible for a famous act of patriotic defiance during a wartime Services match at Lord's when a flying bomb exploded behind the Grandstand: once the other players had picked themselves off the ground and resumed playing, Robertson hooked the first ball he received directly into its crater for six.

By the 1950s I was spending much of my time hurrying round to Lord's (eight minutes from home), or anxiously scanning the press, waiting and waiting for Robertson to relive his glory days, by that time nearly over. How I would have liked to meet him. I asked myself what his speaking voice was like; I wondered how he was with his wife Joyce and his son; what he wore off-duty; did he drive a car or not, garden or not, what music did he like, and, a little later, what was his opinion of Shakespeare? And in a mild way this dapper and modestly stylish figure has never left me: from where I'm sitting today I can see a couple of framed photographs of him which my son Mark, Louis's father, has dug out and presented to me at various birthdays and Christmases. See how JDR leans into that cover drive, whether off the back foot or the front, the sheer aplomb of his hook and square cut, his ease and grace of demeanour, compared to the irritation of the wicket-keeper waiting impatiently for the gift of a mistimed snick off the edge of his bat. Please mourn with me too the injustice that Robertson played so rarely for England – eleven Test Matches only (and none against Australia, though once, in a county match, a bouncer from the notorious Ray Lindwall broke his jaw) – despite averaging 46 runs per innings and making a century against New Zealand in 1949. Absurdly, he was at that moment unceremoniously dropped from the team: England's selectors preferred the opening partnership of Len Hutton of Yorkshire and Cyril Washbrook of Lancashire. Indeed JDR's successful presence against New Zealand was only due to an injury to Washbrook, who was generally felt to be a little better against fast bowling. However, admirers like myself believed that no more elegant pair than Robertson and Hutton had ever opened England's batting, and that the former was our best player of the new ball. And yet, despite having scored 331 not out against Worcestershire in a single day on England's most beautiful pitch – still the highest score in first-class cricket by a Middlesex batsman – JDR never played another Test. Indeed, this self-effacing man loved to tell the story that his pleasure that glorious day at Worcester was comically dulled when, leaving the ground to go home afterwards, he found his car tyres had been deflated.

As you might expect, when not on England duty, JDR always batted (and fielded) in his Middlesex cap – blue with three gold-hilted, Saxon scimitars – and opted for the black rubber-spiked glove rather than the green; and so, naturally, did I. Together with a fair mock-up of the Middlesex cap, acquired I know not where, I earnestly bowled my practice ball against the garden wall, then grabbed up my bat and batted away its rebound in my best Robertson manner. As for the gloves, they were well beyond my means, but in the end my alert parents bribed me to learn to swim with the prospect of the gift of black spiked ones if I completed the course. I did, insisting only on a warm jam doughnut in addition after each lesson at Marshall Street Baths (just round the corner from Carnaby Street) to take away the taste of the chlorine.

Of course, none of the above – my research, the study of idiosyncrasy and the projection of a character into unexpected situations – has much to do with the playing of cricket, any more than my intense study of a waiter in the hotel restaurant when I first went on holiday to France after the War had anything to do with the serving of dinner. And as it happens, through no human agency a small long-term nemesis was awaiting me. As an adult I have, in two separate stage productions, been brought face to face with my own past: finding myself in both plays required to read a period newspaper during a certain scene, I have, on opening the mocked-up copy at the very first performance, found a stop-press account of Jack Robertson's legendary 331 not out against Worcestershire. By the steepest coincidence, there it was, staring me in the face. Twice. And a lifetime later. On both occasions, I hate to think now what must have become of my playing of the next line.

***

Louis however, like his father at that age and unlike his imposter grandfather, was a proper cricketer, though even his quiet rapture over his new bat had a beguiling flicker of mimicry in it. For immediately, standing in his parents' kitchen, he mimed a speculative cover drive from there into the dining-room, feeling completely equipped. His eye over the ball and his fluid action was, I would say, along the lines of Hutton rather than of Robertson, who outside the off stump was often inclined to try a risky square-cut rather than a drive. And then he murmured to himself – and I'm sure it really was a murmur he meant none of us to hear:

"Everything perfect."

Looking and feeling the part of batsman, he had become one, even more than I had; his satisfaction was very much like that of an actor encouraged by his first encounter with his costume.

Louis's air cover drive, like a teenager's air guitar, was only one co-ordinate in his life as a performer: another had been his appearance in a school Nativity Play a couple of years earlier. When I heard about this I'd presumed he'd be playing one of the Kings, so asked him about his casting with some eagerness. To my surprise, he leapt vertically upwards a metre or so, crying the single reply "Sheep!" with, in fact, a vernal satisfaction, as if he was already rehearsing the part of a newborn lamb trying to get the hang of himself. Well, Stanislavski used to say there are no small parts, only small actors, so perhaps this woolly debut, as much as the new bat, was preparing the ground for a future he never pursued. For me of course, a Nativity Play had always been a more self-assertive affair; at Louis's age I was in a homegrown production, but far from sheepish. Annually, on Christmas Day, I would undertake the star part of an unnamed Indian Chief in a play written by myself, also featuring my two cousins, and performed for the older generation after lunch. Rehearsals for this delicate event having taken place before the turkey (the moment the visitors stepped over the doorstep, in fact), the performance was given to an entirely somnolent audience of adults after it. The title of this collector's piece is long forgotten, and many of my family have taken to the grave any memories of my early attempt to hold the mirror up to nature. For my show played only that one performance a year, before being brought back twelve months later, not as a result of public demand but of my own. As I recall, it featured me sitting cross-legged in front of my teepee, philosophising with a certain Chekhovian serenity about the meaning of life, while my cousins Jill and Martin leaned round the proscenium from time to time on a given cue to hand me some vital prop and then buzz off out of it.

Perhaps fortunately, the script doesn't survive, and after sixty-plus years Jill and Martin have – just about – forgiven me. In fact Martin now lets me use his house in Brittany, where to my amazement I once found a large poster with a photograph of myself as an RSC Timon of Athens hanging graciously on his wall. They would come to my shows and never remind me of what I had done to them. I call that generous; the fact that I would one day have the chance of engaging rather more passionately with Indian culture can be, to them, of little lasting comfort.

As Jack in Captain Jack's Revenge *(Royal Court Theatre, 1971)*.

WE CAN HARDLY TAKE CARE OF OURSELVES...

1969–1971

Michael Smith, *Captain Jack's Revenge* (1969)

By 1971 I'd been earning my living as an actor for seven years: first as a barely fledgling Shakespearean for a couple of beginners' seasons at Stratford-upon-Avon, then in a sequence of West End and touring productions, as well as a tour of the US. I'd also proved personable enough to be able to avail myself of some of the rich variety of nightly television drama offered in those days to a reasonably capable young character actor (or "juvenile character" as the terminology went in the casting offices), so I'd made a start there as well. I was twenty-eight and pleased.

Now came what felt, in view of Christmases long past – and perhaps of my son Mark's brief embrace of Indian head-feathers and moccasins as he was growing up – like a serious call to arms. I was being invited for the first time to the Royal Court Theatre in Sloane Square, the crucible of most of what was best in new English playwriting – and in this case American. The offer was to play the title role in Michael Smith's off-Broadway hit *Captain Jack's Revenge*, now to be re-mounted for London.

I certainly had a better script this time than in my parents' sitting-room – though oddly enough the aim could be seen as much the same, to assert what value life might and might not have for an indigenous leader when his tribe's very existence is threatened by the theft of their territory and the denial of his name. The previous year, Dee Brown's *Bury My Heart at Wounded Knee – An Indian History of the American West* had sensationally arrived on the world's doorstep. Its dismal inventory of the violent uprooting of native "Indians" by nineteenth-century settlers in pursuit of their "manifest destiny" immediately sounded a wake-up call that still rings out – the book has sold several million copies and never been out of print.

Brown's stated aim was to persuade his fellow-countrymen, whenever they contemplated their forebears' "westward push", to imagine them looking over their shoulders for the endorsement, easy to find, of an indulgent federal government in Washington; if their Indian victims were to stare in that same direction, they would see only utter betrayal. Brown audits the broken promises and defaulted treaties, the provocations and massacres and condescending diplomacy that have defined America's national shame. Having accounted for one devastated tribe after another, he comes to one of the last major conflicts – the 1873 struggle of the Modocs, a smallish tribe from the Klamath Basin which straddles the California/Oregon border, to hold on to their lands.

Their benighted leader was Chief Kientpoos – known to the settlers, perhaps insultingly, as Captain Jack. Jack probably knew his people were already doomed: theirs was rugged country snagged with ridges and lakes and thus hard to defend resourcefully; in addition, a southern branch of the Oregon Trail ran through its heart like a murderous highway, encouraging every kind of encroachment. For his part, the white man, bewildered that Jack's people were moving on less briskly than he would have liked, had been dropping anchor on sacred Indian ground without any hesitation.

In fact the Modocs adapted to their new circumstance with a certain flair: Captain Jack was, unusually, prepared to see the white man's point of view, and made a good fist of welcoming the incomers, poignantly urging his people to adapt by dressing in much the same way as their visitors. In the consequent push-and-pull, the frustrated settlers begged for government help, which came with a new order that the Modocs must leave their lands without delay and share a reservation belonging to the Klamath tribe further north in Oregon – ignoring the fact that the Klamaths were their traditional enemies. Thrown together, the two tribes did their best to coexist with the settlers, until the First Cavalry moved in to transplant them still further north: in the ensuing struggle, an American soldier was killed and seven others wounded. A Modoc force of sixty then, astonishingly, held off an army many times their strength for five months with virtually no casualties – long enough for public opinion in the East to swing a little in their favour: President Ulysses S Grant now looked for a peace, to be brokered by a commission led by the seemingly thoughtful General Edward Canby.

Canby turned out to be quite the wrong man for the job; he countenanced none of the Modocs' demands. Pressed by the radicals in his own tribe, Jack despairingly drew his gun and assassinated the General and his team; Canby thus became the only US General to be killed during the Indian Wars. Jack was of course tried and sentenced; and so a Chief who had uniquely urged his people to conciliate ended up hanging from an American rope on October 3, 1873. The Modoc tribe have never returned to their homeland.

Nearly a century later, this wretched piece of history attracted the attention of Michael Smith, then working as the theatre critic of *The Village Voice* in New York. The story began to marinate in his own experience as a young American coming of age at the start of the Vietnam War, whose fallout by mid-1968 had included the atrocious My Lai massacre (some five hundred Vietnamese civilians shot by the US Army in cold blood); the assassinations of Martin Luther King and of Bobby Kennedy, and then a pitched battle between tens of thousands of protesters and the police at the Chicago Democratic Convention.

Such century-old images of vicious conflict became the central metaphor of Smith's play, which was located in the present in a run-down apartment in New York's East Village. Here, the aptly named Jack, his pregnant girlfriend Mary and their friend William – a Canadian avoiding the Vietnam draft – are tucked away, living out the Woodstock Dream (even though Charles Manson was rising at that moment like an anti-Christ to destroy it). As the action begins, the trio are woozily readying themselves for a visit from Mary's military father, who is of course opposed to their lifestyle, and determined to reclaim Mary for his.

Smith's inspired idea was to wire these decent but disaffected young people into an historic American scandal. After all, nineteenth-century Indians have always appealed to the hippies of our time in their philosophy, their sense of alienation and their taste in clothes. Confronted by Mary's father (an obvious alias for Canby) they feel ringfenced by American tyranny both past and present: Jack declares that when it comes to mustering a community, they can hardly take care of themselves, let alone assume responsibility for anybody else.

For unexplained reasons, Mary's father is accompanied by a pair of friends in the costumes and with the manners of 1873 California. It happily transpires William and Mary have just written a play set exactly then and there, which they now decide to perform for the visitors. This cheerful embrace of coincidence is part of the self-confidence of Smith's writing: you quickly abandon the whys and wherefores as the Modocs' melancholy tale is re-enacted for the entire middle act by the three young people with, needless to say, the father and his friends as villains. This play within the play (always a powerful mover, as the author of *Hamlet* and *A Midsummer Night's Dream* knew) ends when the young "Indians" rise up and slaughter their perfidious opponents. However, Smith's overall narrative, returning to logic, proposes a strategic victory for the "straights" which uncomfortably suggests that all radical change calls for well-timed violence rather than liberal moderation. While the original Indians killed to preserve their way of life, their new advocates, unable to work up the resolve, capitulate in the shock ending, when a bullet comes anonymously from the back of the auditorium and brings Jack down – an ideal final word on the current licensed killing of American student protesters in Ohio and Chicago.

Though a professional critic, Smith enjoyed friendly relations with off-off-Broadway troupes such as the legendary La Mama in the East Village, the first artistic home of Sam Shepard, Lanford

Wilson and Philip Glass. *Captain Jack's Revenge* premiered at La Mama in April 1970 and got a mixed reception: Michael's successor at *The Village Voice* tutted that the play had a "Godardian flatness" but a few sentences later described it as "amiable, spooky, poky and delicious". Curiously, Captain Jack was played by an Andy Warhol disciple, Ondine (the stage name of Robert Olivo) – a good actor, as far as I know. He'd met Warhol at an orgy, but allegedly claimed that he didn't give "a good flying fuck" for him; in return Warhol, eccentrically magnanimous, gave him a career in films such as *Horse* and *Chelsea Girls*. Later, as Olivo's career flagged, he sustained himself by lecturing on the college circuit on his life as a Warhol Superstar, rather as some *Star Wars* veterans do today.

By the time the play landed on the desk of the director Nicholas Wright at the Royal Court in London, it felt right on the money. Halfway through 1969 the Court had opened a second space, the intimate Theatre Upstairs, and Nick was transforming it from a theatre restaurant run by Clement Freud to one of the most valued black box spaces in town, attached untypically to a mainstream theatre. As now, it had a capacity of ninety, about half of whom an actor could reach out and touch while whispering to the other half. Sam Shepard's very early *La Turista* – an account of two unpleasant gentlemen holed up in a Mexican hotel, both of them named after brands of American cigarettes and looking for a cure for the traveller's diarrhoea that gives the play its title – had premiered there; Howard Brenton had delivered *Christie in Love* (about the Notting Hill serial killer of the 1950s) as part of his group of 'Plays for the Poor Theatre', and also *Fruit*, part of a double bill with David Hare's *What Happened to Blake* (William Blake, that is). Meanwhile Nixon secretly bombed Cambodia, and during the run of the London *Captain Jack* police opened fire at Kent State University in Ohio, murdering four peaceful protesters, one of whom wasn't doing anything at all. Soon, returning veterans would find themselves abused by peace protesters turned violent in their home towns: soon after that, many of the same veterans were flinging their own medals back at the US Capitol Building, aware at last of governmental lies about the progress of the war. These events are a reminder of the vertiginous speed at which anxiety bit deep into the national conscience, traumatising every American of draft age, as did the dishonourable withdrawal in the name of "Vietnamisation". Nixon's and Kissinger's intriguing could certainly be seen as parallel to the hypocrisy of President Grant a century before.

In any event here was Nick, asking me to play Captain Jack in London. As it happened, I'd just come back from a US tour as Laertes in *Hamlet*, directed by Tony Richardson. It had been my first serious trip to the States, the best Shakespeare part I'd had thus far, my first time on Broadway and my first exposure to life on the apartment hotel trail from New York to California. And my first exposure to Nicol Williamson, a stupendous and tempestuous actor whom I greatly admired and who was playing Hamlet. Forgotten by many but something of a legend at the time, Nicol has been quite often misunderstood. Superficially a roisterer on the scale of Edmund Kean in times gone by, he had the undermining wit of John Osborne, and, like him, was everything you didn't expect: very funny, sophisticated, subtly affectionate, wickedly observant, as interested in other people as a brilliant mimic has to be. His work was electrifying, self-lacerating but deft, technically awesome and ferociously disciplined, and in action he looked like a sort of smashed-up cherub. Quite a lot has been written about his unreliability, but it's mostly tosh. He could and sometimes did play Hamlet on a couple of bottles of wine, but he never dropped a stitch (in the 100-performance run Laertes never got a scratch); on another occasion, a few hours after quite a serious car crash (he'd driven a borrowed car off the side of a cliff in Hollywood, dropping squarely onto someone's patio), despite terrific bruising around the brow-bone which made him look like the Mekon in *Dan Dare,* he was all for going to the theatre for a quick lie-down before doing his matinée (and evening) performance as the Dane. At the end of which, as he did almost nightly in New York, he went off to Jimmy Ryan's Bar uptown to sing a respectable selection of Hoagy Carmichael, Johnny Cash, Kris Kristofferson, Perry Como and, at my insistence, Tim Hardin – a genius in his field for all his addictions, and already a significant influence on me as I hoped he might be musically on Nicol.

As Hamlet Nicol could be scary, but almost the best of the performance were his generously humorous scenes with Roger Livesey's Gravedigger and the First Player. He could also speak faster than any actor I've known apart from John Gielgud – try to catch him doing the Beckett monologues or some of *Inadmissible Evidence*, of which clips exist, or read Kenneth Tynan's account of his subsequent Command Performance in the White House for President Nixon. He was also everything a certain kind of bolshie young actor wants to be: resentfully romantic, oddly nonchalant, but heroically committed to his job. As one such, I drank with him and often dealt the cards till dawn – bridge was his game – and I kept up pretty well, even if professionally I was to take another turning and I suppose a less self-punishing one; I'm forever grateful for his heart, his grit and the unforgiving standards he set.

Not that there wasn't sometimes a downside: I once watched Nicol turn over a couple of restaurant tables at some imagined slight. But by then I'd become something of a useful chaperone for misfiring talent. In 1968 I'd worked on television with Ian Hendry, another great but intemperate actor – on the screen he bore an uncanny resemblance to Humphrey Bogart – and once found myself failing to dissuade him from going from table to table in a fashionable Chelsea restaurant with a basinful of washing-up, offering it around as if it were a dessert trolley.

The only time Nicol really disappointed me was on the cricket pitch. In Berkeley California the *Hamlet* Company played cricket on the campus against a local team: in alarm the mystified police turned out and very nearly moved in on the action. Flushed with success, in Los Angeles we then made the mistake of challenging another local team to a match, forgetting that cricket had thrived there since the Hollywood Cricket Club was formed in 1932 by the British actor and cricketer C. Aubrey Smith (he'd been a fine fast bowler for Sussex, and once captained England). We'd also overlooked that we would be playing that day – in front of the TV news cameras, there to cover the odd ceremony – against a team of West Indian players of at least county standard. I nevertheless nearly had the brother of the legendary Everton de Courcy Weekes caught at first slip – would have had, in fact, had Nicol not been a shade too slow to raise his catching arm high enough and fast enough. This disappointing moment was the nearest I ever saw to him having a hangover: in every other way he was an inspiration.

Coming home with an American clockwork bus for my Mark, now three years old (he still has it) I was resigned to crouching in my dispiriting little flat in Bayswater (of which I still unhappily dream, usually of being found squatting in it by a fierce subsequent tenant). I had leased it from a fellow describing himself as "high up in Sellotape" (a picturesque image) who had therefore bequeathed me an attic full of the product, which by then had uselessly dried out – or, more frustratingly, had not *quite* dried out.

I wasn't quite useless, but I could have done with some drying out myself. The US had left me with the remains of a moderate dependency; not quite the full-blown Habit much feared by the parents of narcotic-users (and unusual in our profession), but a liquid version that often suggested determination rather than spontaneous Dionysiac excess, and in any case mildly alternated with the snowier substances.

***

> Would you find me on the day of doom, look for me
> In the dust of the wineshop's door,
> I drink so much wine, its aroma will rise from my dust when
> I'm under it;
> Should a toper come upon my dust, the fragrance of my corpse
> Will make him roaring drunk.
> – *Rubaiyat of Omar Khayyam*

Part of the above I suppose was due to spending so much time with Nicol. Returning to base I realise now that I was determined at all times to promote him (who needed no promotion), not least because he'd told me that he spotted a tentative kinship between me and his younger self. That was fine by me: my alliances in those days had a good deal to do with trying to find a more convincing model of myself – some bigger drinker who nevertheless kept his wits – and I liked to make friends with anyone who sensed something of this. In this skewed way I gave and received friendship by the exchange of mutual emulation.

I also wanted to resume what I normally took to be my place of a Saturday lunchtime. This was in the saloon bar of the Queens Elm pub in the Fulham Road. I'd be alongside Dudley Sutton (*Lovejoy*) in his usual corner with his pint of so-called milk and his features like Nicol's; or with Mike Pratt *(Callan*, skiffle player and friend of Lionel Bart) with whom I shared a birthday; with the fabulously pugnacious-looking but brilliant Ronald Fraser (my first, and near-enough definitive Bardolph in *Henry IV* at the Old Vic in 1955), with Bunny May (*Birds of a Feather*) who had been at the Old Vic as a boy actor at the same time as Ronald (Moth in *Love's Labour's Lost*, Falstaff's Page), together with my true friend Clive Graham, whom I'd manage to get cast in our *Hamlet* as Guildenstern when the original actor dropped out in mid-rehearsal (Clive also understudied Nicol and went on for him for a couple of nights after Nicol drove off the cliff), Jimmy Villiers (*The Ruling Class*, and a drinking companion of Peter O'Toole – who didn't come to the Elm); he was rumoured to be about eighteenth in line for the throne of England. And sometimes with Robert Stephens. I had ample Nicol stories, Sharon Tate stories (I was nearly an accidental witness to the slaughter in LA). I also brought back from LA some of director George Roy Hill's stories (he'd wept on my shoulder in despair at the disastrous final edit of a movie he'd just made – I had to force out of him that it had "a stupid working title – *Butch Cassidy and the Sundance Kid*").

It was all part of coming home, I suppose. The response to my glowing tales of Nicol – to the very idea of Nicol – made me realise something typical of a generation of English actors who probably drank as much as he did: though there was genuine admiration from some such as Dudley and Bob Stephens, there was some scorn from the rather right-wing contingent who had heard with relish that Nicol was unreliable and out of control. Had he not once stopped a show and gone back to the beginning? Disgraceful. Was he not pissed as Hamlet? Unprofessional. Had he not punched the Broadway producer David Merrick? I realised that drinking actors come in all shapes and sizes and I liked only the most tolerant. The others reminded me too readily of public schoolboys I'd known who prided themselves on sneaking off to the pub and sinking six pints and most of a bottle of port, each without the slightest sense of liberation, let alone creativity. There were certainly a lot of this kind in the theatre, who got more and more jealously resentful the more they lost their balance. If you ever worked with such, you knew the ones with a thirst straight off: in rehearsals, they smelt so strongly of aftershave in the afternoons that you realised why they'd piously declined to come to the pub for lunch with the rest of us for a routine glass of beer (normal), but stayed in the rehearsal room with their own discreetly pungent little flask, the potent bouquet of their aftershave masking its contents.

Back home after four months, I suppose I was something of a malcontent. Not that my own concerns were of much particular consequence, but I would complain to anybody who'd listen that London's village-like preoccupation with fashion, or the predicted arrival of decimal currency, or even the likelihood of a Rolling Stones concert in Hyde Park, hardly compared to the preoccupations Americans woke up with each morning, above all Vietnam. In this I ignored the actual political realities – Harold Wilson's partisanship with the US over the war ("you can't kick your partners in the balls" – although at least he kept us out of it), his fall and Heath's rise; Margaret Thatcher's regime lay just round the corner. All the same, in LA, which seemed the best place to see it on TV, I had watched a man walking on the moon, giving the US a respite from the violence and loss of faith that characterised 1969. Concorde had completed its first flight, and human eggs had been fertilised in a test tube. At least London's mothers weren't receiving letters from some jackass rejoicing that their "pinko" sons had been murdered by the police on a university campus, as the family of one of the victims at Kent State had done.

On the other hand, I'd returned to England on the arm, for the time being, of Francesca Annis (who had taken over as Ophelia from Marianne Faithfull) – enough to make any man walk tall and creating an envy of me comparable to that caused by the recent news that Robert Stephens had got together with Maggie Smith. This gave me some bar-room *éclat*, or at least an affectionate audience, as I could recount how I'd fallen off my horse on our recent holiday though sheer incompetence, or bought opium rather than hash in the souk in Marrakesh. Correction about the horse: I didn't fall off, just began to slide and recovered: Francesca, a good horsewoman, turned round anxiously to help and fell off herself. So confident of her was I that I sometimes didn't get home till dawn, because I was playing cards with Nicol, sometimes quietly singing Tim Hardin's 'It'll Never Happen Again', with its wonderful ambiguity about whether the thing that would never happen again is the lover's thoughtlessness or the relationship that he's being so thoughtless about, now lost for good.

Well, she made sure of that when she fell for Jon Finch while shooting Roman Polanski's *Macbeth*, and serve me right. She remains an heroic figure in my life, too little glimpsed these days but a great enrichment.

In a bid for grace, I'd pack all this in every couple of months and devote myself to Mark, three by then, with whom a magistrate, with as much instinct as sagacity, had granted me ten unencumbered days of access every two months (and three weeks in the summer). This was part of a divorce settlement agreed with my wife of five years, Katharine Barker, now one of my best friends again but then enduring with me one of the very final divorce cases to be heard before the law changed its emphasis from criminality to mutual agreement.

In other spare moments I was working my way through every concert I could find at the Rainbow, a now forgotten venue near Finsbury Park, mostly by American artists – Jefferson Airplane, Country Joe Macdonald, Delaney and Bonnie, Crosby, Stills, Nash & Young and Joni Mitchell, seeing *Midnight Cowboy* three times, and being (out of hours) generally disorderly. Throughout I always found someone to celebrate with, including a future West End mega-producer, an air guitar virtuoso who liked nothing better than adjourning to his room at the end of the evening to mime along to Pete Townshend in *Tommy*. I even got to know Tim Hardin, who'd moved to London to take the Methadone cure. I was friends with women, not quite as you might assume but because I truly preferred their company to men's. Still, there was also a fair bit of mutual hit-and-run I suppose, or less tentative alliances which lasted many years before perishing on the vine.

As a sort of finale to all this, one weekend in September 1970 I went to the Isle of Wight Festival dressed up (at his suggestion, as he couldn't go himself) as Tony Palmer, then a friend of mine and the rock critic of *The Observer*, to see Jimi Hendrix and Leonard Cohen. I'd met Hendrix briefly in New York and been charmed by his courtesy and soft-spoken modesty, but those were not of course the main qualities I was looking forward to catching at close quarters in the Press Enclosure at the Festival. To achieve my end I looked as much like a down-at-heel journalist as possible – snooper's mac and trilby hat – and showed the pass Tony had given me to a sort of Hell's Angel at the door. I said I was Tony Palmer from *The Observer*, to which he pointed out that I wasn't. I insisted that I was; with an ever-broadening grin he said I absolutely wasn't. Finally (note the magic three of comedy) he pointed out that he himself had had lunch with Tony Palmer the previous week. The best part of this story is that even then I felt I could, like any good actor, force a truth out of fiction, and so I declared "Yes, now I recognise you" and of course we did – and was about (I suppose) to say that the main course had been particularly good, when he cheerily waved me through: "In you go, motherfucker". Thus it was that I was a few feet from the stage with several hundred thousand people behind me, watching what turned out to be Hendrix's last major gig: a week later, by a stroke of bad luck with some barbiturates, he was dead, choked by his own vomit.

***

By 1971 *Captain Jack's Revenge* felt right up my street, not only in terms of the casting but of cast of mind. At the very least I would now be sitting in stupefaction playing another heroic Indian chief, listening not so much to his inner leadership voices but to Jefferson Airplane at taxpayers' expense. One way and another, I reckoned, I was for the time being an honorary American, and probably a better bet for Captain Jack than an Andy Warhol superstar with only one name. I'd also just done a good TV production playing an off-duty Nazi officer in the Somerset Maugham story *The Unconquered* for ATV – I'd warned the producers that I couldn't ride the requisite motorbike, thinking that would be more welcome than actors who notoriously boast about the fictional extra skills they say they have: juggling, horse riding, a language. However, it was a warning the director, Gilchrist Calder, irritably ignored, with the result that on two successive days I drove a priceless Zundapp into a ditch on location, thereby disposing of the only two available for hire in the UK; after the first occasion a company runner had to find the second at the other end of the country while I calmly slept. I was playing a confident young Nazi on his way to perform a rape in a French farmhouse – you never, in the fleeting close-ups, saw such a nervous one. I was punished by being lightly bitten by a farm dog as I eventually safely got off the bike in the courtyard; the wrangler laughed at me, attempted to control the dog and got a far more savage bite from it that removed him from the set indefinitely. As for me, I was glad to have screwed up not because of intoxicants but incompetence; and I may have viewed the Royal Court offer as a welcome return to a more manageable medium.

***

Captain Jack's Revenge turned out to be eminently actable. Patricia Quinn was Mary (and my girlfriend onstage and off, where, being a devoutly Method actor, she had briefly and graciously accepted the role of Francesca's successor). A deeply original and intuitive performer, she was on her way to her wonderful Magenta in *The Rocky Horror Picture Show*; and then she became Lady (Robert) Stephens and I lost touch with her apart from an occasional 3am call from Robert (clinking glasses behind him), taking me gently to task about what he felt was missing from a performance of mine which he'd seen, usually that very evening. Far from being infuriating, I enjoyed this a good deal, since Robert, the very finest of actors, was infinitely generous, and a lifelong enthusiast for the job. Anthony Higgins (startlingly handsome and soon to move to another level working with John and Anjelica Huston in *A Walk with Love and Death* and in Peter Greenaway's *The Draughtsman's Contract*) was William the draft-dodger, and Edward Jewesbury, whom I was later to work with at the RSC, was General Canby.

In practice *Captain Jack* allowed for stretches of loaded silence, and at other times of polyphonic chaos: there are periods when the record player, the slide projector, the movie projector, the telephone and the doorbell are all running at the same time as the dialogue, or in place of it, the multimedia effect accompanied by Bach's *B Minor Mass* and the Jackie Gleason show on TV. There are also times when the two central lovers either hate or adore each other – you can't tell which because they are, technically, stoned. There's a dreamlike quality in their trips: LSD for hallucination, marijuana for comfort; and some of the dialogue tilts towards a slightly self-conscious Theatre of the Absurd:

> WILLIAM: This is my life.
> JACK: And mine and hers and theirs.
> MARY: What do you mean by "this"?
> WILLIAM: Has there been a misunderstanding?
> JACK: It's all a misunderstanding.
> MARY: Apparently so.
> WILLIAM: What was the password?
> JACK: What was the payment?
> MARY: What was the return address?

Elsewhere Smith puts a classically authentic surge beneath the simplest lines, as when Jack denounces not only the "paper words" of the white man but also the violence within his own people:

I can save them from death, but they would have me lead them forth to meet him. My heart is hiding in a cave. I am becoming the rocks that bruise and bite me … here is my homefire, but where are my trees and laughing waters? I will not go. I will sit here until the spirit comes and wakes me from my dream.

There's also a dose of the family miseries of Osborne and Albee. Acknowledged from the start as the Company's rock'n'roller – there wasn't much competition – I set about influencing matters without waiting to be invited by Nick, who was directing. Bach's *Mass* and the Pergolesi *Stabat Mater* were swiftly replaced by Crosby, Stills & Nash, until I declared on reflection that their too-close-harmony was also too cute for the play. Likewise Eric Clapton's solo on George Harrison's *While My Guitar Gently Weeps* was too showy and virtuosic. Inclining towards Stateside as usual and as befitted the writing, I introduced Jefferson Airplane at full tilt in *White Rabbit*.

The end result of our labours was rather good, successfully evading the temptation to split the cast into good and bad guys: I had to sense the helplessly anxious love for his daughter that underlay Canby as my overbearing father-in-law, and the flaccid thinking that underpinned the hippies' philosophy, however much they idealised themselves into the figures of Captain Jack and his displaced tribe.

We were warmly greeted by the London critics, though a few were offended by the hubristic comparison whereby the new stoned young were said to be persecuted for their lifestyle as cruelly as the Indians had been for theirs. *The Times* praised my own "splendid stoic dignity" as Jack and, as one rave is all a good new play needs, it came from an unexpected quarter, *The Guardian*, where Nicholas de Jongh, never an easy critic to please, went right against form in his praise of what he called

> an extraordinary play … wavering between fantasy and fact, between idea and vision … its dislocated language confounds meaning as often as asserts it: chatter, persistent talk of illness

invading the bodies, mysterious telephone calls ... it drifts and wavers with an unnerving and uneasy pulse. The sense of disorientation is palpable... the older generation's intransigence is their glory, while the young have the Indians' pride and obstinacy... Nicholas Wright, in the finest production he has achieved for this theatre, beautifully paces and controls... Michael Pennington's Jack, though too young, is ideally disturbed.

Well, "ideally disturbed" had come quite easily.

***

Captain Jack was still not the last of my dealings with the disinherited American Indian. Three years later I went downstairs at the Royal Court for perhaps the real deal, in the form of Christopher Hampton's *Savages*, in which I played an anthropologist decisively on the side of the Indians, with Tom Conti.

And Paul Scofield.

If Nicol Williamson had been an example of Anti-Hero Worship, Scofield was its acceptable face. And now I was side by side on a sofa with him as he played a liberally-minded British Ambassador fascinated by the culture of the Brazilian *indians* – I was the activist who'd lived among them and despised the Establishment's failure to do anything substantial to help them. My defence of the indigenous Brazilians took the form of continuous passionate argument with Scofield: in fact that was the entirety of my part. This certainly left enough space for me to observe him and goggle at his heroic daring. In the familiarly righteous argument of my two scenes, of course, I didn't stand a chance. At one weekday matinée a woman near the front turned to her friend and complained at the beginning of the second of them: "I don't *like* that young man." They'd just finished their interval tea-tray, which in those days was still – just – the fashion in the West End (we'd transferred by now from the Court), and, in the same conservative vein, she wasn't having any youngster criticising the much-loved star of the show. Attacking Paul Scofield? Hadn't I seen him in *Ring Round the Moon*? Had I no respect?

As the director Mike Nichols once said of Al Pacino, part of Paul's greatness was his ability to "consult somewhere else". This gift in an actor goes far beyond the normal practice of playing a particular moment in a pre-planned way or even exactly as directed or rehearsed, but rather of subsuming all the available information and advice until there's no alternative but to take each line completely freshly, in an imaginative freefall. Then you're not so much acting as being, spontaneously embodying rather than suggesting – and always healthily surprising yourself. In Act Two of Hampton's play, Tom Conti's revolutionist, who is holding the well-meaning ambassador hostage, has a brief exchange with him that marks a truce on their political hostility and the beginning of some human curiosity:

CONTI: Are you married?
SCOFIELD: Yes.
CONTI: Happily?
SCOFIELD: Well … you know…
CONTI: Children?
SCOFIELD (after a brief pause): No.

In his five monosyllables, the momentary crotchet before "Well … you know…" was then lengthened to a minim before the "No" about the children. By those brief deferrals of the natural beat in his lines, Scofield peopled his silent world of regret and self-justification: the ambassador's hinterland of marital misery was made fully visible by declaring its opposite. Scofield always had a sweetness in his smile, which he used in this case with the greatest courtesy, to stop further questioning. At the end of the play Conti in fact shoots him dead: as Scofield saw the gun pointed at him, his one verbal reaction was a simple "Don't!" while he gently waved his hand this way and that at the gun as if he could expunge it, disarm it, shove it away, or perhaps civilly say goodbye to it.

Elsewhere, with a mischievous showmanship, he managed to tie a bow tie onto himself as if he were in front of a mirror when in fact he had none – he was downstage centre, and his only view was of the darkened stalls. Try it. He accomplished this as if it was an automatic daily occurrence, as no doubt it is with ambassadors going to receptions, but at the same time he was conducting a stilted conversation with his melancholy wife about something else. This was a great technician at work; elsewhere he made more numinous magic. Towards the end of the play Ambassador West has a monologue about how humans mythically stole the fire of the jaguar, with the result that

> Only the reflection and the memory of fire
> Burn in his eyes

What happened here was not like acting at all but definitely the consultation with somewhere else that Nichols attributed to Pacino: all you could see or imagine were the flames and the murderous redness of the jaguar's eyes.

So Paul Scofield had brought a jaguar onto the stage, its reality excluding any other thought; but it didn't surprise me. Back in 1965, I used to watch him nightly at Stratford on my first job, as he suddenly made a thousand people see a unicorn. I used to crouch in the wings then: he was Timon of Athens and I was the Fourth Creditor's Servant from the left, Titus by name, which I hoped made people briefly wonder if I was the young Titus Andronicus. He occasionally made the metal on the front of house lamps sing with some supreme tenor note which he would never repeat the next night, however much I willed him to. I was in an unapologetic, flat-out spasm of hero-worship. Timon's furious departure from Athens halfway through the play, once he has seen how he has been exploited, lands him not in the defeated life of a vagrant that he expected, but ironically makes him rich again (his first discovery is a hoard of gold) and a newly articulate witness to the world around him. In his cubbyhole on the seashore he sees at last the interdependence of every living creature:

> If thou wert the lion, the fox would beguile thee,

he advises a visitor; on the other hand

> if thou wert the lamb, the fox would eat thee, if thou wert the fox, the lion would suspect thee, and peradventure thou were accused by the ass,

but on the other hand again:

> if thou wert the ass, thy dullness would torment thee, and still thou livest but as a breakfast to the wolf.

Need he continue? Yes, because as the wolf,

> oft thou should'st hazard thy life for thy dinner.

His hands and face were dirty and his gown as torn and bedraggled as it was elegant before. But Timon is full of a new rapture, his eyes literally wide open and his face pouchy and battered; looking into some far region he sees everything he's not noted before, especially that:

> If thou wert the unicorn, pride and wrath would confound thee, and make thine own self the conquest of thy fury.

We'd witnessed Timon's fury before, as he cast his Athenian robes aside, excoriating every false thing they stood for. But the unicorn? Who knows anything about unicorns, except that they may be another name for the narwhal, that strange tusked Arctic whale with its canine teeth, or perhaps no more than an inherited heraldic device which could impale us with its horn? Meanwhile Scofield was there for the studying, though I never was on quite such comfortable terms with him as to ask him about it. I only knew that it was a moment of Shakespearean genius: this greatest of actors made his audience almost look over their shoulders to see the animal. Whatever it was, they saw it in his startled eyes – the idea has come to him in a moment – and felt it above their heads in the stalls, because of his unique gift for enticing them into his visions. This was Scofield in 1965, some years after his King Lear, ploughing his bitter imagination once again. I might be out of work in the future, but I'd seen the unicorn, and so had a thousand others a night: the exact same thing at the exact same moment, and I at least haven't forgotten it in the fifty-five years it has taken me to find a way of describing it.

And what neither I nor the RSC knew then was that they would not be doing another main house *Timon of Athens* for thirty-six years. Or that then it would be my turn.

As Estragon in Waiting for Godot *(Guy Slater as Pozzo and Jonathan Lynn as Vladimir, directed by Stephen Frears), winner of Best Fringe Show at Edinburgh Festival in 1963.*

THE MAKING OF MICHAEL

1955–1964

The figure in the box-brownie print stands in a scratch wig that looks more like a little Russian *shapka*. In his right hand he has a diminutive plastic sword that, were it not for its size, could have come out of a Christmas cracker, and a matching little round plastic shield; in his left he carries a helmet with a plume, equally diminutive. He wears on his shoulders a blatant blanket which has been blown by the wind back between his legs, and something resembling a counterpane lies on the grass beside him. He is in Wellington boots and a surprisingly good pair of tights, surely found at a theatre costumier of the day (which has passed now), as close-fitting as ballet tights but woollen, and typical of Shakespearean productions of the 1950s – always assuming the actor had good enough legs to grace them (which, by the way, even Laurence Olivier never did). The whole posture – right leg straight, left slightly bent in imitation of the kind of actor who used always to place one foot up a step to look commanding – is respectable enough. This looks like a quite presentable Hotspur in *Henry IV* but for the giveaway dimple in the cheeks, which conveys merriment and satisfaction rather than revolutionary hostility.

Until, that is, it dawns on me that this may not be Hotspur at all but a far less familiar figure – the Bastard Falconbridge in *King John*, who at one point in the Franco-English wars cheerfully decapitates the Duke of Austria, whom he suspects has killed his father King Richard I (the Lionheart); so maybe the helmet stands for the head and the counterpane the abandoned body of his victim.

The relative obscurity of the part and incident gives us some clue to the begetter of this strange photograph. But then so does the image on the next page, which is of a very self-satisfied gentleman in a judge's wig and on top of it a sort of pillbox hat. This time he has on a passable white beard from Bert's Wigs (now, thankfully, long forgotten). He also has a voluminous sweater and his arms could be described as akimbo (he has driving gloves on the end of them), except that his left arm is not at his hip but resting on top of some great growth or bundle worn underneath the voluminous sweater – perhaps a goitre, or a huge bosom that descends easily to his waist. Well might he rest that gloved hand on it like a shelf. Falconbridge's tights have now been abandoned for flannel trousers suggesting the golf links; the Wellington boots are still there, but seem designed for someone bigger: they crinkle up loosely and so end at half-mast, well below the knee.

Clearly the precocious eleven-year-old has given up his Christmas cabaret as an Indian chief and is widening his range. But what are the flailing imaginings of this young man? With the premature instincts of a canny character actor, he has exchanged a very little-known incident in an unfamiliar history play for a major part in a famous one that at his age he couldn't possibly undertake – Falstaff in *Henry IV*. And as an instinctive impresario he seems to be embracing the current policy of the Old Vic Theatre in London, which between 1955 and 1960 performed every single Shakespeare play with a more or less permanent Company, but no public subsidy or private or commercial sponsorship, achieving its 80 per cent of capacity on box office alone – a feat inconceivable today. One of the things they mastered was tactical variety, so rarities like *Cymbeline* and *King John* were scheduled with caution in the repertory amidst crowd-pleasers such as *Hamlet* and *Twelfth Night*. What this remarkable Company certainly did was inspire a generation of audiences and actors, even some at age eleven (I still run into them).

Flicking further though the pages of this photo album I find Henry V touched by his destiny the night before Agincourt, a tremulous Andrew Aguecheek *en garde* in *Twelfth Night*, presumably about to duel with Sebastian and therefore brave against all odds, and Parolles, mocked and humiliated for his vanity in *All's Well That Ends Well*. As if in sympathy, despairing plants with drooping heads wilt in the garden pots behind this young hopeful's repertoire.

Meanwhile, what can be occupying the mind of the paternal figure up in the top corner of some of the pictures, watching quietly aghast from an upstairs window? Perhaps in heaven's sanatorium there's a special ward for parents who worried overmuch about their children: perhaps there are also secure private rooms for double-first lawyer-scholar fathers whose only sons and heirs have joined the motley. What is wrong with my boy, this one may have wondered; I thought he was obsessed with Jack Robertson, but now here he is in the garden wearing tights and his mother's pillbox hat. Worst of all, this is hallowed ground: he's posing exactly where he used to stand at an imaginary crease while I bowled him adequate off-spinners so that he could be more like JDR; we had the cricket net up behind the bowler's arm, so that he could do a bit of good driving, and I was careful not to bowl fast enough to cause damage to our patio if he missed the ball.

And now…? The Christmas Indian play for his cousins was bad enough, with all its endless soliloquies, not to mention his recent enthusiasm for the filthy comic Max Miller, currently playing nightly at the Metropolitan in Edgware Road, as short a walk away from here as Lord's. Far more palatable for a parent are Jimmy Jewel and Ben Warriss on the radio, but he seems to have abandoned them completely. And now this, presumably the result of the unofficial season ticket we seem to have these days at the Old Vic. I know what I'll do – I'll build him a model theatre of unprecedented size, with miniature lighting circuits (with dimmers) and a fly-tower (as

I think it's called), and a practical rouched red curtain to go up and down. So many technical aspects to it in fact that it should, he not being a mechanically-minded boy, put him off this obsession.

And he did. And it didn't.

And having known successive Christmas lunches lurching not into a welcome nap but to renewed embarrassment that his only son was becoming a fully-fledged prima donna, my father may have drawn comfort from the fact that Arnold House, where I was at school, though having no particular leaning towards the performing arts, did hold an annual Verse Speaking competition. I had recently done Wolsey's farewell to power in *Henry VIII* for the occasion:

> I have touch'd the highest point of all my greatness;
> And, from that full meridian of my glory,
> I haste now to my setting: I shall fall
> Like a bright exhalation in the evening,
> And no man see me more…
> Farewell! a long farewell, to all my greatness!
> This is the state of man: to-day he puts forth
> The tender leaves of hopes; to-morrow blossoms,
> And bears his blushing honours thick upon him;
> The third day comes a frost, a killing frost,
> And, when he thinks, good easy man, full surely
> His greatness is a-ripening, nips his root,
> And then he falls, as I do. I have ventured,
> Like little wanton boys that swim on bladders,
> This many summers in a sea of glory,
> But far beyond my depth: my high-blown pride
> At length broke under me and now has left me,
> Weary and old with service, to the mercy
> Of a rude stream, that must for ever hide me.
> Vain pomp and glory of this world, I hate ye:
> I feel my heart new open'd. O, how wretched
> Is that poor man that hangs on princes' favours!
> There is, betwixt that smile we would aspire to,
> That sweet aspect of princes, and their ruin,

More pangs and fears than wars or women have:
And when he falls, he falls like Lucifer,
Never to hope again.

I would say now that these speeches perhaps need a little cutting here and there, but they struck me at the time as the most beautiful laments I had ever heard, and I'm sure I offered them in their entirety. I doubt if many of my audience knew the lines, or their surrounding play; but the Arnold House judging staff were so astonished that they awarded me the Prize, my first and thus far only outright Award for Acting.

***

I've lost count of the times I've hoped my father and mother would feel compensated for all this in due course. Between the Cardinal Wolsey and my Mum writing to her sister, in sorrow rather than anger, about my fully-fledged "mania for the stage", they rather rashly sent me to Marlborough College in Wiltshire (too far from the Old Vic or indeed Stratford, I felt). In a way it was their one mistake – or must have seemed so as I rebelliously grew my hair, read Gerard Manley Hopkins (and by contrast Jack Kerouac), and took the piss out of John Betjeman (an old boy of the school) at end of term concerts. This spirited impersonation was greeted with feigned disgust by the staff (actually it was generally cheered as quite a good portrait, though a bit too camp).

I had taken with me to Marlborough, to make it all tolerable, not only my copy of *Shakespeare at the Old Vic* (an annual dossier of action photos and essays on the season's shows) but an adoration of panto – so much so that while I was still living at home I had kept insisting that I'd seen Nat Jackley and Arthur Askey on the bus after a matinée I'd been at (they were of course busy in the theatre getting ready for their second house). At the age of eleven, I had been enraged at my parents' refusal to let me see Max Miller live at the Metropolitan simply because the BBC was banning him at the time. I punished them by mounting an uncut *Coriolanus* (yes,

Coriolanus) specially for them on the model theatre my father had so devotedly built for me. From this event, if nothing else, I got a sharp lesson in the value of vocal pace in such a play: there are some audiences on whom you have such a tenuous hold that you have to get on with the job at all costs.

On a brighter note, around this time my parents started taking me as a special treat to the Ivy for a Tournedos Rossini or Bombe Alaska, mainly perhaps because of its proximity to two West End Theatres, the St Martins and the Ambassadors – at least once I believed I saw Richard Attenborough and Sheila Sim in the restaurant, even though just the other side of the Art Deco windows they were in the middle of a performance at the Ambassadors of the original production of *The Mousetrap*. If I had been told that the show would still be running when I was seventy-six and writing my memoirs, and showing no sign of giving up before me, I would have found the idea difficult to grasp. I also loved (and listened and listened to when not living the high life at the Ivy) *Guys and Dolls* and *The Music Man*, from which last I could do a creditable version of 'Gary Indiana' and 'Seventy-Six Trombones'. Oh, and *West Side Story*, which opened on Broadway in 1957 as I first left for Marlborough, but surprisingly didn't win the Tony for Best Musical that year (*The Music Man* did) and came to London in 1958, kindling an almost unbearable yearning in me to play the character Tony some day.

Once at Marlborough I saw that everyone has an obsession of some kind – for girls, for boys, for rugger, or for pub-crawling. By the time I was nearly out at the other end, I had published, on a friend's printing press, a camp version of the school magazine *The Marlburian*, which I re-christened *The Marlburienne*. I saw it as a righteous outlet for what I had seen as the sheer mass of homoerotic poetry, which, though not particularly reflecting my own impulses, I had seen produced by many of my friends. This Wildean revolt against censorship almost got me expelled, but those you would expect to be the most disapproving (the Master and my Housemaster), once they'd located, studied and officially disowned the finished article, veered into something very like a guarded admiration. This, I learned, was the technique of limited tolerance practised by a moderately fair-minded wing of the English Establishment of the day – official censure jostling with private acknowledgement. After all, these men worked at a school in which one Housemaster, fingered for paying too much attention to one of the prettier boys in his charge, took his dog and his gun out into Savernake Forest one day and blew its and then his own brains out. As for me, my subversive project, which brought quite a few of my friends out of the closet, probably made me feel like John Calder, who had in a sense discovered Samuel Beckett, or Richard Neville, later of *Oz*.

More officially, I did play Prospero in one of the frequent School plays – in a great cloud of dust that, as I moved, came billowing out of a dilapidated magic cloak that had already been much hired out by the Shakespeare Memorial Theatre in Stratford but which had originally been worn by John Gielgud to work his spell in the part. What the hell, it was his mantle and now it was on my shoulders, gently sliding off me again as I laboured through my I'm sure stodgy performance.

This and other practical theatrical experiences were engineered by the German teacher, Kenneth Keast, with whom I had no other contact at all and whose speciality language I knew no word of, but who spotted my zeal and fully indulged it. He directed most of the school plays and gave me all the opportunities I could hope for – before *The Tempest*, in his *Saint Joan* I had got my first good part at Marlborough, as Chaplain de Stogumber, largely because I didn't mind playing old and crying. We also did Patrick Hamilton's 1929 classic *Rope*; *Dear Delinquent* (West End comedy); and made the adventurous avant-garde choice of Karel Čapek's 1920 *RUR*, in which I played the intriguingly named Alquist, chief architect and supervisor of construction at Rossum's Universal Robots. Alquist is important to the play because he's a builder, and being so handy he survives the overthrow of all the other humans by the new race of robots he has helped bring into being. So, a sort of hero; the range of what Kenneth Keast allowed me to do, I am sure, began to turn me into that (to me) precious thing, a character actor. As an impresario, I also myself staged, with my lifelong friend Michael

Elwyn, Sophocles' *Philoctetes* with ourselves in the main roles, and likewise Pinter's *The Dumb Waiter*, very soon (and probably without approval, let alone purchase of the rights) after its West End run in 1960. In all these adventures, how heady the excitement and how terrible was the day after the show; how weirdly intense it had all been, like real living, musky and erotic in a way I didn't quite understand, and how grey the Monday.

***

My parents suffered not because of this but as the result of their three-weekly Sunday visits, the permitted limit in any single term. The rule was that you could joyfully meet your parents after morning Chapel, spend the rest of the day with them until about 6pm, then wave them goodbye until their next visit nearly a month later. If they'd arrived the previous night they would probably have stayed either at the Ivy House or the Sun Hotel – "Old World Comfort and Charm" – or, if the school fees weren't hurting too badly, at the handsomely colonnaded Ailesbury Arms on the southeast corner of Marlborough's oddly sloping High Street. It's now residential flats, but it started life in George III's time as the Duke's Arms (the Duke of Wellington perhaps?).

On the other hand, if your visitors arrived on a day trip you'd celebrate their visit with hideous brevity by having tea at the Merlin or the Polly Tea Rooms. Either way, by the end of teatime darkness was falling over the soul as well as the town; my parents told me that they often then drove back to London in complete silence. I interpret this as their shared acceptance that they had probably made the wrong choice of school, compared to Westminster perhaps, where I could have continued life as a theatregoer as much as some kind of scholar.

My Dad was eased momentarily perhaps – well, I know he was – by seeing me lurch onwards to his old Cambridge college, Trinity. As encouragement, he recalled for me that he used to dine with Anthony Blunt in Trinity Refectory, that he'd eavesdropped on Aleister Crowley disputing with Ludwig Wittgenstein in the Copper

Kettle Café on King's Parade (not quite historically possible), and Michael Redgrave and Vladimir Nabokov discussing *Uncle Vanya* outside the Arts Theatre. He did a good job and I felt thoroughly motivated. Meanwhile I tumbled out of school into the National Youth Theatre for the summer holidays of 1961 before going up. I had never seen so many winkle-pickers, leather or corduroy Norfolk jackets and heard so many enormously confident baritone voices. And I hadn't imagined that I would within a couple of minutes of arriving make two lifelong friends, John Shrapnel and Robin Ellis. Nor had I expected to find myself playing not only the doomed Earl of Salisbury in *Richard II* in the West End, but also, as an extension to the season, Cinna the Poet in *Julius Caesar* at the Schiller Theatre in Berlin – where one afternoon between performances I and some buddies crossed at Checkpoint Charlie for a quick look round the Eastern Sector only two months after the Wall had gone up: I marvel we don't feature in one of Don McCullin's extraordinary pictures of precisely such a moment, gazed at by lethally-armed East German guards with itching fingers. At least they laughed at my passport photo.

Arriving vertiginously at Cambridge (together with John and Robin), was like being dipped in a barrel and immediately leaping free of it. My father had secured a double first in History and Law, but I barely doffed my hat to his old college, insisting instead on living in a room in town rather than some musty staircase in New Court. For one thing that made it easier to shuttle between my lodgings in Jesus Lane and both the ADC, the undergraduate-run theatre, and the professional Arts Theatre where we occasionally played – both of them quite a long way from the city's libraries, lecture halls and other scholastic centres. I was emphasising – to myself as well as anyone interested, including my tutors – that I had serious work of my own to do in the next three years apart from getting a degree: in fact I was choosing my Jesus Lane digs as if I was already in a provincial repertory company. Inevitably there were melancholy moments over the next three years spent trying to explain to my Dad that Uni was nowadays a dedicated training ground for actors, journalists and politicians rather than for naturally gifted scholars like himself who could fly through their exams *en route* to tea at Grantchester. Instead I drank vatloads of coffee at the Copper Kettle, and ate most nights just along the road from my digs, at The Corner House, run by a Greek family, where like-minded rebels could gather for moussaka and apple pie. This is where the beautiful Jill Corner, who was currently playing Myra to my Simon Bliss in *Hay Fever,* threatened to slap my face for some impertinence or innuendo, despite my warning – lifted directly from *Look Back in Anger*:

> JIMMY: I hope you won't make the mistake of thinking for one moment that I am a gentleman.
>
> HELENA: I'm not very likely to do that.
>
> JIMMY: I've no public school scruples about hitting girls. If you slap my face – by God, I'll lay you out!
>
> HELENA: You probably would. You're the type.
>
> JIMMY: You bet I'm the type.

The offence – if any – is long forgotten. What can it have been that I said? I wonder if I should get in touch with Jill now to apologise – Miriam Margolyes has stayed in touch with her, I know. Was I angling for the chance to return the slap in order to become more like Osborne's anti-hero? Quite possibly, for the truth is I longed for the part but it never came up.

***

I just about justified my parents' faith by slipping in a weaselly way into a 2:1, intriguing the examiners (like the staff at Marlborough) with a kind of literary showmanship and a not-quite-sacrilegious criticism of the most popular classics. This in an exam is like the bravado of a performance, particularly on a first night: it depends on hinting that you know what you're doing even when you don't, not entirely. It also meant keeping my English tutors at bay, thus returning the contempt with which they generally, in those days, regarded any form of theatrical interpretation of world drama (as opposed to literary study of it), as entirely irrelevant.

Such was my dereliction – quite a close friend told me that I was undoubtedly going to fail my degree entirely because I hadn't studied F. R. Leavis on *Othello* – that I found myself on the night before my Nineteenth-Century Literature exam for the Finals of the English tripos grimly contemplating the lively nocturnal scene outside my room while opening a copy of Alfred Lord Tennyson for the very first time. This being a matter of hours before I was inevitably going – by a remorseless examining logic which stipulated that one subject only was to be written about from each of the paper's three sections – to have to write an essay about him. In the absence of any knowledge apart from what I'd rapidly assembled overnight, I did this by making my handwriting deteriorate rapidly as I started the Tennyson essay (having just covered W. B. Yeats at excessive length) to the point that I trailed off while quoting the only line I knew by heart – "Break, break, break on thy cold grey stones, O sea..." and with a briefly scribbled postscript – "Sorry, time ran out" – leaving my paper on the desk and quitting the exam a good hour early. I may not have known Leavis on *Othello*, but I was good at decoys and unreliable implications. I also knew how to turn every paper I sat into a discussion of the current state of affairs in the theatre. Even Chaucer. Even Existentialism.

I was also working on a project of another kind: I had been at a single-sex school, and I couldn't even dance. So I needed to find a female safe haven or havens by some other means. I remember persuading Jill Corner (before the slap) to take a long walk after a show late one night and ending up on a bench outside the ramshackle little pavilion on the cricket field on Parker's Piece. There, where I might once have waited my turn, padded up to bat (and in the right kind of gloves), nothing so vigorous happened now, except that I do remember reclining with my head in her fully-clothed lap – as in a Pietà, she seated, me stretched out, ruminating about Life. Now I think of it, this was often the position of choice for not-quite-successful wooers in those days: I remember groups of us congregating in Michael Butcher's room to listen to Joan Baez's first album as if in church, and I think it was Michael who adopted the Pietà position for his girlfriend then, or maybe it was John Shrapnel or Richard Eyre. It makes sense – that way, the girls stayed in charge, even though as Rakes and Ramblin' Boys we were pretty harmless. Those were the days of virginities carefully treasured until cast aside on a momentary impulse, to be followed by grim male visits to pharmacies to secure abortifacients of a risky kind; their purchase being accomplished by a sequence of pseudonyms for the drugs and hints at how advanced the "problem" might be. The streets sometimes seemed to be full of young men intent on diverting the course of nature by the cavalier pursuit of ergot-based migraine medications called Moulin Rouge, and other racy IDs.

I fell in love more or less continuously, more or less hopefully and more or less deludedly. My most considered choice was Gillian Goodman, a striking young tragedienne who knew more professional theatre *polari* even than I did after the Youth Theatre. She often played my mother on the stage and my teacher off it. We were together only for my first year and her third, at the end of which she got hired by Derby Rep: a move which then involved me in a number of heave-ho cross-country train pilgrimages via Bedford, and brought me to realise that Derby was a bad choice of girlfriend-site for a Cambridge undergraduate because of the tricky and mostly unpredictable nocturnal route. Sure, on the outward journey there was the excitement of the enterprise, mixed with trepidation as to what nasty surprises might be waiting when I arrived at 41 Empress Road in the middle of the night. For by then nasty surprises were what Gillian represented; this was a newly professional actress with admirers, and she needed to put childish things like an undergraduate flame behind her. As she hesitated over any longer-term decision on her love-life, her concept of a welcome was eccentric: this visiting undergraduate felt well out of his zone having to share sleeping quarters not only with the brand new (and first) Beatles album he'd brought for her, but with the character man from the acting company as well as herself. He and every other professional I met in the company were, however, extremely warm and welcoming in a way that I have come to take for granted in the profession.

The rest of Cambridge is for me a list of names and play titles: Jack Gelber (*The Connection*), Jean-Paul Sartre (*Huis Clos*), Jean Cocteau (*The Infernal Machine*), Shakespeare (*passim*), John Webster (*The White Devil*), Noël Coward (*Hay Fever*), Carlo Goldoni (*Servant of Two Masters* before it re-morphed as *One Man, Two Guvnors*, which is a great improvement), and so on; and a dazzling list of contemporaries – actors such as John Shrapnel, Robin Ellis and Miriam Margolyes (who, once Gillian had left, often used to play my mother), John Cleese (already a genius, together with Graham Chapman, Bill Oddie and Eric Idle) and Simon Perry, who went on to run the National Film Finance Corporation; directors such as Stephen Frears, Richard Eyre, Michael Apted, Michael Newell and Trevor Nunn – then in his last year but as prolific as he is today (*Macbeth, A Doll's House, Much Ado About Nothing*); writer/actors such as Carey Harrison, Guy Slater and John Grillo.

It's hard to describe plausibly the headiness of it all. As I've implied, undergraduate theatre was fuelled by tutorial indifference going on disapproval: to play Willy Loman in *Death of a Salesman*, John Shrapnel had to assume a pseudonym drawn after lengthy research by us all at a furniture shop on King's Parade, which stocked a multitude of chairs: he thus became Lloyd Loom, allegedly appearing by special arrangement between the ADC and his alma mater, the Actors Studio in New York. On the same show, I became quite excited at knowing that my own tutor had uncharacteristically deigned to come and see the performance. We were preparing for my Tragedy paper, but he dismissed the production at our next session as being unconvincing, like all "theatrical representations" of great plays. As evidence, he cited that during her housework Linda Loman had, on the night he was there, failed to tuck in a small section of the blanket on the downstage side of her bed.

As an acting generation we were internally riven by the young, mostly male need to establish categorically where you stood on doctrine. So the Copper Kettle was thick with factions, propounding the righteousness of Stanislavski, Brecht, Erwin Piscator and Antonin Artaud (*The Theatre of Cruelty*), and God help you if you were wrongly placed on reputation's variable tide. Then you might find yourself walking angrily home, only to have a colleague shout at you across the street that he'd really disliked you in your show last night. Some of us thought Shakespeare and Ibsen were what mattered, others Chekhov and Miller, but never all four. Another time Tony Palmer, in those days something of an impresario, hired the Guildhall to put on *Oedipus Rex* – a cast recording exists, in which a number of quite well-known-to-be actors appeared, or rather spoke – somewhat reedily, in a vocal range that suggested a guitar short of a couple of strings or a trumpet with one blocked valve. We went to the Edinburgh Festival two years running, the first time to do a Trevor Nunn production of Ibsen's *Brand* on a stage the size of a postage stamp, and Cocteau's *Intimate Relations*, in which Miriam Margolyes played – yes, my mother again. The second year at Edinburgh was startling in that it involved us building a revolve in a Presbyterian church hall and premiering Henry Miller's only play, *Just Wild About Harry*. Described by the author as "a melo-melo in seven scenes", this single excursion into theatre is pure Miller, welling up from the same abundant love of life and freedom from convention that made its author the dean of writers dedicated to human liberation. Admittedly inspired by Eugène Ionesco and The Theatre of the Absurd, his tragicomic slapstick is nevertheless as American as the Marx Brothers and the blues. I played a back-street doctor, let's call him; the Lord Chamberlain, who had the right to do such things in those days, said my main speech had to be removed because it suggested the medical process of an abortion (not so: in fact it was written in an onomatopoeically suggestive gobbledygook). We responded by putting the whole speech on a blackboard headed by the word "Censored", and left the audience to read it in silence. More orthodoxly, we won the prize for the Best Fringe show for Stephen Frears's production of *Waiting for Godot*, which presented Vladimir and Estragon for the first (but far from the last) time as circus clowns – Jonathan Lynn like Grock, me like a whey-faced Harpo Marx – and played James Darren's 'Goodbye Cruel World' on the soundtrack. Having seen this, one of my fellow-actors confided in Stephen that although I was a nice fellow he felt I had chosen the wrong profession, but that's how Cambridge was in those days. I hugged myself in the knowledge that Harold Hobson of the *Sunday Times* had declared he had never seen an Estragon before who so convincingly saw himself as Christ (not my intention, but what the hell).

All in all, it was at the ADC rather than the Arts (which was reserved for the Footlights and the annual Marlowe Society production, our professional showcases) that I did most of what I already called my work rather than my recreation. I had my first shot at Hamlet there early in my final year (1964), and no less than George Steiner announced approvingly in *The Guardian* that I had "abandoned John Gielgud's musicality for the rush and flow of real thought"; I was pleased of course, but it was actually Gielgud's remorseless speed of thought that I would have liked to emulate rather than his vibrato. At the end of the same term I played Shakespeare's Troilus at the Arts Theatre, so alarming Professor George "Dadie" Rylands, doyen of Shakespearean acting, mentor to Edith Evans, Michael Redgrave and John Gielgud and friend to Anthony Blunt, that he declared concern that I was so emotionally extravagant that if I didn't start to discipline my feelings by learning some technical control or at least an equilibrium, I would surely die young.

O Cressid! O false Cressid! false, false, false!

I continued to howl regardless, pinned against the stone proscenium at the Arts (it was still there when I played Lear there fifty years later), and it's possible that I looked less like Troilus betrayed by his lover than a premature Archie Rice as played by Laurence Olivier in *The Entertainer*, betrayed by his son's death for Britain, for which he chose exactly the same rather out-of-date posture for his grief.

It was Georg Wilhelm Friedrich Hegel who declared that all great historical phenomena appear twice (Karl Marx felt he didn't go far enough, and should have added that the first time is invariably as tragedy and the second as farce). I don't accept this, as I would rather not condemn fifty per cent of my own work as being less good than the other fifty per cent, and I might have to spend my life deciding which: Hamlet in 1964 or 1980; King Lear in 2014 or 2016, Berowne in *Love's Labour's Lost* in 1965 (I went on as the understudy for a stretch) or 1978; Angelo and the Duke in *Measure for Measure* (1974 and 1978 respectively), the 2020 *Tempest*, when I added Prospero both to my Marlborough version and to my 1974 Ferdinand. Two Ronald Harwoods (*Collaboration* and *Taking Sides* – both twice), two Eduardo de Filippos (*Filumena Marturano* and *Il Sindaco del Rione Sanità*), two Alan Bennetts (*The Madness of George III* and *Single Spies*), two *Seagull*s and two *Three Sisters* but no *Vanya* or *Cherry Orchard*, two *Timon*s, three *Troilus*es if you include Cambridge, two *Winter's Tale*s, two *Macbeth*s, three American Indians, including the Christmas specials, and two prolonged RSC residencies.

However, to reduce Hegel's grand image to scale, I do say that in my profession you truly can be said to walk in your own footsteps, sometimes feeling their incompatibility: at any rate a career is perhaps only credible if it, and the account of it I'm attempting here, is more circular than chronological: you keep revisiting plays and hopefully doing them better. At that time such an idea surprised me: I had no idea that not only *Hamlet* was going to be a regular stop (five productions) but that *Troilus and Cressida* (three, for all its difficulties) was also to become a travelling companion for most of my working life, never far from reach. For the moment, *Troilus* Number 1 had got me my first job: the RSC sent their casting director (Maurice Daniels) to Cambridge to see our production and he declared himself delighted as he presented me with an offer. Intent on delivering their seven-play History Cycle *The Wars of the Roses* in Stratford that year, Peter Hall's and John Barton's Company had run out of spear-carriers (the historical drama's equivalent of a *corps de ballet*) halfway through the season. Would I care to join for its second half to be one of the imports thrown into the ensemble pool, with nary a word to say but at least breathing the same air as Ian Holm, Peggy Ashcroft, David Warner, Donald Sinden and the rest? I understood that I would have, rather than lines to speak, a multitude of quick changes and not much movement (except an occasional rush off to deliver a message to my Lord of Something), but with ample scope for mute face-pulling in response to the ever-changing action – all the more so since I was one of a group that for purely practical reasons swiftly changed loyalties from scene to scene, from the red rose to the white, from archbishop to bolshie citizen – a mimetic test for a beginner forbidden to open his mouth. I jumped at it, while my contemporaries made more orthodox professional debuts (proper parts with speeches) around the country in various of the still-vibrant seasonal repertory companies: John Shrapnel began as Claudio in *Much Ado* at Nottingham Playhouse under the directorship of another of my heroes, John Neville; Robin Ellis was at the Everyman Cheltenham as one of Tamburlaine the Great's warlike sons – having so much trouble with his over-loose tights, he now tells me, that his agent commented after the first night: "Robin – do wear a jockstrap tomorrow". (That Company was led by Dorothy Reynolds – in *Salad Days* – and her husband, Angus Mackay, and they were known as the Lunts of Cheltenham.) Robin then went to Salisbury to play Jack in *Charley's Aunt* and stayed for eighteen months, before arriving in the West End as Jack Absolute in *The Rivals* at the Haymarket with Ralph Richardson. By October of that year John Cleese would be in the West End and on his way to Broadway and the Ed Sullivan Show with the Footlights Revue *Cambridge Circus*; at the same time, Trevor Nunn (who'd directed it) was joining the RSC as an assistant director after a stretch at the Belgrade Coventry, beginning his four-year progress to artistic director, under the tutelage of Peter Hall. He started with a life-changing production of Tourneur's (authorship now disputed) *The Revenger's Tragedy* in 1965.

So mine was hardly a big break, but at least I followed my lifelong habit of bouncing from one thing into the next over a weekend (from prep school to Marlborough to the Youth Theatre to Cambridge to Stratford), arriving by the Avon a couple of days after graduating to become, without much anxiety, approximately sixteenth supernumerary from the left.

In fact I was very ready even for the banalities of minor employment. Did I not now have Katharine Barker, a professional actress, for a girlfriend? And already in the West End; having graduated just recently she had been playing at the Phoenix Theatre opposite

Kenneth More in Giles Cooper's *Out of the Crocodile* while I was still at Cambridge. We would meet at Valotti's Café, opposite the theatre at the Holborn end of Shaftesbury Avenue, whenever we could; I fell in with the crowd of very kind and friendly actors in there who were working up and down the Avenue and came in for pre-show eggs and bacon after a long day at home – in which, they always seemed to say, they had been "doing their accounts" – a muskily agreeable hint of the professional life to a neophyte such as me. This was the moment when I suddenly thought I might be able to survive in this world and make a life out of what had once been a game in my garden.

It helped that before leaving Cambridge I had had a truly Damascene moment with a play that's now more or less forgotten. *The Connection* by Jack Gelber had been a big hit in 1959 for the Living Theatre, already legendary for pioneering Brecht and Cocteau in New York and more or less defining off-Broadway. Edward Albee, Norman Mailer and Allen Ginsberg were huge fans of the play; Ken Tynan raved about it, declaring that audiences kept coming back to the production like a Moscow audience dropping into the Art Theatre from time to time to see how those three sisters were getting on. However, on its arrival in London in 1961 *The Connection* had been sturdily booed by its West End audience. Then it filtered down into rep and to students. I doubt if the reps wanted it, but at Cambridge we jumped on it. Self-governing undergraduates, we, like the Americans, had done our Cocteau and Brecht and Henry Miller too, so we reckoned we were nearly as cool as the Living Theatre.

But *The Connection* was something else again. It had a perfect Aristotelian Unity: it was a single evening – shockingly for the time – given over to the apparently random ramblings of a group of New York junkies holed up (literally) in an attic waiting for their connection (the Cowboy) to arrive with the magic bag of heroin and other variants. It was a big long wait in real time, with lengthy jazz improvisations: we had remarkable players like Lionel Grigson and Paul Zec at Cambridge then. A couple of times a character silently came on with a phonograph and played two minutes of Charlie

Parker and then wordlessly left again. The play was a little ahead of its time, and would have done better later, in the freeform late 1960s – like *Captain Jack's Revenge*, only weirder. I was thought fit to play the central role and honcho junkie Leach: Warren Finnerty had won an Obie for his performance in New York. Me, I was bona fide qualified in the avant-garde: after all, I'd done *Death of a Salesman* (as Richard Eyre's brother and John Shrapnel's son) and *Waiting for Godot*, so, as a Lee Strasberg devotee, I was ready for the enigmatic Leach.

The Connection had a light dusting of Pirandello on it. It opened with a film crew arriving to film the local junkies, whom they'll pay in dope – the latter were there as the audience came in, glaring and hostile. I had bought myself a cowboy shirt, as like Finnerty's as I could find: it still hangs like a piece of papyrus in my wardrobe. I sloped around Cambridge muttering like an addict on the loose; I barely washed. I regaled relative strangers in the Copper Kettle Café with Leach's stoned delight that man just might be transparent, his shadow created by different shades of black. Leach comes tottering on first, cutting up a pineapple and wincing at a bad boil on his neck, so of course I developed (and was) a distinct pain in the neck myself. I came to understand how junkies self-fictionalise. Though all Leach wants is "that taste, that little taste", the one thing I didn't do was the main(line) thing about him – nobody had tackled shooting up on the stage in those days – but I learned how it was done and did a thorough impersonation. I re-read *On the Road* and thought of myself as a real gone cat – maybe Leach was a little like Dean Moriarty – and I was completely and unchallengeably hip for a month. We achieved a fainting a night when, unable to get his "flash", Leach overdosed, his "frail line of life and death swinging in a silent breeze".

The reviews thundered that the play was "boring and unnecessary", but I was rather sternly commended for "facing up for the first time at Cambridge to the full responsibilities of a serious part" – as if I already had a career worthy of retrospection. In very truth though, I began to see what being an actor would involve – a completely alternative life generated from within yourself but based on people you really know nothing about and carrying echoes of people you do – and that I hadn't made a mistake in choosing it. I was in heaven with my feet on the ground: oddly, as I squeezed my boil, whinged and strapped my arm, I discovered the perverse dignity of my job. The local rag may have called it A Play We Could Do Without, but I'm certain my twenty-year-old acting self couldn't have done. At the very least, when within ten years I came to do *Captain Jack's Revenge*, though I was still heroin-free, I was well prepared for drinking illegal hootch by the neck.

I think too it was at Cambridge, while failing to attend to my studies, that I first heard about the Moberly-Jourdain Incident. This is not like the Higgs boson or anything of such broad human consequence, but the story of two middle-aged Oxford academics, Charlotte Anne Moberly and Eleanor Jourdain, who took a holiday in Versailles in 1901. After their return, they claimed that while walking in the Palace Gardens they'd gone back in time to the period of the French Revolution and even encountered Marie Antoinette, sitting sketching on the grass in her summer dress. Ten years later they wrote a book about it (why so long?), under pseudonyms (why the shyness?), and *An Adventure* became a bestseller despite (or because of) the inevitable ridicule. It was even adapted for television, with Wendy Hiller.

Readers learned that, unimpressed by the Palace and finding the Grand Trianon closed, the ladies had set a course to the Petit Trianon, a small château in the grounds. But they got lost (despite their Baedekers – how?); then, starting down a lane, Charlotte noticed a length of cloth being shaken out of a window as if just washed, and Eleanor encountered an old deserted farmhouse with an ancient plough in its yard. They realised that they had experienced a phenomenon which is nowadays taken quite seriously, a timeslip; whereupon a feeling of oppression and dreariness came over them. In fact they don't seem to have enjoyed themselves very much at all this extraordinary afternoon. A couple of men looking like eighteenth-century palace gardeners told them to keep going straight on. They passed "very dignified officials, dressed in long greyish green coats with small three-cornered hats", and noticed a woman offering a jug to a girl in the doorway of a cottage – this bit is quite painterly, and indeed Jourdain was to describe it as a living picture – which begins to give the game away.

Moberly didn't see the cottage, but certainly sensed an unnatural and unpleasant atmosphere: the trees flat and lifeless, like wood worked in a tapestry, no light and shade and no wind. Close now to the Temple of Love, they found a man of "dark and rough complexion" seated beside a garden kiosk, in a cloak and large shady hat. Moberly thought his appearance "most repulsive… its expression odious". Turning to them, he revealed a face marked by smallpox, its expression evil and unseeing. Then another man in a sombrero showed them the way to the Petit Trianon and there was Marie Antoinette, sitting on the grass. At first Moberly thought she was a tourist, but since her dress looked old-fashioned, she realised that of course it must be Marie Antoinette. Jourdain, however, didn't see her at all.

The couple then had tea at the Hotel des Reservoirs before returning to Jourdain's apartment. One would imagine they would have had quite a bit to talk about, but they later claimed that they didn't discuss the incident at all until a week later. For three months, they then compared notes and did a little post facto research, coming up with the already known facts that in August 1792 the Tuileries palace in Paris was besieged, the King's Swiss guards massacred and the monarchy itself abolished in short order. They later went back to Versailles but found nothing out of the ordinary, and were never able to find the mysterious path, the kiosk or the bridge.

When *An Adventure* was published various theories made themselves heard amidst the cries of mockery. Perhaps the ladies had stumbled across a private (modern) Event: but it transpired that nothing had been booked that afternoon. Perhaps they had strangely visited an equivalent ancient one: the political philosopher Charles Montesquieu had lived nearby and reportedly gave parties in the grounds in which his friends performed *tableaux vivants* as part of the entertainment. Perhaps the Marie-Antoinette figure was a society lady or a male cross-dresser, and the pockmarked man Montesquieu himself. It was acknowledged that such a gathering of the decadent French avant-garde of the time would have made a sinister impression on two imaginative middle-class Edwardian spinsters unused to such things.

More recently a theory has edged to the surface that the whole thing was a shared delusion arising out of a lesbian folie à deux between the women. Or at least an "hallucinatory experience", embellished over time after the fact. They had certainly chosen a good historical moment for casting their list of characters, with Marie Antoinette as the star. On the other hand, in 1903, an old map of the Trianon gardens had been found showing the bridge that the two women claimed to have crossed: interestingly, it had not been seen on any previous map.

The identity of the authors of *An Adventure* was not made public until 1931. Meanwhile, it had emerged that Moberly had also claimed to have seen an apparition of the Roman Emperor Constantine in the Louvre in 1914, noticing him to be a man of unusual height in a gold crown and a toga; he was not observed by anybody else. And during the First World War, Jourdain, by then Principal of St Hugh's College Oxford, became convinced that a German spy was hiding among her students.

At this point one begins to lose faith; still, I've always wanted to believe this story. Obviously, it tells us as much about the psychological dynamics of the pair as about the paranormal: I too have read J. W. Dunne's *Experiment With Time*, and I'm quite comfortable with the thought that this overlaying of one picture over another, one time over another, becomes a more insistent habit the further your memory is able to stretch. For me particularly though, it touches one of the vital nerves from which theatre is generated. You can see the same adventurousness in Tom Stoppard's *Arcadia*, and more or less every time a ghost appears in Shakespeare to bring images of the past to perturb the protagonist, without disturbing his sense of the freezing battlements around them in the present or the nature of the argument he is having with his mother, or the regal Entertainment he is hosting. For of course the story has a tremendous sense of theatre, or at least theatricality. Leaving aside the possible criminality or hoax element, the whole story makes the couple sound like two actors researching for a *mise-en-scène* of three hundred years ago, maybe for a TV series, as they seek ways to get every little bit of the story authentic, having seen under its skin and into its bone.

It's what we all do, all the time; you are at liberty to substitute your own favourites here, but I offer you my own preferences from way back: how did McKellen and Dench convince you that they were the Macbeths, or Bob Peck that his children had been murdered in the same show? Or Scofield that he saw the jaguar, also acknowledging the possibility of a happy marriage to a woman he admits he is unhappily bound to? Or Michael Redgrave as Uncle Vanya giggling at himself like a wayward child as he contemplates his failure to kill his enemy at point-blank range or dreams of cuddling up to Yeliena precisely because it is impossible. We all dig deep for this, and since there's no pecking order here and as this is after all my book, I will propose myself as having persuaded Lyric Theatre audiences nightly that I was indeed the murderous Raskolnikov in *Crime and Punishment* (1983) or the ruminative old horse in *Strider* (1984) while simultaneously at some collusive level reminding them that I was nothing of the sort. Every time we succeed we are in charge of time, and our job becomes to nurse and guide our audience. We may not have the same outrageously vivid imaginations of these two ladies, who saw no limit to what it can achieve, but in this sense too I do often have the sensation of walking in my own footsteps or a little in front of them, of a perpetually adjusting déjà vu.

Time was nearly up. What really had I been doing in the privilege of Cambridge? I went to very few lectures, and then usually because I was interested in the physical mannerisms of the lecturers – Leavis's advancing senescence or Raymond Williams's ardent socialism – rather than their views on George Eliot. In my final year I relished going to see my supervisor in his home: he was young and recently married, and I enjoyed teasing him about his obvious exhaustion when I arrived just before nine in the morning. But I didn't go dancing, or rowing, or even socialised much; and I started to work for my exams each year at the last available moment. I wasn't terribly sociable, except with a chosen few – John Shrapnel, Robin Ellis,

Carey Harrison. No wonder my father was hurt. I don't think I ever dined in Hall, as he had with Anthony Blunt – I must have been permanently out of pocket at the Corner House. Unfortunately he had passed away by the time I came to play Blunt in Alan Bennett's *Single Spies*.

The answer of course is that I was trying to make Cambridge as much like a drama school as I could. By my third, graduating year, what it couldn't provide I was looking about for, such as going to a freelance voice teacher in London to learn how to laugh technically when I might not feel like it. University at that time was never a form of drama training and undergraduate actors who'd spent most of their time performing rarely went on to drama school; the one example I know of then left RADA after the first year because he already knew all he needed to after twenty productions at the ADC. But, for all that, the doing of the plays, the love affairs, the impassioned conversations were very much as I might have had at Drama School, albeit they were conducted in a relatively remote part of the Fens rather than in the West End.

So did I waste my time there, and if not, what had I learned? An instinct both for stage realism and for deep digging into myself in order to play realistically in *The Connection*; appreciating the sheer theatrical aspect, were it ever to be exploited, of *An Adventure*, both of which helped rather than hindered me in developing some sense of stage improvisation.

Autodidact and *Guardian*-reviewed actor with a 2:1, I was ready to get going in another sense too. Latterly at Cambridge I had developed the habit of staying out of my digs and dossing at the house on Parkers Piece of the Stage Manager of the ADC – not an undergraduate but an experienced professional, Michael Vaughan, as good at his job as his cricketing namesake. He and his wife also put up actors passing through Cambridge to play at the Arts for the week, such as Joan Littlewood's Theatre Workshop Company, and I became able not only to understand a good deal about stage management and lighting (which many actors don't) but to sense in the talk of Brian Phelan and Victor Spinetti, say, the serious but lightly borne responsibilities of the job, more akin to the work of a carpenter than a dreamer – or perhaps a carpenter scrupulously reconstructing a dream they once had. And in that cherished aim, as Nina says in *The Seagull*, you can never cheat.

I had also by then finally parted with Gillian, in a melancholy *Brief Encounter* farewell ceremony at King's Cross Station: as, after a brief visit, she steamed away into the arms of Derby Playhouse's character man, I found myself so upset that I travelled twice around the Circle Line before I could bring myself to get off, go home and raise a smile of greeting for my parents, who lived only a few stops away from King's Cross. But what the hell, I'd got a job. I'd started. So there you are, Miss Diva of Derby Playhouse:

With Paul Scofield in Savages *(1973)*.

A TOUR OF MOUNT RUSHMORE

It's sometimes said that a much-loved performer is "inimitable": it's up there with "magnificent" and "superb". It's also improbable. Paul Scofield, Laurence Olivier, John Gielgud, Ralph Richardson, Alec Guinness, Michael Redgrave, and Peggy Ashcroft, Sybil Thorndike and Edith Evans, generally seen as the Olympians of my lifetime (which I roughly measure as the post-Henry Irving but pre-Mark Rylance years), are highly imitable (the first four especially), and any impersonation is usually done with profound respect rather than satirically. A passable Olivier or Gielgud is a commonplace; as it happens I do the best version of Paul Scofield that I know of. I even ventured it at his Memorial Service, where it was well appreciated, and I hope he didn't rotate.

Among living Olympians, Ian McKellen is a bit trickier to catch, which is no reflection on him but maybe the trend is changing. On the other hand, Ian himself is fascinated by his predecessors. Once he and I were part of a large celebration of John Gielgud; Scofield was topping the bill with Prospero's great invocation of the elves of hills, brooks, standing lakes and groves, at the end of which he breaks his staff and drowns his book. I'd happened to turn up at the theatre a couple of hours before the show, and came upon him rehearsing his piece. I heard him before I saw him: and the hairs on my neck rose as they had when I used to crouch in the wings watching him play Timon at Stratford forty years earlier.

Come showtime, everybody – contributors, drama students acting as dressers for the evening, stage management, McKellen and I – packed the wings to watch Scofield, all of us drawn to the flame. As the latter stepped with his peculiar delicacy but vast presence onto the stage, Ian turned to me and said in amazement: "He does just the same thing as we do – he checks his flies are closed at the last moment before he goes on." It was completely charming and entirely genuine: for a moment, Ian, for all his tremendous achievement, was looking at Scofield as something close to God; the checking of the flies being a beguiling touch of nature that truly does make us all kin.

These are memories that extend over what Leontes in *The Winter's Tale* calls a "great gap of time" and you'll note that they're not of big speeches. In fact, Paul Scofield was a giggler: one night as Timon, he momentarily slipped into a speech of similar rhythm from *Hamlet*:

> There's ne'er a villain dwelling in all Denmark
> But he's an arrant knave…

This is Hamlet embarking on his feigned madness, having discovered the crimes of King Claudius. Timon, rather less impressively, dispatches the Poet and Painter, who've visited him in his seclusion, with:

> There's never a one of you but trusts a knave
> That mightily deceives you…

However, in his high-speed extrication from trouble, Paul for this one night instinctively favoured Hamlet's version, simply substituting "Athens" for "Denmark". As he corrected himself, he playfully tut-tutted the audience as if they had made him do it. It didn't matter at all; he was working at such a depth that we could even absorb the idea of the actor momentarily playing Hamlet by mistake. I for one took my hat off to him: it left me wondering if, if ever my time were to come, I would have the same chutzpah.

And just to season my admiration, I did notice many years later, during the run of *Savages,* that he was having a little touch of stage fright. So he was human, and I marvelled at his occasional frailties. And there were nights he looked a bit like Danny la Rue – he did tend towards slightly old-fashioned make-up, such as an orange base and mascara. This made him somehow more not less admirable in my eyes.

***

When Scofield did in fact play not one speech but the entirety of Prospero in *The Tempest,* in 1975, it was very much disliked by John Gielgud, himself a famous and quite frequent interpreter of the part; he confided in me later that he had slipped away from the theatre without going round to see Scofield afterwards, apparently much to the latter's ire – it is indeed rather unusual among Mount Rushmore figures not to pay their respects to each other, come what may. And in fact Gielgud's feelings about Paul (who was, like Chekhov, universally loved for his niceness), were ambiguous: he felt the younger man had a high level of vanity and touchiness (who doesn't?), and warned me not to be deceived by his spectacular and apparently saintly amiability. I could see that: clearly Scofield the Complex Man had invented a character called Scofield the Nice which he then played to perfection, and which gave him ample protection from all sorts of slings and arrows.

This kind of dissembling, if that's what it was, is not unusual, though very unlike Gielgud himself, part of whose charm was his complete inability to counterfeit in civilian life: his greatest talent apart from acting was putting his foot in his mouth while dropping a multitude of bricks. To my great good fortune, he took to me: his friend the playwright Charles Wood had told him that mine was the Hamlet (1980) that he, John, would most have liked to see after his own repeated visits to the part over the years; he was happy to accept Wood's judgement as a friend without coming to see it, so everyone stayed happy.

I had been introduced to Gielgud in 1978, when Natasha Parry, Peter Brook's wife, took me for Sunday lunch at his country headquarters in the South Pavilion of Wotton House, near Aylesbury. He would live there till the end of his life in 2000, but when I went he'd been in residence for a short time only; perhaps because of a momentary lapse in the Hollywood section of his career, he complained continuously about not really having "the dough" to keep the house going – a problem his successors Tony and Cherie Blair don't seem to have had.

Gielgud was extremely funny, though his view of his contemporaries was even then tinged by a certain *méchanterie*. He chuckled at the memory of Edith Evans (allegedly) refusing to make love to her husband on any night when she had a matinée the next day – I don't quite know how Gielgud would have known that, but any gossip delighted the little boy in him. Having revealed this, he suddenly turned to me – it was a little like seeing a water pistol swivel in your direction – and asked what I was playing that season at Stratford. I listed the parts with a certain pleasure – Euripides' Hippolytus, Berowne in *Love's Labour's Lost* and the Duke in *Measure for Measure* – only to hear him declare that each was quite unplayable, and to name those he remembered to have been the greatest failures.

If this was unnerving it was slightly assuaged ten years later, not only when we were Oedipus and Tiresias in *The Theban Plays* on BBC TV, but when we played a comedy together, John Mortimer's *Summer's Lease*, also on television. He was quite unwell by now, and had to return from the Italian location to England for surgery during shooting. He looked rather worse when he returned to the set (for a scene at the Palio in Siena) until the moment when "Action" was called, when he suddenly blossomed as if in time-lapse photography. And he continued to advise me on a list of parts he thought I should propose myself for to Richard Eyre, then the Director of the National Theatre. These included Goethe's two-part *Faust* – oddly enough a pair of plays I'd made a tentative stab at adapting myself. I pointed out gently that he had grown up at a far less crowded time, when a leading actor could, to some extent, offer his performances to a buyer rather than the other way round. Nowadays, I pointed out, should Richard want to do *Faust*, he'd make a longish list of leading men and work his way through them until he found one who was available.

Apart from his rejection of Scofield as Prospero, jealousy was less common in Gielgud than in any other Olympian I've known. Laurence Olivier died while we were shooting *Summer's Lease*, and nothing could have been more sincerely touching, when we went for a long walk that evening adjusting to the news, than John's appreciation of Olivier, who he felt had a far wider acting range than he did; it was an unforced compliment paid to someone not much noted for his own compliments.

Back in the early 1980s, when I was still playing my Stratford Hamlet, I had been taken to meet this other great predecessor. Olivier, though frail by now, came with that rolling gait of his round the corner of his house in Haywards Heath towards the front garden to meet me. Without noticeably raising his eyes he declared in greeting that he'd spotted that I had blond highlights in my hair to play the part, just as he had in the film: he registered this piece of guile long before face or voice. The fact was of course that I was already a light ash-blond, while his had been a complete makeover of his dark hair. I subdued a retaliatory instinct to hint that my adjustments were much more subtly done than his had been: I may have imitated some things in him, but in that one small detail I was an improvement. In another way, this was a gesture of affable partnership from someone to whom partnering didn't come easily, and it was a great way to break the ice. We had a good talk together – in which he was extremely honest about the aspects of Hamlet he felt he'd never got right. At my admission that I found the graveyard scene tough, he declared his surprise: even Nicol Williamson, he said, who was not half the actor that I was, had found that scene quite easy. It was only on the way home that I realised that not only had he not seen me in the part, but to my near-certain knowledge he hadn't seen Nicol either.

R.I.P. to all these gentlemen. Trekking through the not very vicious brambles of *schadenfreude*, I see now that all in all, I've been lucky in my advocates. Peggy Ashcroft was a champion of a less complicated kind, and was so ever since Stratford in 1964. In the 1980s, she, together with Gielgud, eagerly became a patron of the English Shakespeare Company, which I was setting up with Michael Bogdanov. I was neither surprised nor offended when she called me a few months later, the day after seeing our opening production of *Henry IV*, to say that she and John had greatly admired the acting, particularly the verse-speaking, but they really didn't feel they should be publicly associated with such an iconoclastic modern-dress Company at this point in their lives. This element of touchiness about their own reputations was much more typical of their generation than of ours. Trade approval of innovation comes far more easily these days, carrying little hint of the Establishment approving of the Revolutionary. It's certainly not newsworthy; and Peggy, a great campaigner and a sort of moral force similar to Judi Dench now, may really have been covering for John, who just didn't want to break the news himself and was, ever so slightly, hiding behind her skirts.

I feel gratitude to all these people for their interest, and have also been much entertained by them for life; for instance, there was a day when Gielgud mused to me that he didn't know why he'd never got married; as I drew my breath to remind him why, he added "I never met the right girl, I suppose," which apart from the obvious evasion was no more nor less than the truth. This was his equivalent of Olivier's admitted inability to have a row with his beloved Joan Plowright because he could never resist turning it into a bit of acting, complete with moves.

I owe most to Peggy especially because she confided in me about her loneliness – she was always in love, but rarely settled – and her need to have her transistor radio within arm's length during the night so she could listen to the World Service instead of struggling to sleep. Now her ashes are under a mulberry tree in New Place in Stratford: she, who in 1964 (as we shall see), having directed a brief showcase for me of Lorenzo in *The Merchant of Venice*, strode upstairs to tell Peter Hall that there was a sixteenth footsoldier from the left that he really should keep an eye on for the future. She who years later I took to a modern-dress production of *Troilus and Cressida* at the Barbican by which she was so outraged that, in a voice that filled the theatre, though I was only sitting next to her, she declared she was going to call Trevor Nunn that very night to complain about what he was allowing in the RSC's name (it wasn't his own production). My happier memory of her at the Barbican was when I did the Proposal Scene from *The Importance of Being Earnest* at some fundraiser, astonishingly with her as Gwendolen Fairfax; so I can say I was her Jack Worthing for a few minutes. The last time I saw her was at the campaign to save the Rose Theatre on Bankside, when she presided over the soon-to-be-destroyed site like Queen Canute but in a comfier chair. The drivers charged with demolishing the ruins were delighted, stood themselves down, autographs had to be signed, and all parties came to terms in short order.

I met Alec Guinness only once, in 1967, when I was sent to audition for him for a revival of T. S. Eliot's *The Family Reunion*. The appointment was in his dressing room at the Wyndham's Theatre between his matinée and evening performances of Simon Gray's *Wise Child*, in which he played a hardened criminal forced into drag because he's being blackmailed by a young victim who promises not to reveal his identity if he, Guinness, agrees to impersonate the boy's mother. The play was soon to be thrashed in New York, where it closed after four performances, but it did well in London, whatever that tells you about English and American audiences.

I like to think that Guinness had his dress on as well as his blonde wig when I saw him, but I'm not sure. He was charming, enquiring if I'd ever seen *The Family Reunion*. I had to say no with a simulation of regret, while thinking secretly how much I'd always despised the post-war pre-John Osborne phase of verse plays led by Eliot. I would be surprised if I didn't regularly rail against it in Cambridge at the Copper Kettle or perhaps in Robin Ellis's rooms, and perhaps even denounced it in my final exams to fill out my non-essay on Tennyson, let's say. The interview continued well, and I had no idea anything had changed, until, being as a great actor an expert at detecting falsehood but at first choosing to ignore it, here's how Guinness handled it: he suddenly broke off and apologised for having suddenly, as he thought, become distant those few moments ago – it was only that he'd had a big success with *The Family Reunion*, and he was always startled and unreasonably disappointed when a new generation weren't aware of the fact. This was especially skilful, as I hadn't noticed the cooling-off at all. He went on to be equally honest about the basic condition of being an actor with treasures in the past – even though he also had plenty of them in the present. In a way, he turned *schadenfreude* inside out. On the other hand, I didn't get the job. And as you see, I've remembered it.

Peggy Ashcroft and me in a reading of
The Importance of Being Earnest.

STRATFORD

1964–1965

Ah, but I was so much older then,
I'm younger than that now...
– Bob Dylan, 'My Back Pages'

April 23rd 1964 marked what's commonly seen as the four hundredth anniversary of Shakespeare's birth. On the same day fifty-two years after that, I'd be marking the four hundredth anniversary of his death – thought also to have been on April 23rd – on tour by playing a matinée and evening as King Lear in Northampton; but back then I had arrived in Stratford to do no more than step silently onto the RST stage with the King's crown on a regal cushion for David Warner's Richard II to surrender to Eric Porter's Bolingbroke – the very stage that I had been gawping at almost as intensely as at the Old Vic's for nearly ten years previously. My parents had accompanied me until I left school: my father would take us on the A40 and A41, through the Chilterns via Aylesbury and Banbury (no M40 then, no hint of Coventry); you would come over the crest of the surrounding hills, just glimpsing Stratford in the distance, my father now hoping we had our booking secure at the Shakespeare Hotel, which named its rooms after Shakespearean characters. The oldest of the current staff at the hotel told me not long ago that he remembered me from those days as they've never since had a bespectacled early teenager so longing to be billeted in "Othello" or "Andrew Aguecheek". I've forgotten many of the visits – not the plays but the circumstances – except that I know we drove home from the South of France one year with me suffering a nasty dysentery all the way, recovering just in time to demand a full fry-up on the Channel ferry, as a booster to the immediate prospect of going to Stratford to see *Titus Andronicus,* of all dead-cert nausea-triggers the champion, you would think, even with Laurence Olivier and Vivien Leigh in it. Needless to say I can never thank my beloved Mum and Dad enough for these patient pilgrimages (my father had a particular scorn for Shakespearean comedy). If we went to Stratford on a Saturday we might go for lunch at the Mulberry Tree on Bridge Street before the matinée and once noted that Peter O'Toole was at the next table with friends, and running late; my father felt he was pushing his luck as he was due on stage at 2.30 sharp as Shylock or Thersites, I forget which, and he was still on his steak and wine. It must have bolstered his view, which he occasionally shared with me, that actors were less responsible humans than attorneys such as himself.

In 1964, I spent my first morning in town on the terrace outside the theatre's Green Room (home-made pies and crumbles in those days, nothing rotating at 750 watts) waiting to rehearse and looking across the Avon at the pavilion which housed Richard Buckle's huge but temporary Shakespeare Exhibition, made for the anniversary. It featured mostly recorded speeches, not necessarily written by Shakespeare or even performed by actors, some life-size cut-outs of the plays' characters, and laborious guesses as to what daily life in Shakespeare's Stratford might have felt like. It was heavily criticised for its ardent emphasis on the tourist trade, just as David Garrick's ambitious Shakespeare Jubilee had been in 1769. As for me, I was thinking what luck was mine to be part of the live events on my side of the river, albeit with only my crown and cushion, struck dumb and almost motionless by the great events of Shakespeare's history plays around me – murder and mayhem, realpolitik and usurpation, delivered by the best. The RSC were doing near-enough the lot that season, from *Richard II* right through to *Richard III*. Of all the plays of Shakespeare, the three parts of *Henry VI* (plays five, six and seven in this sequence) were the only ones I hadn't seen at the Old Vic in the 1950s: they had had a short run during one Marlborough term-time and the Headmaster informed my father that he couldn't "set a precedent" by letting me dash up to London for the weekend to see them. Perhaps he imagined the school suddenly emptying as its pupils likewise raced *en masse* to see the least well-known of Shakespeare's plays; or perhaps he thought it would turn me into a murderous insurrectionist like Jack Cade in *Henry VI Part Two*.

By now, the effect of joining the Royal Shakespeare Company untrained and very wet behind the ears was to feel a mix of reckless self-confidence and maximum shyness. While Robin Ellis and John Shrapnel were hard at work in manageably small regional repertory houses, here I was in this army – or two armies, Lancastrian and Yorkist, in rotation from scene to scene – silent but helpful-looking, doing what the kings and queens required. Everyone around me was going about their business when I arrived at rehearsals – some took a moment to greet and encourage me and get the new name right, others ignored. Some friendships were quickly formed, and many nodding acquaintanceships. Professional camaraderie being what it is, there was kind protectiveness everywhere, as if I'd just jumped onto a fast-moving bus between stops. What startled me most in this baptism was the relative playfulness of such a crack troupe, which included a fair amount of corpsing, even in the most tragic or complex *mise-en-scènes*; I was exchanging the earnest humourlessness of most student actors for the apparent frivolity of far more famous ones, serious artists who still liked a joke, who got on with their quotidian lives up to the very moment they stepped transformationally onto the stage, and which they resumed once off it. So much so that the notable Nicholas Selby, a kind and paternally inclined man playing the villainous Cardinal of Winchester in *Henry VI* in a great prelate's gown, had made an art of it: I was tipped off that he always wore long costumes like that, whatever the part, so that he could under-dress in his own civilian trousers and thus make a quicker getaway at the end of the evening. Imagine my shock. It was the same Nick Selby who, answering a query from another newcomer as to why he wore such elaborate make-up as the Cardinal, replied that the rulebook said he had to be in his dressing room by the half-hour call like everyone else, and it gave him something to pass the time. Imagine my mixed feelings too that in the wings of the set for *The Wars of the Roses* were a number of large loudspeakers that conveyed Guy Woolfenden's score powerfully through the house; on the stage right speaker, during *Richard III*, Ian Holm generally saw an opportunity for doing some courting between his endless taxing scenes as Richard, and would be perched on this speaker with his current *innamorata*, whom he subsequently married.

He also took his mischief onto the stage, sometimes in the interests of his own high standards. There's a scene in *Richard III* when Richard appeals to a large group of citizens who he hopes will support his claim to the crown. For better effect, he wears a cassock and comes across as a holy man as he goes walkabout among them. It was determined one night that everyone he'd murdered up till that point should reproachfully mix in with the crowd of citizens, also dressed as monks. The main intention was to get Ian to corpse, an unprecedented thing for him; however, he spotted the trick in a flash, strode up to each of the newcomers in turn, plucked back their hoods and revealed Charlie Kay, Roy Dotrice and Janet Suzman. Ian didn't turn a hair (he never did); he had just smoothly taken over the trick, and we all admired him even more, especially we newcomers.

Elsewhere, being so used to fighting callow sectarian battles with other university aspirants and going sulkily back to my digs (but rarely to a lecture), I now had to adjust to being on the same stage as workaday professionals of every age, gender and persuasion, many of whom had spent a lifetime in the service and who had families (or stubborn solitudes) and seemingly limitless experience: Brewster Mason, Hugh Griffith, Clifford Rose, John Normington, Janet Suzman, Patience Collier. And many others who are now dead, less famous but notably kind to a beginner, none more so than the gay ones (the UK was still three years short of legalisation) who were without exception the warmest and most tolerant members of the Company – and invariably extremely butch on the stage: this, after all, was *The Wars of the Roses*, the world of Young Clifford and Sir John Talbot, of Jack Cade, the monstrous Queen Margaret and the bottled spider Richard III, to which I would be returning more purposefully twenty years later with my own company.

The greatest benefit of joining such an outfit so early and in such a very junior position was the immediate after-care involving in-house re-auditions in front of the directors and subsequent "studio" work behind closed doors that every newcomer was busied with, having once got the job. This was a means of assessment by the management of an apparently inert rump of (possibly talented) walk-ons – not all of whose names the resident directors necessarily knew, having ordered them in bulk via the casting department. For our part, we could stretch our wings a bit in the hope of dropping a broad hint about our future usefulness to the Company. I did one such audition for Peter Hall himself, who responded to my rendition of Troilus' final speech about the death of Hector, still fresh in my memory from the undergraduate production that had got me the job:

> Hector is dead… There is no more to say.
> Stay yet; you vile abominable tents,
> Thus proudly pight upon our Phrygian plains,
> Let Titan rise as early as he dare
> I'll through and through you;
> And thou great-sized coward,
> No space of earth shall sunder our two hates;
> I'll haunt thee like a wicked conscience still
> That mouldest goblins swift as frenzy's thoughts…

– by proposing that, no question, I should stay with the RSC and work my way up through its ranks indefinitely, as Ian Holm and Roy Dotrice, their current stars, had done. I later did, as part of this process, the showcase rehearsal of Lorenzo and Jessica in the garden at Belmont that I mentioned earlier, directed by Peggy Ashcroft – the start of a friendship that lasted till her death in 1991, and in which she championed me at every opportunity. Oh, and was briefly directed in another showcase by John Barton – who many years later directed me as Hamlet, for which he'd fought heroically for over ten years – as Alcibiades to Tim West's Socrates, and also a bit of Aeschylus' *The Persians* directed by the legendary Michel Saint-Denis. Oh, and delivered myself of some of John Donne's raciest love poems. Before I left eighteen months later I had also worked with Peter Brook for the first time, and felt his unique mix of affection and rigour in a public reading of Peter Weiss's *The Investigation*, about the Frankfurt Auschwitz Trials, which was perhaps the most grown-up thing I did (as Nazi Defendant Stark) in that first period, though we played it for only one evening.

And I did attract a certain amount of minor glamour from the start as a result of already going out with the resident Princess of France in *Henry V*, who was genuinely popular. While I was still at Cambridge, Katharine had been more or less a rumour to my friends (a real professional actress – what street-cred for me); in fact she had already scored her success opposite Ian Holm as King Henry, so I could bask a bit – much as I had tried to do with Gillian at Derby, but without having to sleep beside some new boyfriend, though I was privately a little suspicious of David Warner's attentions in relation to Katharine. Initially she was installed to the east of Stratford in digs in Tiddington, while I had a little cottage at a tactical distance due north up the Birmingham Road (91 Oakfield Road) which cost 50 per cent of my £12 a week salary (it was suddenly raised after a few weeks to £14 for no declared reason) – thus breaking my father's unwritten rule that your rent should never be more than a quarter of your income. Before long we conceived the idea of a wedding in the autumn, perhaps in Holy Trinity Church to please our parents.

Stratford was very different then, a market town with considerable charm and nothing like so much tourism. Baileys the family grocer (all local produce), and their rival Pearce's, who still used weighing machines with weights, the Ann Hathaway Tea Rooms, where sitting almost permanently we could find and gossip over apple pie with the wise and wonderful Madoline Thomas, an Abergavenny girl who took up acting on the death of her husband in her fifties (she lived till 99); walks along the river, the great singing teacher Denne Gilkes (and her cats), who'd arrived in Stratford from Scotland in 1936, remaining for her further thirty-six years to teach voice production and singing for what was then not the RST but the Shakespeare Memorial Theatre. In the large panelled music room in her "ruined palazzo" over a grocer's in the High Street she taught Laurence Olivier, Vanessa Redgrave, Ian Richardson, Diana Rigg, Paul Scofield and Donald Sinden. Musically, she couldn't do anything much for me though.

In that October of 1964 Katharine and I were married over Shakespeare's dead body in Trinity Church: the great Roy Dotrice told me fifty years later that he still remembered the price tag on the soles of my new shoes when I knelt, submitting to my vow, on the altar steps, as well as recalling that his daughter Karen sang *Where Have All the Flowers Gone* instead of *Jesu Joy of Man's Desiring* during the service. Anthony Gooch, a Cambridge friend who later went into MI6, came up on the Friday with perhaps my best friend by now, Robin Ellis, who was therefore cast as my Best Man, and slept on the floor of my little suburban cottage. On our big day Robin delivered a very good Best Man speech – so I'm told: Kate and I had to leave before he'd finished as we were nearly at the half-hour call for the matinée of *Richard III*. This we followed with a weekend honeymoon at the Welcombe Hotel, out in the fields towards Warwick. Charlton Heston was staying there too and was at the next table for the torrentially wet Sunday lunch, but he didn't say he'd been at the wedding. Or the theatre. Kate and I were rather silent too, happy enough if a little reflective: we were 22 and 21, and nobody gave us a chance. They were wrong in the short term and right in the long. In due course, twenty months of it, I was to become a father: Mark, conceived in those enchanted days by the Avon, and born a fortnight after we won the World Cup (of which more later), has illuminated my life ever since.

Soon we moved to a flat by the river, which we rattled around in, listening to the Beatles and warmed up by Katharine's lamb stew; but I felt like a fully paid-up pro, observing the last moments of Alec Douglas-Home before Harold Wilson slipped into power on 15th October on a majority of four seats.

Meanwhile, watching Ian Holm in action (I mean onstage as

Richard III), bunched like a street fighter and pulling off the trick of mixing absolute realism with an impassioned swing in the verse in a way that I'd never witnessed till then and would not often afterwards, formed a large part of my education. This astonishing actor, with the instincts of the great film performer he was to become, and a devastating vocal power in the theatre, was an absolute model. In fact, I came to know him quite well, not at the time but later, when oddly enough *Savages*, which I'd been in with Scofield, was done again on radio – I reprised my part and Ian played the lead. As we worked, he invited me to the country for the weekend but as it happened I couldn't go and he never asked again, so he had a star's sensibility all right. He later suffered the kind of devastating nervous breakdown that seems to be reserved for the most dependable great actors, topped off with a persistent claustrophobia. There followed a phase when I quite often played squash with him, and I noticed that he had to leave the door onto the court, which normally sits flush to the back wall, slightly open, or off the latch; he also played as close to that rear wall as possible instead of rushing forward and sideways to score his points. The anxiety that caught hold of him on the squash court – and I suppose elsewhere – reminded me of nobody so much as his own Richard III at a moment I've never forgotten. This was when Richard, finally arriving in his tent the night before the climactic battle of Bosworth, and despite his apparent brash self-consciousness, glanced round at the small battalion of storm-troopers he had surrounded himself with and suddenly seemed strangely frightened by them, scanning each one in the tent as if searching for a friend, rather than foes he'd simply bullied into submission. The silent anxiety he conveyed in this – you would have thought – impervious character was the final resolution of an already brilliant performance – a triumphant example of playing "against" character in order to deepen it – and heartbreaking. And now here he was with me, frightened of the door of the squash court and the world on both sides of it.

Female friends of mine who have been chatted up by Ian do report that he always said the same thing as they trudged through the fields on a first date: that he was tired of being everyone's favourite "quality" actor but still not a star. So he was available for confession – with women at least; he was thought a little taciturn by many men. I did get to know him better at the Harold Pinter Festival in Dublin in the 1990s, when (now married to Penelope Wilton) he came round after a performance of *One for the Road* and asked me how I had achieved a particular vocal effect he'd noticed – as if he was a drama student. Believe me, that'll do for me: being asked for advice by God is sometimes how friendship works in the theatre.

Right at the end of 1964 *The Wars of the Roses* was filmed by the BBC. If you look at this TV version, which lay unreleased for half a century but is now available, among other scheming Dukes you will witness Donald Sinden and particularly Brewster Mason, a giant of a man who could still a riot by simply appearing at it; in his role as Warwick the Kingmaker he wore soft boots which gave the lie to his considerable bulk and allowed him to move in complete, riveting silence. If you watch the DVD please allow yourself to imagine the night during the run when he gained my affection for life by the subtlest of errors. As you watch the TV, when he defies the Yorkists on one battlefield, you hear him roaring:

> I am the head, the body and the limbs
> Of Lancaster…

It was a chilling moment, but on this occasion he got in a tangle, thus:

> I am the bod,
> (An indecisive pause for thought, followed by great firmness)
> The heady and the limbs of Lancaster…

By the time we filmed *The Wars of the Roses* that November I had also made eternal friends of Charles Kay and Janet Suzman, who taught me to play bridge – the unofficial RSC Green Room game of choice, far more so than poker or chess: there were those, Roy Dotrice among them, with such *sang froid* that they could hear their entrance call coming through on the tannoy, calmly bid and indeed play a hand, before jet-propelling onto the stage as Hotspur or Edward IV or Jack Cade.

Best of all in a way was to watch my new friend Peggy Ashcroft. On the same backstage loudspeaker as that on which Ian Holm did his courting, on the nights we were playing *Edward IV* (John Barton's condensation of *Henry VI Parts Two* and *Three*) Peggy could be seen instead, seated in a deep reverie as she prepared to pull off one of the nastiest and most challenging scenes in the entire Shakespearean canon – when Queen Margaret captures the rebel Duke of York (Donald Sinden), places him on a molehill, smears his face with a handkerchief dipped in his murdered son's blood, puts a paper crown on his head and torments him before executing him. It is one of Shakespeare's earliest triumphs: such is his descriptive range that you can almost see York's tears mingle with the blood on the handkerchief, the one thinning and diluting the other like soiled laundry under a tap. At the same time, there are passages of super-Marlovian rhetorical violence as the pair slug it out that anticipate the Shakespeare of *King Lear*. The master playwright is announcing his arrival, fully equipped to compete in heroic poetry but also touching in the most intimate human detail as nobody had before, and perhaps nobody since.

This being my first job and being somewhat Method-inclined, I assumed that Peggy's raptness as she sat on her speaker was a profound Stanislavskian preparation for the challenge ahead – until the day I noticed on her John-Bury-designed encrusted leather armour, just at the neck, a telltale clip. On further observation I saw that it was a transistor radio – no headphones in those days – on which she was listening to the third Test Match against Australia at Headingley, before stepping insouciantly into the Shakespearean bullring. Her raptness may have been at the fact that Australia was unexpectedly winning even though Ken Barrington narrowly missed a century and Middlesex's Fred Titmus took a bagful of wickets. Because if there was one thing Peggy loved even more than the right kind of gentleman, or listening to the World Service in the smallest hours of the night, or being one of the greatest actresses of her time, it was cricket.

In the light of which, I hope that at some point or another in our ensuing friendship I told her of an event in my last prep school year when my chances of directly emulating Jack Robertson were ruthlessly spoiled. I had been cheated out of a school prize annually awarded to the first young player to score a 50 by my dastardly team Captain, Quentin Livingstone by name, who declared our innings closed ten minutes *before* the tea break (normally the agreed time to declare), when I was on 42 not out; in the next match he went on to score the prize-winning 50 himself. It's no fun to be the runner-up – I've spent my life in a profession that thrives on Awards ceremonies – which is why I have always liked the nearly-famous. So I dragged the bitterness of this stitch-up away to boarding school, where I shortly gave up the game altogether. Peggy would have been outraged – she might have hunted Quentin down and stuck him on a molehill.

Fortune favours the brave, or the stoical, or at least the bloody-minded, and I at last scored 50 for some showbusiness team one Sunday afternoon in the 1970s (clinched by that tricky stroke, an on-drive for four). On the other hand I know that Peggy appreciated the moment when my long-rehearsed performance as JDR was eventually seen by millions. In fact I would have titled it *Robertson Redux*. This was in 1982, when with Paul Eddington, Jonathan Lynn and Maureen Lipman I filmed Richard Harris's cricket-and-adultery comedy *Outside Edge*, directed by Kevin Billington, in which I had to bowl and also bat in the village match. On the first day of filming, I bowled my first ball. Kevin almost ruined the shot by crying out jubilantly "Fred Titmus!" – the name indeed of Middlesex's star spin bowler from the 1950s to the 1970s. I had to admit that was not by chance – that elbowish, slightly splay-footed action he (and other) off-spinners have had was quite easy to imitate.

A few set-ups later I went in to bat. I was supposed to be bowled first ball, but what was delivered to me on "Action!" was a full toss, and I smacked it away for four. "Cut!" I apologised for using up film stock and promised to be clean bowled in Take Two, but pointed out that some unrepeatable opportunities have to be taken. The full toss had been such a pleasure; you might as well have dissuaded

Jack Robertson from such a stroke. Kevin immediately understood the significance of this, perhaps sensing that I was perfecting my impersonation of my hero after thirty years' rehearsal; it was pretty good, and the camera had caught it.

Back at the end of 1964, I said goodbye both to Peggy and to Roy Dotrice; but I would not only be seeing Peggy a great deal thereafter (she ultimately became a close neighbour of my widowed aunt), but I was to work with Roy in 2000 in Hugh Whitemore's *The Best of Friends*, when he would spend an hour putting on an old-man make-up as Bernard Shaw each night, though he was in fact himself older than the character by then and could have saved his time.

An *au revoir* also (disguised as a goodbye) to Donald Sinden, and to Eric Porter; and a candid *au revoir* to Ian Holm as well. A continued R.I.P. to them all, and an easy passing to Ian.

I'd been asked to return to Stratford for the 1965 season, this time with a following wind pressing me a small step up the casting ladder. If you look at the season's programmes you can see a pudding-faced boy in rehearsals in brown suede, in photos in which the living only just outnumber the now-dead. He looks personable and attentive enough, a little like the young William Blake I now think; more than politely interested, but somehow rather blank, compared with the intentness of William Squire, Jimmy Laurenson, and John Barton around him. I would like to find some sign of inner activity, as if I was absorbing rather than loyally listening, like a Leonardo drawing that is at first sight blank and unforthcoming, but under the influence of ultraviolet light reveals a muscular system of breathtaking complexity and interest. This revelation of inner life is what happens with Paul Scofield's face in almost any photograph you see of him, but not with the young man here. On the other hand he is only in early rehearsals for the first fairly good part in his career – Dumaine in *Love's Labour's Lost* – and perhaps feels the burden of proof on him. I hope it was all right on the night.

Katharine (who was playing one of the Princess's ladies) and I continued to live in wedded happiness on the bank of the Avon in Tiddington Road and attending to the Beatles (I had long before

As Hamlet, ADC Theatre Cambridge, January 1964, with Sue Best (Gertrude).

As the Little Monk in *Galileo*, with Robin Ellis (Galileo) and Simon Perry.

As Dumain in *Love's Labour's Lost* (RSC 1965), with James Laurenson (Longaville), Charles Kay (King of Navarre) and Charles Thomas (Berowne).

As Mathias in *The Jew of Malta* (RSC 1965), with Eric Porter as Barabas.

As Mathias in *The Jew of Malta* (RSC 1965), with Peter Geddes.

As Mercutio in *Romeo and Juliet* (RSC 1976), directed by Trevor Nunn.

As Mercutio in *Romeo and Juliet* (RSC 1976), with Ian McKellen as Romeo.

Diary of a Madman (RSC 1977).

Mirabell in Congreve's *The Way of the World* (RSC 1977–78), with Judi Dench as Millamant.

As Berowne in *Love's Labour's Lost* (RSC 1978), directed by John Barton.

Four studies of *Hamlet* (RSC 1980).

Wedding to Katharine Barker (10/10/1964) at Holy Trinity Church, Stratford-upon-Avon: L to R: Robin Ellis (Best Man), Vivian Pennington (my father), Gladys Barker (mother of the bride), MP, Katharine, Fyfe Pennington (mother of the groom), Peter Barker (father of the bride), Diana Chappell (witness and friend).

Mark Pennington in Middlesex kit as a compliment to Jack Robertson.

Above: Mark and my mother and father in their garden.

Left: As the Bastard Falconbridge in *King John* in the same garden, aged about eleven.

Below: My parents, Fyfe and Vivian.

As Chekhov in the one-man show *Anton Chekhov* (Cottesloe Theatre at National Theatre 1984).

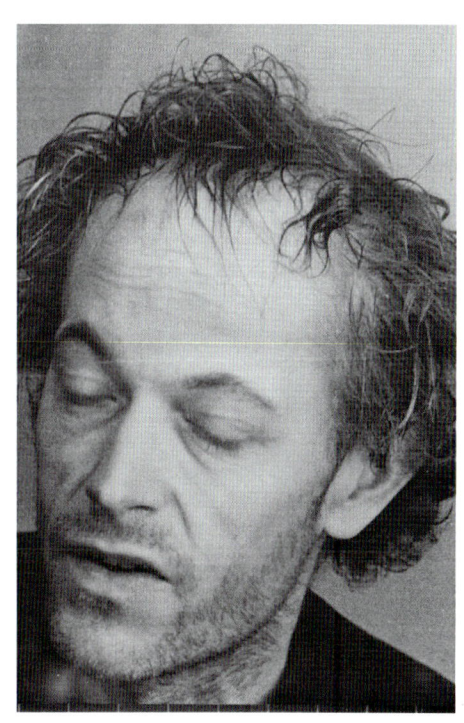

As Raskolnikov in Yuri Lyubimov's production of *Crime and Punishment* (Lyric Theatre 1983).

As the Duke in *Measure for Measure* (RSC 1978).

As Moff Jerjerrod in *Return of the Jedi* (Lucasfilm 1983).

As Timon of Athens (RSC 1999–2000).

declared that I couldn't marry anyone who didn't love them, and *A Hard Day's Night* had just come out). After a so-so performance as Dumaine, (a so-so part which carried with it the understudying of Berowne, and I got several performances out of this when the principal developed vocal nodules), I moved on to Mathias, the earnest juvenile lead in *The Jew of Malta*, where I had my first opportunity to study and indeed to talk with a star at first hand, wondering how it was that even the mighty Eric Porter, so confident and experienced, could forget his lines so regularly (now, at his age, I know). Or how it was that I was able, with some natty improvisation in blank verse, to save him each time from the pit that then opened at his feet… "I do believe thou sayest…", etc. He rewarded me with a confidentiality that he knew would please me, saying that the two of us shared a problem – a tendency to run out of breath after four or five lines of verse and therefore struggle to reach its main point. I was thoroughly and subtly flattered: it was the kind of bonding offered by someone comfortable with forty years of fame and it hugely pleased the tyro recipient: I've never forgotten it.

Then Scofield arrived to play Timon, as did the to-me legendary Paul Rogers, whose Macbeth at the Old Vic in 1955 had had such a lifelong effect, and who was now to be Apemantus, the next best part in *Timon*. I ended this two years' initiation with (I suspect) a tremendously narcissistic performance as Fortinbras in Peter Hall's production of *Hamlet*, starring David Warner. I tried to find a different voice – chilly, unfeeling, eminently self-confident – for the glacial Norwegian prince that Peter declared he wanted, intent as he was on showing nothing but self-satisfaction in the character and certainly no compassion for the massed dead of the Court of Elsinore when he arrives at the end of the play (apart from a special snide assertion for form's sake that Hamlet would have "proved most royal" had he been given the chance). However, having seen me do this for a couple of previews Peter entirely changed his mind about how to play the part – Fortinbras should now be genuinely warm and affectionate towards the stricken Danish court – if only for the sake of the handful of stockstill dead principals finishing a long evening's work and wanting to get on to the curtain call and home for dinner or to the Dirty Duck for drinks.

I failed to understand this, and three months later, after the show's transfer to the Aldwych, I got my cards and was on my way out of the RSC – for the time being. In a sense I'd already gone, having been symbolically seen off the premises by a disappointed John Barton when I had taken over Berowne from Charlie Thomas for that stretch in the summer. I had assumed that Fortinbras was the first stage on the golden path once described to me by Peter Hall, but was left in no doubt that his enthusiasm for me had now, frankly, lapsed – also for the time being. Indeed he said that I'd disappointed his hopes in me: I had a surprising amount of technique for an untrained actor, he said, but no personality in my work, and I should go away and do some living to balance what he saw as my over-studied performances.

Whatever I thought of that, the whole two years had provided an extraordinary launch for me and some obvious changes in my life. Whether John and Peter were proveably right or not, I had been tossed hither and thither and picked myself up only part damaged, and perhaps more bloody-minded, more of a cuss, more looking about for an Establishment to buck. And by the time I came to work very much more profitably with those two directors, I knew I had been blessed, and that they *had* forgotten all about the past.

Meantime it was on one day during *Hamlet*'s Aldwych run that I found myself in a call box off the Marylebone Road, ringing Kate in our newly acquired London home to ask how things were going with her that afternoon, to be greeted by a well-judged little pause (what a pro she was) before I heard the words: "we're fine". And this perfectly rendered greeting is how I first met Master Mark Dominic Fyfe Pennington.

As Angelo in Measure for Measure *with Francesca Annis as Isabella (RSC 1974).*

AN UNVICIOUS CIRCLE

1966–1973

> Come, poor babe… Blossom, speed thee well!
> There lie, and there thy character: there these;
> Which may, if Fortune please, both breed thee, pretty,
> And still rest thine.
> – William Shakespeare, *The Winter's Tale* (Antigonus)

If you weren't in front of your television it's hard to imagine what happened to the nation on 30th July 1966 at Wembley Stadium, when Geoff Hurst won the World Cup for England. Won it twice in quick succession, if you recall: an extremely doubtful goal as an English equaliser in the very final moments, necessitating extra time, in which Germany and then Hurst scored again. At which point it became such stuff as dreams are made on, even more exciting for the nation than the prospect of the BBC's lengthy adaptation of Galsworthy's *The Forsyte Saga*, then in production and due to be on our screens the following year: already there was a slight promotional hum in the air, although it was only two thirds of the way through its filming schedule. Above all, I was surprised that Mark – who wasn't due for a couple of weeks yet – didn't burst forth to join the Wembley party with Kate and myself and the nation.

As for *The Forsyte Saga*: disappointingly, I just didn't get cast, though I was hungry as hell to be either Jolyon (Martin Jarvis in the end) or Michael Mont (Nicholas Pennell); either would have done, and I had excitedly read the three novels that comprised the twenty-six episodes. But ex-RSC or not, I had no calling card for TV at that point – I petitioned, sometimes even bypassing my rather gentlemanly agent John Cadell, who also felt I must build up a TV CV as soon as possible but wasn't having much luck planning it: after barely two years, the only reputation I had was as an ex-Peter Hall debutant. Reflecting on this and ignoring all etiquette, I made one extraordinary gesture in making use of one's contacts: I invited Eric Porter to supper. He had secured the hugely coveted central role of Soames Forsyte, and I felt he might put in a word for me (after all, he'd already put a warning word in my ear at Stratford about my and his verse-speaking). We had a nice evening, and he behaved impeccably, even though he'd been one of the voices at the RSC who felt Kate's and my marriage was a disaster waiting to happen; but I'm sure he didn't put in the word on *Forsyte*, why should he? Nevertheless I did feel the serial needed me – I certainly needed it, standing impatiently as I was on my precarious launching-pad into the open market.

In truth, things had been going rather slowly as soon as I'd finished at the Aldwych in March, liberated from Fortinbras, my eyes on the horizon. I'd even been turned down for the notorious soap opera set in a motel, *Crossroads*, which starred Noele Gordon; Bill Kenwright, now a major producer but then just another thesp, got the part. I'm inclined to say he stole it from me, but he then, as an impresario, repaid it in the nineties and noughties with some pricelessly enjoyable projects, as if making up for it.

We had a lovely new flat in Paddington, but after her confinement Kate's professional luck wasn't in either. And now there were going to be three of us. Mark arrived on the 12th of August, and moments after making his acquaintance that morning I darted off to keep an appointment at the BBC with John Gorrie, more or less the doyen of TV drama directors at the time (and still around), who, perhaps out of kindness, or a mild recommendation from someone, was proposing to me a non-speaking Russian informer who haunted the action of a Georges Simenon story *Les Gens d'en Face*, adapted as *The Consul*: he was about to direct it for the BBC as part of a series called *Thirteen Against Fate,* all stories by Simenon but entirely without Maigret.

Peter Hall sometimes used to get good actors to play very small parts by saying their effect on the audience would be to make them marvel that the intriguingly flimsy character was always there but "refuses to speak". Well, John Gorrie had assembled a cast that needed no such dissembling: it included Jonathan Burn as Adil Bey (a Turkish consul working in Moscow), Michele Dotrice, John Ringham, Heather Canning, Madge Brindley, Geoffrey Beevers, Ray Smith and John Savident, all extremely willing to speak at length. Most of it was shot in Bristol. As for me, I was called simply "Youth" and tried, not for the last time in my life, to look Russian, quite often somewhere in the shot but uttering never a word. I list the other actors because they represent a time in TV drama in which it was possible to secure more or less continuous employment without necessarily being stars. Over the next few years I would work again with each and every one of them.

***

In 1966, TV was moving in two directions at once – towards more and more civilised, classical, somewhat theatrical high culture on the one hand, and the necessary exposing and fixing of society's vital questions on the other. Much of this latter was thanks to a Canadian, the remarkable Sydney Newman, who as the BBC's Head of Drama initiated both the hugely popular *Avengers* and *Doctor Who*, and a number of groundbreaking social realist dramas in series such as Armchair Theatre and The Wednesday Play.

In November of that same 1966, *Cathy Come Home* (audience twelve million) provoked an immediate debate in Parliament (as well as launching the career of the great Ken Loach), out of which Shelter got a huge boost and Crisis was formed the next year. British TV had emphatically woken up, even if the directors still tended to have first names such as Claude, Gilchrist, Herbie, Cedric and Basil.

Ken and his like would not have wanted much to do with *The Forsyte Saga* – it certainly belonged in the highbrow world. However, had

I been in some of its black and white twenty-six episodes, perhaps I'd have had the pleasure of re-encountering Robin Phillips, who played the Byronically disillusioned Wilfred Desert, and who had befriended both Kate and me when he briefly came to the RSC in 1965 as an assistant director for Peter Hall. He had also become pally with Glenda Jackson (Ophelia) and Murray Brown (a New Zealand-born actor who only walked on but made up for that by becoming Robin's loyal long-time partner), cooking for us all when we climbed the stairs to their Mayfair rooftop for visits throughout 1966. Robin meanwhile always had the latest stories of Joe Orton and Ken Halliwell, the talk of the town but as yet unshadowed by their tragedy of the following year: in our minds Murray and Robin somehow became embodiments of the pair of them as we feasted and gossiped.

It was an enriching period, if only because of all the daydreams. Glenda and I had mock-blazing rows about what constituted good acting – she specially despised my enthusiasm for a quality of vulnerability (such as Robin's) in a good actor. However, by the end of the year, Robin had retired from acting as far as he could, and had secured an invitation from James Roose Evans at Hampstead Theatre to direct a play that he had himself found, *The Ballad of the False Barman*, by Colin Spencer.

Spencer was certainly an interesting figure: the author of *Gourmet Cooking for Vegetarians* and then a further eighteen cookery books, he was described by Germaine Greer as our greatest living food writer. As if that weren't enough, he was a published novelist and short story writer of some standing, and, later on, the author of the much appreciated *Gay Kama Sutra* (with illustrations). His first novel, *An Absurd Affair*, he still feels can be sensibly ignored, but nine followed including satirical black comedies: *Poppy, Mandragora and The New Sex*, and, set mostly in Vienna, *Anarchists in Love*; he has been credited with a Dickensian breadth of characters and social settings, and by Sir Huw Wheldon, the first presenter/producer of *Monitor*, as a writer "of serious purpose; affecting, hilarious and grave ... unforgettable characters in all their seaminess and sadness, their idealism and desires." For the theatre Spencer also wrote

Spitting Image, which played at Hampstead and then in the West End, Vienna and New York – the play concerns a gay couple who discover that they're expecting a baby, and society's reaction to them: John Russell Taylor, in his book, *The Second Wave: British Drama of the Sixties*, remarks "for all the play's cheery light fantastic, [it] contains altogether more truth than is quite comfortable." Further, a couple of stage comedies: *The Trial of St George*, a satire on British justice when it deals with the kind of sexuality inspired by the *Oz* Trial, and *Keep It in the Family*, about a happy incestuous family, staged by the Soho Poly.

The Ballad of the False Barman, wherever that quite fits in his CV, was a musical fantasy set in a beach bar (surely in Brighton) run by a bald-headed lesbian proprietor known as The Duke (Caroline Blakiston in the event) and peopled by whores of various sexes (most strikingly perhaps Penelope Keith as Big Molly) and their clientele, which included a transvestite thieving vicar (James Bree). My Kate played the put-upon heroine trying to survive and then capitulating to the world around her, embracing it indeed, and it all seemed extremely racy at the time and quite funny. I no longer have the script, but I know that as Bimbo the Barman I belly-danced on the counter in my skintight jeans a great deal, and generally shimmied about in a shirt tied in a knot under the ribcage to expose the entire central area of the body. So it wasn't much like Fortinbras. However, I apparently appealed to an entirely new fan base with a character who, when the whole Company was arrested, presented a dilemma as to whether he would be better sent down to Holloway or to Wormwood Scrubs. Murray and Robin felt the whole thing would do my reputation no end of good; and in fact we had a whale of a time, even though Colin's fellow-playwright Hugh Leonard, in reviewing the show, declared himself sorry for the actors, "for whom it must have been like trying to ascend a cliff face on a bicycle".

Not at all. The only anxiety Kate and I had was for baby Mark, now three months old; not for his moral fibre to be sure, but what were we to do with him during rehearsals? Hampstead had immediately and most kindly invited us to bring him in his pram to the then rather cosy and friendly box office of the theatre, where they could keep an eye on him and we could rest and feed him in our breaks. From this he caught the smell of the greasepaint early, and Kate and I proved to each other that we could both work and parent all at once – just as we had when, one night during the late summer, John Gorrie had persuaded us to bring Mark along to be in one shot in a *Tale of the Unexpected*, making his debut as an infant apparently abandoned on a doorstep somewhere in the Home Counties. It was very bracing, especially as his character then grew up to be played by the splendid Nigel Stock, and in another way was a good preparation for *Ring Round the Moon*, which Kate, her tide now turning, was about to do in Coventry after *Barman*, while I, house-father, stayed home with Mark. We thus exemplified what actor couples always take pride in when they manage to pull it off, and Mark seemed to enjoy the Hampstead foyer, to judge from his gurgles – but then a Company of actors, however unfamiliar, are innocently great huggers of children in rehearsal breaks.

The approach of the unexpected but very attractive script of *Barman* had already had a magical effect on another area of my work, as if a switch had been thrown. Before ever we went into rehearsals, a second TV drama had cropped up, its dates fitting perfectly, in which I improved my casting from "Youth" to "First Youth" in a thing called *Don Quixote Go Home*: also featured were Brenda de Banzie, who had played the mother of Laurence Olivier's Archie Rice in *The Entertainer* (but wasn't talking about it), Charlie Kay (friend for life since the RSC spell), Richard Pearson, Anne Stallybrass and June Watson (friend for life and founder member of my ESC twenty years later). The plot, by Alexander Baron, centred on an ex-Army officer being persuaded by the young daughter of a soldier to join the Ban the Bomb movement, and it was beautifully directed for ATV by Graham Evans, on a level of skill with John Gorrie. And it led to another new experience – the pleasure of immediately going after its recording into a very hirsute piece of medieval warfare by Brian Rawlinson called *The Conquest* – I played someone called Wolfnuth, Barrie Ingham was Harold Godwinsson, the Earl of Wessex, and Janet Suzman was Edith Swan Neck – all this before I began rehearsals for *Barman*.

Retrospection sometimes makes a fool of me, or a little vague about long-lost TV scripts. The whole period – call it 1964 till the beginning of 1967 – has for me an obvious pattern of cause and effect, but it would make a lousy plot: keen student joins glamorous theatre company, not having quite enough to do in it but mixing with some who certainly do; he tumbles out of that into the arms of TV drama, at its apex at that time by any standard. He barely says a word in the medium at first – and would never be part of a long-running serial – until he pretends to be a sort of CND proselytiser and next some variety of hairy thug from the Middle Ages. Then, since Ken Loach still hasn't called, Fate, seeing no forward logic in hand, hurls him back into the world he knows best and always will – the live theatre – but In a small playhouse in Hampstead in a not particularly profound part, which nevertheless makes him reflect on all the gay people he knows, especially from Stratford – not so much how they, responsible professionals, behaved themselves, but what amused them when they contemplated the extremities of others of their predisposition. And to deliver that not only authentically but with all necessary delicacy and humour – this is not the tragic persecution of Peter Wildeblood or Oscar Wilde, but an extended camp joke, as old as *polari* (indeed this was the moment that Kenneth Williams and Hugh Paddick ruled the airwaves as Julian and Sandy in *Round the Horne*.)

What was I learning, aside from being a good and adaptable parent? The inherent conflict between portraying a state of mind, lurid, detailed and precise on the one hand (what research he's done! What an actor!) but on the other serving the advancing story and not outstaying your welcome – which may involve editing the interesting behavioural symptoms down a bit for the sake of moving the plot forward, which is the only thing an audience or viewer will stay in their seats for and understand in the end. Fascinating personal transformation and the bracing pace and variety of narrative thus have to accommodate each other.

Where would I be able to apply this idea next? My life in the theatre now broadens as well as deepens because, after the usual rigmarole of auditions, recalls, discussions and questions, I suddenly, with a great leap, secure a West End lead – one of the three in John Mortimer's new play, *The Judge*; indeed I achieve good billing — not above the title, not being an established star, but down at the bottom of the poster/programme page, printed in the much cherished slightly bigger point size used down there, where the magic word "and" immediately preceded my name, as if I was a special treat in store. O frabjous day. And thank you to John Cadell, the gentleman agent who had persevered with me ever since my graduation and was for the moment, I hope, heaving a great sigh of relief. He had certainly been busy.

An enormous TV star with a classical background (including the RSC), Patrick Wymark (*The Planemakers*, *The Power Game*), was to be Mortimer's eponymous Judge, and Patience Collier, a senior and formidable character actress whom I'd known a bit at Stratford, where she was rather kind to Kate and to some extent to me, was a provincial antique dealer, an old flame of the Judge's whom he re-meets on his tour of Assizes in somewhere like Chard in Somerset, accompanied, as was the practice, by an ambitious young Judge's Marshal, in my case called Trapp, as if he was a character out of Samuel Beckett, it now strikes me, rather than Mortimer.

In the play, the Marshal proves a bit smarter as an advocate than either the judge or the dealer – and was rewarded with, to be candid, rather better notices than either. There was some trouble in rehearsals when Stuart Burge, who was directing, and apparently tiring of my tendency to be Methody and physically lacking in authority, called Michael Codron, the producer, to ask him to sack me and find someone more upperclass. Part of the reason Codron was and is a great producer is that he was having none of this (in those days you could be fired without compensation up to about halfway through rehearsals). So he popped into the theatre one day, went away, and the next morning called me to insist that I get a short haircut (you're in the Army now), and always to wear a suit to rehearsals. He then, and only then, emphasised that he was completely delighted that I was playing the part. And he'd made an appointment for me at his own barbers – I think it was a salon in Swan and Edgars. I bridled of course, but he rightly insisted, and so we got through the scrape.

Having nabbed the notices, I was bannered in the trade paper *The Stage*: on their weekly Chit-Chat page (which that week also carried news of Martha Graham's upcoming Aaron Copland season and also of the London premiere of D. H. Lawrence's *The Daughter in Law*), they devoted their central spread to this month's "Rising Star" under the banner "Limelight" by announcing my arrival on the scene, accompanying this greeting by a picture of me at my most grudging. My Mum kept the cutting until she took her own final curtain call in 1987, whereupon I rescued it from crumbling like an old papyrus into dust, and now I've got it upstairs.

After a reasonable run at the Cambridge Theatre for *The Judge*, maybe three months, what do I do? Go back onto the telly; like an engine kicked into life, I bounced, unstoppably it seemed, from one reasonably interesting project to another, from one director to the next. First into *No Hiding Place*, Season 10, persuading the legendary Raymond Francis that I didn't do the crime, and Anne Stallybrass (later of *The Onedin Line*) that I was a good catch. Snip, Snip and fold: my Mum got busy with her file of reviews and scrapbook again. Then I played another "Youth" in *The Order* (one night's filming and a couple of lines I think), with John Neville as the leading man. Neville had been my hero at the Old Vic in the 1950s as Richard II and Hamlet, even more than had Paul Rogers as Macbeth.

From my Mum's point of view this unfolding hit-and-run TV riff, so different from the stubborn labour of a stage play, was a permanent gift in that she got immediate phone calls from all her neighbours and could bask in my supposed prowess; and my father, having once scorned all actors as sexually dubious, got the same kick when he lunched at the Garrick, which as a good lawyer he had joined. So they had a good year, though they didn't know that I was slightly fouling my own nest in the process. I was certainly prey to all sorts of head-turning and indeed -swelling influences as if in a great souk; from *No Hiding Place* into a wheelchair for an episode in Granada's *Escape* series titled *Five Men for Freedom* as an unpoetic character called Byron who'd been assaulted by an Afro-American (a good dingbat deep-Southern accent for me, this one). It gave me the honour of working with Calvin Lockhart as my adversary – I would say the most prominent and gifted (and most strikingly handsome, his skin the colour of brown velvet) Afro-Caribbean actor – he was in fact Bahamian – working in this country at that time (1967). Calvin's subsequent on-screen heyday in the 1970s would include prominent roles in *Cotton Comes to Harlem*, as a smooth-preaching con-man; he was greatly admired by Sidney Poitier, who directed him in the comedies *Uptown Saturday Night* and *Let's Do It Again*, both of which starred Poitier and Bill Cosby. "Calvin had wonderful range as an actor," Poitier rightly announced to the press, "He really had such enormous promise." And then he died, much too young. At that time I also met the veteran director Julian Amyes, who not only did a fine job on Byron but fifteen years later cast me as Anton Chekhov, thus provoking a very large development in my working life in relation to the great man (my own solo show, still alive and kicking after thirty-five years, and a book). Julian's brief for the time being was briefer – he had dramatised the triangle that existed between Anton, his sister Masha and his lover-becoming-wife Olga Knipper. It was ideally cast with Prunella Scales (with whom I'd done *Three Sisters* by then) and Isabelle, Julian's very gifted daughter with whom I briefly but delightedly stepped out thereafter.

For the present, still bouncing like a ball from one project to another, I stayed in Manchester (with the director Mike Newell, who had been at Cambridge with me) for the first two episodes of a short-lived comedy series about the generation gap (with Malcolm McDowell and Timothy Dalton, and Roger McGough as the voice) on ABC TV; for me the big pleasure in that was to work with the director Jim Goddard, a sort of early version of Mike Leigh in his belief in improvisation and the unpredictable, which I thoroughly embraced. I liked that Jim had special empathy for actors, who duly both respected and loved him: "Show me what you can do" he would say before rehearsing each scene. He seemed to have an encyclopedic knowledge of our abilities, mannerisms, gifts and faces, matched by an extraordinary ability to place regional accents, both British and American. He went on to direct *Reilly – Ace of Spies*, the original TV version of the RSC's *Nicholas Nickleby* and *Boys from the Blackstuff* as a Wednesday Play before it was serialised. Then he died – youngish – without, alas, hiring me again.

Having, I suppose, got over his feeling in rehearsing *The Judge* that I should be replaced, I was then reclaimed at last by Stuart Burge in the first real cracking TV lead I'd had. This was *The Single Passion,* a beautiful play by Ronald Eyre about the abortive revolution attempted by Lenin's brother Alexander Ulyanov when Vladimir Ilyich was a child, perhaps giving him some big ideas.

Like all but a very few recorded BBC dramas of the time, *The Single Passion* was erased soon after transmission and the tape re-used: to make matters worse, director and writer are dead, as are many of the cast, so I've no written record of the event, apart from one flattering review. What I remember is Rosalie Crutchley playing my mother and Alan Webb my father at one end of their careers, and co-conspirators Nigel Terry and Chris Timothy at the other; and that I may at one point have sounded vaguely reminiscent of Paul Scofield in the Trial Scene of *A Man for All Seasons*. This was pointed out to me by a young actress at the Wrap party – she called it an echo or perhaps, she said wryly, even a conscious impersonation. She just about escaped with her life, but on the other hand I knew that I had been found out, accused by this maddeningly observant young colleague. Stoutly as I defended myself, hoping to cast the criticism into outer darkness, it can now be revealed that she was right. Imitation is typical of the first couple of years of a career, and after that heroes don't help: self-respect will serve you better, together with growing self-belief. I hadn't got quite to that point, but I like to think I gained fuller independence not long after; and I perversely rejoiced in the otherwise disappointing fact that, the tapes having presumably been erased, nobody would know of my plagiarism. Now of course I remember only one line in the film, and I suppose it is possible that

> A revolutionary is a doomed man

might have been in the same key, or at least had a smack of one of Paul's greatest performances at Stratford:

> Timon hath made his everlasting mansion
> Upon the beached verge of the salt flood…

I also recall that Alan Webb, a brilliant but rather forbidding actor, asked me, between rehearsals of a croquet game on location, how long I'd been an actor (three years) – it turned out he'd been one for forty-three, which is as intimate as he got. For some reason I felt slightly offended: I was obviously developing *a jeune* premier's myopic temperament.

***

All in all, it was to be a year between *The Judge* and my next theatre job, now that I'd thrown Alec Guinness's *Family Reunion* out of my pram. The replacement came about in the oddest unhappy way, which caused me to re-assess the past and try to take some charge of the future. One day I was eating a sandwich, lovingly prepared by Kate for when I got back from a meeting at the BBC. As I chomped I became aware of a tall pinstriped figure standing unsmiling at or slightly behind her shoulder, like an usher. I asked him who he was and what for; he told me that Kate had instructed him to start divorce proceedings. One decision, he said, had to be taken immediately – either I or she had to leave the premises before this day ended. I volunteered, in a rather gallant way, if I may say so. We certainly had been wrangling – having married in hope and good heart, all the clichés had asserted themselves: by the time the West End break was exhausted, the marriage was beginning to show fractures for familiar causes. But this possibility, divorce, had never come up. I called Robin Ellis, who immediately offered me a temporary bed in Pimlico; before I left home, I went in to see Mark asleep, this being the middle of the afternoon, and then took my leave. I never saw the apartment again, and had to fight to see Mark, to forgive the method employed and, as I saw it, the stage management of Kate's sponsoring mother, who I knew viewed me with great suspicion. As it turned out, ours was to be one of the last pre-reform divorce cases redolent of the criminal law – someone had to be found guilty of something, and there was no such thing as mutual agreement. In due course, "mental cruelty" was tried out, the evidence being that I tended to play my little and rather feeble record player at unseasonable hours, such as back home again after the show – it was no more powerful than a dansette; eventually good old adultery had to be (inaccurately) conjured or at least hinted at and in the end contrived. I came across the decree not long ago, and the only guilty party was said to be the girlfriend whom I eventually involved, also about to become a divorcee. I can make fun of all this because Kate and I are of course as thick as thieves now.

But no sooner had I got to Robin's that fateful day than I had a call from John Cadell with a proposition. A major production of Oscar Wilde's *A Woman of No Importance* had ground to a halt during its pre-West End tour; the director had walked or been fired, and some of the cast had quit as well. Fortunately Tony Britton and Phyllis Calvert, the show's stars, had remained. A new director, Malcolm Farquhar, had been swiftly hired and they were re-casting all over the place. Would I go to Liverpool a.s.a.p and take a look at it to decide if I would care to take over the part of young Gerald Arbuthnot, start rehearsing the next day, and begin playing at the next touring date the following week? Quite apart from the learn, it was bracing to find myself wanted on the day I had proved unfit for purpose at home, especially as someone who'd always promised themselves a proper balance between work and life if possible.

The show was a mess in Liverpool, and when the house lights came up at the end, I told the Company Manager, who was hosting me, that I was tempted to give him my car keys so that I wouldn't be able to wake in the night and flee back to London. However, I charged in the next morning in what I suppose was rather a Methody (and fast-studying) frame of mind. James Hayter, Pauline Jameson, Agnes Laughlan, Tony Britton (father of Jasper) and Portland Mason (daughter of James) enveloped me in their protection and Malcolm Farquhar set about directing with apposite pace and decisiveness – except that he would describe Portland and myself as "the juves". Phyllis Calvert, in the lead, Mrs Arbuthnot, whose secret lovechild Gerald was, was welcoming in a detached sort of way. There was, however, a moment that gave us significant trouble from start to finish. The philandering Lord Illingworth (Britton) comes stumbling onto the stage, evening dress askew, straightening himself out while Portland, my fiancée whom he has just endeavoured to ravish in the garden, appeals to Phyllis and me:

> he ... he tried to...

But she couldn't bring herself to complete the crucial sentence. Phyllis was then to intercept me as I catapulted myself onto Tony, meaning to fell the philanderer to the ground:

> GERALD: What?... I'll ... I'll ... I'll...

At which time she had to interrupt and restrain me with a line made satirically famous by Noël Coward in *Hay Fever*:

> Stop, Gerald, Stop, He is your own father!

Shock and horror at this sensational *coup de théatre*, and down comes the curtain on Act Two. But surely, I felt, Phyllis needed at least to act/mime some gesture of physical restraint of me or I would have proceeded to kill Illingworth. No chance: Phyllis never once touched me or made any such gesture, not in rehearsals or throughout the run; she remained all dignified restraint herself, declining to intervene. So I had to stop of my own accord (presumably having a sudden change of heart) as the curtain descended. She was much praised in the press for showing "how beans could be spilled with style" and I suppose this was the moment that proved it; me, I couldn't quite understand why a colleague, albeit quite grand, was entirely declining to act *with* me: it had never happened to me before. For the first time professionally I felt disappointed by someone I admired and wanted to collaborate with: Phyllis was a movie star, a national treasure and extremely talented stage actress, but she was on this evidence a determined soloist. How was it she had simply declined to act with a newcomer, especially under the circumstances?

I'll tell you why. Because she felt she was on her own, and at other points in the play she was right. There came a moment when she sat downstage left, looking diagonally across the audience to her right, and shedding silent, genuine tears. I was upstage centre watching and I could see the silver tears dropping in profile against the dark background of the house – they fell from eye to lap, no bumping into the nose. Also, they came every night at the exact same moment, and they were unmistakably genuine. I was amazed always; it was always on cue, always real. I thought only John Gielgud could do this; it was brilliant, though in another way it seemed to belong to the (unofficial) Peter Barkworth School of Acting, very popular at the time, that insists that only technique really matters. However, at this moment the technique sparked with genuine emotion exactly at 8.20 pm (if that's what it was) every night, and at 3.20 every matinée day.

I don't think Phyllis thought much of me; in fact I was warned by colleagues that I'd made a powerful enemy in her, and I should be less openly critical. Well, R.I.P.; and (truly) my compliments to her surviving family. You so rarely meet difficult people in this game that this story is worth telling, not least because there had been another difficult star in *The Judge*. Patience Collier had, in 1956, played opposite Paul Scofield in *The Power and the Glory* at the Phoenix Theatre, and the same year given a "delightful vignette" opposite John Gielgud in Noël Coward's *Nude with Violin*. As I have said, she was kind to Kate, playing Alice to her Princess in Act Five of *Henry V* – and in a way to me too, except that on *The Judge* she did have her moods: convinced I was upstaging her, and – I suppose as her equivalent of what I might call Calverting – making an eventual 8am phone call the next morning to me. As I crouched dripping after the bath, this was to inform me, as if in a national newsflash and quite uninvited, that if she were to tour the world with a Company of her own with two chosen actors, she would *not* have me in it, certainly not, or John Hurt either, but would take dear Gary Bond or dear Barry Justice (both good actors by the way and charming fellows – and rapturously gay, so you can see her drift). They were her ideal, her perfect Company, and I had had a narrow escape.

A Woman of No Importance featured oddities all round. Jacqueline Pearce, whom I was seeing a little by now, was spotted in the audience on the first night and my solicitor reported this to me next day referring to her as "the co-respondent in the case". Who did the ID, I wondered, and who cared? Was it the same type of private detective who might burst into a double bedroom with a camera in a grand hotel in Brighton, according to legend? The next oddity was to be the last-ever show at the Golders Green Hippodrome on our way to the Vaudeville in the Strand; it then closed its doors as a theatre and became home to the BBC Concert Orchestra until 2004; it's now at the centre of a controversy as a Grade II-listed building, bought by an Islamic charity earlier this year. As for the London notices for us, *The Stage*, so enthusiastic about the previous year's *The Judge*, said that my Gerald was "thoroughly convincing and surprisingly natural": did this "surprisingly" mean considering it was – who…? Wilde? Me?

Anyway I now wanted most of all to get back onto the telly: I liked it. I'd moved on from Robin's, my parents were fuming about the imminent divorce, though not against me, Kate had taken Mark back to the Wirral where her parents lived – it turned out that she was going to go on to work with the Stables Theatre Company in Manchester, a job I agreed she shouldn't lose. The marriage was clearly shot, not so much for any infidelity but for mental cruelty with the record player (this charge came not from her, but from her acquisitive lawyers, earning a dollar). I'd subsequently hung my hat in a few places, including a bedsitter in Welbeck Street, as if I was an overflow consultant from Harley Street. But then I was parked at the east end of Shaftesbury Avenue, opposite the Phoenix where Kate had done *Out of the Crocodile*, looking longingly at Valotti's Café next door – I was in a spare room belonging to Robert Dean, a kindly fellow-actor who'd spotted that I was spinning in the wind a bit and who said I could help myself to anything in his fridge – except the yoghurt, I think it was. All other routes had been quietly blocked, mostly by myself I dare say.

However, it strikes me that everything I did in 1968 was of interest in itself, regardless of my sometimes unhappy participation in it: I was no longer trying to make silk purses out of sows' ears, TV was continually expanding and I was blessed. First of all, one of the great director originals, Claude Whatham, hired me to lead in a Wednesday Play with an unpromising 1950s title – *Anyone for Tennis* – which was not in fact about summertime house parties but one of J. B. Priestley's "time plays", in which one timescale continually alternated with another, as did one setting too, and dream and reality interacted. I don't think this had ever been done before in any medium – certainly not by Claude's method, which included such hair-raising novelties as 360-degree panning shots which involved the physical removal of part of the set once the cameras were off it so that a new structure could be in place when the camera returned to that angle a few moments later. These moves, by the by, being undertaken by operators who were already struggling to keep out of each other's line of vision. Actors darted out of one scene to turn up in a different set, in a different decade and a different mood, in different clothes and confronted by a camera they hadn't seen before. It was, as you can imagine, one hell of a learn for me, not only of the lines but of the geography and timeline; it was also as formally complex as anything I've ever seen done in a TV studio (certainly for its time).

Claude also planned to record the play in one take (ninety minutes, unprecedented), an ambition that was slightly compromised by an unfortunate dry towards the end of the recording evening from one of the older actors, suddenly unable to remember the place or time he was entering – but it didn't seem to matter. He has taken his secret to the grave as far as I know, and was in any case entirely forgiven by Claude. As well as a kind man, the director was a genuine original whose natural successor in the stretching of TV's technical limits was inherited by Don Taylor, who many years later was determined to do such plays as *Oedipus Rex* in one take – which we very nearly managed; however, because of a noise leak from beyond one wall of the BBC studio, where a car park was being built, we were obliged to come back the next day and do it all over again: and second performances are rarely as good as the first or the third.

In My Own Footsteps

***

And now Clive Graham greets me: I already know him because he was a friend of Janet Suzman's and used to turn up in Stratford sometimes. He asks if I'd like "the one", viz a cocktail after rehearsals for Episode 1 of *Middlemarch*, in which he is Sir James Chettam, enamoured of Dorothea until she's entrapped by the dreary Casaubon, and before Will Ladislaw finally wins her when she's widowed. I am to be part of the love interest as Ladislaw – a good part, a sort of hero in fact, but without the obligation to drive the whole show; Casaubon's young cousin, he is an idealist descended from two generations of rebellious women, his paternal grandmother having married a Polish musician (causing her wealthy family to abandon her); his mother has run away from her family after finding out their pawnbroking business was based on theft, instead pursuing a career as an actress. Will inherits this rebellious spirit; however, despite his passionate nature and engagement with politics, he can be restless and struggles to commit himself to pursuits that don't "come easily".

For this reason, Ladislaw I suspect is a better part in an adaptation than in the original book, where all the above is only sketchily suggested: meanwhile my record of lecture attendance at Cambridge was too poor for me to have benefitted from F. R. Leavis's inspired interpretation of the novel. Henry James calls Will a dilettante, Nietzsche takes the trouble to despise him. Virginia Woolf's and Emily Dickenson's enthusiasm are not quite enough to still those who feel that Dorothea has finally married someone beneath her. So the actor needs to invest something of his own in a not-quite-finished character, on the honest presumption that Eliot would have liked it if she'd known about camera lenses. All good actors know how to do this, just as they usually know when their best take is in the can. I didn't bother with an accent despite the plot's musky hint of Polish blood in Will (two generations back), any more than Lydgate (probably a more interesting character for us novelistically) and Dorothea used the accent of Coventry, which is probably where Eliot's "Loamshire" is meant to be.

It seems to me now that I had one scene in most episodes and was absent from two. Will turns up on Dorothea's honeymoon when she's married to Casaubon, in a Roman art gallery; he works as a local newspaper editor to be nearer to her, he causes her to run the risk of being disinherited, but in the end their love prevails, and he is thus the nearest thing the show has to a romantic lead.

I believe our seven-part serial was the first drama to be done in colour by the BBC, and no production department, including Lighting, had quite caught up: the sky cyclorama glimpsed through the French windows was a violent turquoise, faces looked orange and hair a little green, eyebrows unaccountably blue, and I had lips of a lascivious red which Mick Jagger might have envied. I kid you not. The camera looks shyly at as many people as possible, like a modest intruder at a rather interesting party, similar perhaps to that approached by Jourdain and Moberly at Versailles. Half-breaking the BBC rule of instantly wiping the tapes after transmission, random sections of the series sometimes surface at the NFT: I'm not sure they're worth the trouble, though a comparison with the hipper later version of 1994 might be interesting. As Dorothea in ours, *Middlemarch* was really Michele Dotrice's show – she'd been in *The Consul* too – and Clive was a drinking companion and true friend to me for the rest of his life, till the former quality finally did for him. At least by then I had got him the job of understudying Nicol Williamson's Hamlet in Hollywood in Chapter One.

***

> When I am dead, scatter my dust,
> And make my condition an example to men,
> Moisten my dust with wine, to make the seal
>   on a vat,
> Out of my corpse, wash me in wine when I go;
> For my burial service, use a text concerning wine…
> – *Rubaiyyat of Omar Khayyam*

And then, out of the blue, there indeed was Tony Richardson, auditioning actors for *Hamlet* with Nicol at the Roundhouse in 1969. I was supposed to be testing for Horatio, but instead sat in my donkey jacket with my legs dangling into the orchestra pit of whatever theatre we were auditioning at, and told him that I only wanted to play Laertes. He invited me to give him a taster, so I did Laertes' initial advice to his sister, which has a strong sense of elder brother bossiness, and is a degree more sexually explicit than you might expect. Tony immediately gave me the part and the following week screen-tested me for the lead in his movie of *Ned Kelly* (I did the test but was somehow pipped by Mick Jagger – perhaps he'd heard about my Middlemarch lipstick). I'd also given Tony an idea, and Marianne Faithfull (when she wasn't loyally trying to persuade Eric Clapton to do the music for *Hamlet* – dream on) and I were urged towards quite a bit of groping that was more than fraternal. More and better.

At this point, I imagine my Mum closes her scrapbook for a while. We did film *Hamlet* during its Roundhouse run, but it didn't come out for a while after, so wasn't much reviewed, even though it was marketed as "from the author of *Romeo and Juliet*, the love story of Hamlet and Ophelia", with a picture of Marianne flat on her back and tumescent; and we also went on tour to both the East and West Coasts of the US (New York/Boston/Berkeley/LA), so there wasn't much for Mum to collect from that either. The process of knowing your lad was on TV tonight, then watching the programme and reading reviews for it first thing the next morning while the phone rang or the post thickened with praise from your friends and relations, must have been far more satisfying for her than postcards from Boston about what unexpected thing happened in the show last Wednesday. Skype or Zoom would have been invaluable for the ambitious Mums of actors in 1969.

For the US, as well as Francesca taking over Ophelia, Patrick Wymark relieved Tony Hopkins of Claudius. Patrick then did me the kindness one night in Jimmy Ryan's Bar on 42nd Street (the best whisky sour in town) of telling me that he'd personally refused to let me be cast in the later TV version of *The Judge* because the stage success had left me too big for my boots. Such were my thanks for having got him out of trouble whenever he dried, which was quite a lot. It was humbug, it seemed to me, akin to what he did on the current opening night when he got to Claudius's line just before the crucial duel between Hamlet and Laertes and in declaring "In the cup an *union* shall we throw", said *"onion"* instead, indignantly claiming later that "onion" was a little-known Folio reading. Yes, maybe the 99th Folio. Or more likely, an old schoolboy's joke. Francesca and I laughed at this from our newly-formed Love Island, then fell into melancholy at how a fine actor had let himself down. And indeed Patrick's life's work really was done; he was drinking for England in New York and died soon after, by which time I was in Marrakesh with Francesca, often negotiating a price for the day's hashish but on one occasion finding that I'd bought pure opium instead and nearly overdosing, I dare say.

***

Perhaps good luck, like tragedy, comes not in single spies, but in battalions, and another was on its way. If I've given the impression that bouncing from one TV to another - "then I did this – or that" – which I had been lucky to do before going to the US, was a matter of picking up a phone every five minutes and consulting my diary, well, that's a different level of fame. Rather, an acting life is generally quite fitful: you're often waiting for a decision from someone and aren't sure if you should nag your agent for an answer – or even to nag the production company yourself; hoping, after doing a good interview, that someone somewhere has put in a good word for you. You don't get the jobs you think you will, and are offered the ones you don't really want. It's a rocky, helter-skeltering business, and you endure as best you can. And it remains that way, even if you've achieved a fair amount. Only last year I was invited to meet a young Swedish film director to do a cameo part as Winston Churchill. I had once almost been Churchill, in the 1972 movie *Young Winston* – the producer, Carl Foreman, was all for me but the director, Richard Attenborough, wasn't; the young Swede now made me improvise for a full hour in the character before flinging his arms round my neck and declaring "You *are* Winston!". I never heard from him again, and when my agent nagged the casting director, who sounded about 16, she said that I probably hadn't "blended", as if I was a hair gel. Those who love to hear such stories I refer to my book *Let Me Play the Lion Too*, where I tell the story of another casting director who declared I was by far their favourite actor in the world, and then greeted me at the interview as Geoffrey.

However, I was now called by the mighty Jack Gold, whose contemporary equivalent among auteur directors is perhaps Peter Kosminsky. Jack was one of the few directors Nicol Williamson respected, ever since they did *The Bofors Gun* together, and so he should. Jack now cast me as Robert Graves in *Mad Jack*, a TV story about Siegfried Sassoon (Michael Jayston) and his struggle with his growing pacifism in 1917. Graves was a friend of Sassoon's, and in Tom Clarke's script spends his time cynically observing other officers, coming into his own when he arrives to persuade Sassoon to go before a medical board to avoid having to return to the front. Graves was still living in 1970, so as we trudged along the Dorset beaches arguing, my character was concealed from all of the crew under the name of another friend of Sassoon's, Geoffrey Cromlech.

It's also known that Sassoon and Graves/Cromlech together had a taste for mischief. There are stories of them pounding along the beach working out their differences as two rather different proponents of pacifism, a conviction which Sassoon always disingenuously denied. Eventually Graves turns on Sassoon and charges him with making his protest for personal reasons, because he has a martyr complex. Back in the hotel, the two of us, Michaels off-duty, went excitedly from table to table at dinner, lecturing the other guests on the differences between 18th and 19th century humanism. I was reminded of my tour of the Chelsea restaurant with Ian Hendry (*qv*), though perhaps the talk was brainier; and Michael and I got into the habit of further mimicking our characters by tampering with the other patrons' breakfast orders when they'd all gone to bed. Fortunately, this being out of season, the "patrons" were mostly our own colleagues on the unit, and I think we were forgiven.

I then went on to another working friendship, with Dennis Waterman, doing a love triangle with Susan George called *The Root of all Evil* (at that time Dennis and I liked a drink too, and thought nothing of consuming through the night and still being on first call and efficient on the set in the morning); with Ian Hendry, as described, in *The Tycoon*, in Guy Slater's *No Easy Walk*, and in *A Rogue's Gallery* (for Granada) with Judy Geeson, written by Peter Wildeblood.

***

Had I known it, five years after his *Hamlet*, in 1974, Nicol Williamson and I were about to head back to Stratford, he with his eye trained on Macbeth and Uncle Vanya, and mine on Angelo in *Measure for Measure*; I stayed for eight solid years, becoming a regular, with my own place at table and licence to reminisce about the old days – should I want to.

The more I look back on it, the more of a serendipitous marvel this was. Here's how it came about. I'd known Peter Gill for a long time, since his early days as an assistant, then associate director, at the Royal Court, best known there for his realisation of three hitherto underrated plays by D. H. Lawrence, which he presented as a group in 1968. While I was in the US in 1969, the Court had also presented two of Peter's own early plays, *The Sleepers' Den* and *Over Gardens Out*, which revealed that he could evoke his Cardiff boyhood with great economy of means and lyrical skill.

I was glad to have an appointment with him now, as he was to direct *Twelfth Night* as a guest at the RSC. He was curious to know what I'd been at in the last half dozen years, curious too as to how I'd got along with Nicol, who was now going to play Malvolio for him. I told him everything I've been telling you, and added my Nazi rapist who couldn't stay on his motorbike in *The Unconquered*, and *The Dolly Scene* with Sinead Cusack – largely because of the fact that the great John Hopkins had written it. A *Public Eye* with Alfred Burke, a *Callan* with Edward Woodward and Jane Lapotaire (I was called Monsieur Lefarge), a Thirty Minute Theatre for the BBC with Penelope Wilton which contained a rather tame but baptismal first naked scene in a bed (but without activity) for both of us, *No Exit* with John Gregson, a Sunday Night at the Court called *Pretty Boy* (a first play by Stephen Poliakoff), an unknown Sam Shepard at a time when his work was barely known here, called *Chicago*, which had stopped me smoking for life as it contained a lot of vigorous gym work in the action. Dürrenmatt's *Portrait of a Planet* for Kenny McBain at Prospect, *Savages* of course – and – heaven for me – a Russian play, *The Promise* by Alexei Arbuzov, recently a London hit for Ians McShane and McKellen and now revived in Sheffield; then – hoopla! – Andrei in *Three Sisters* for Richard Cottrell, which was everything I could have hoped for and aspired to, and to which I'll hope to return, dear Reader. Also *Trelawney of the Wells* and *Captain Jack's Revenge*. Around that time I'd also had a fascinating TV documentary encounter with James Mossman on dissident Soviet poets – I even went on a cheery date with him, he flirting harmlessly before, very shortly afterwards, taking his own life for other reasons. He had recently lambasted Harold Wilson on *Panorama* and given Peter Shaffer the central idea for *Equus* by telling him of the blinding of a horse near his home in Suffolk.

My update didn't sound bad to me. Or to Peter. His problem now was that the obvious part for me in *Twelfth Night* was Orsino, but he'd cast it. Would I accept Curio (my agent had warned me about this and advised me to tell Peter to stuff it, but I didn't have to because he did it himself without asking). After we'd gossiped a while further, Peter felt that he'd serve me better by commending me to Keith Hack, who was casting his (parallel to Peter's *Twelfth Night*) guest production of *Measure for Measure*.

He did, and after a couple of audition sessions on Claudio, Keith brushed that idea aside and conceived the notion of my playing Angelo – younger than usual, confused about his desires, and not without vulnerability. It was such a startling break with tradition that Trevor Nunn came down to the final audition to check, for this was now his RSC. Trevor offered me Ross in *Macbeth* as a makeweight, but I did with that what my agent had advised me to do with Curio.

So in a way Peter Gill was responsible for what I'm tempted to call my Golden Age with the RSC from 1974 to 1981 and beyond. And not only mine – thus it was that I, Francesca Annis, Richard Griffiths and Ian McDiarmid came to go to Stratford and stuck there for quite a while: we were initially not homegrown RSC graduates but guests hired and imported by guest directors on the open market who then stayed a long time – as did neither Peter really, nor Nicol Williamson.

Ion Caramitru as Hamlet (1985).

BREAKFAST IN BUCHAREST

Michael, do you get stopped in the street?
– Ion Caramitru
Only by the police, not by the fans…
– Michael Pennington
A fi sau a nu fiiata-ntrebarea:
– *Hamlet*, Actual III Scena 1

When Ion Caramitru did his sensational Hamlet ("To Be or Not To Be" in Romanian above) for the Bulandra Company in Bucharest – approximately the equivalent of London's Royal Court – in 1985, not many people knew it was his second shot at the part, and even fewer that he was coming to it five years after Michael Pennington's second Hamlet, at Stratford. Ion's first had been as a student in 1964 at the National University of Theatre and Film in Bucharest, just when, by a lovely coincidence, I too was doing the part as a student at Cambridge. (Later I was quick to tell him how wise it had been of him to wait a full five years after my maturer version, and he laughed in the explosively and companionable way I had come to recognise.) But his Hamlet shouldn't really be the subject of such badinage: it was a vital element in the Revolution that finally overthrew Nicolae and Elena Ceaușescu. The production boldly based Claudius and Gertrude on that wretched couple, and Hamlet's Ghost was simply played as a roving spotlight hugely amplified as it called for Revenge. Ceaușescu's bureaucratic Cultural Committee, having heard rumours from rehearsals, crawled all over the previews of the show, damning it as "too modern", a peculiar judgement that threatened not only its future but the actors' personal liberty – it was perhaps comparable to the moment when Shakespeare's Company found itself nearly being jailed by Queen Elizabeth I (who was terrified by the idea of revolution) for presenting her with a performance of *Richard II,* a masterpiece on the subject of the Deposition of a reigning monarch.

Richard Eyre saw the Bulandra *Hamlet,* preliminary to inviting it over to his National Theatre in London in 1990:

> Predictably the Cultural Committee found the production too provocative; but they advised their masters: "You can't stop Shakespeare, or at least you can't be seen to." Surprisingly, this worked: the Committee's fear of becoming the laughing-stock of the public outweighed their official fear of subversion.
>
> The audience sat on uncomfortable seats or crouched on the edge of the stage swathed in scarves and overcoats. They were enraptured: line after line was greeted with the applause of recognition. This was their story; Hamlet's oppression by Claudius mirrored theirs by Ceaușescu, and if Hamlet vacillated or accused himself of cowardice or cursed himself for his inaction, it only reflected the audience's own feelings of frailty and submissiveness.
>
> Allegory and metaphor are part of any theatre syntax but at that time in Romania they were its essential core. There was a shared language, a code in which thoughts could be spoken, ideas asserted and passions voiced; it was the only medium in which dissent could be expressed. It provided solace and inspiration, and it was not coincidence that in the imminent 1989 revolution it was to the Hamlet, Ion Caramitru, that students and teenagers turned for a leader and, following their example (an actor's dream), a general said to him: "My army is at your disposal. Tell us where to go."
>
> Following his instinct, Caramitru directed them to the TV station where, after fierce fighting, he found the TV News studio guarded by only a single Securitate man, too frightened even to raise his hand in a salute. From there he and a poet friend made

an announcement to the nation: "We're free, we've won. Don't shoot anyone. Join us."

***

So, his second *Hamlet* had only been the start: Caramitru could be seen standing on the Palace balcony in the 1989 Revolution as an obvious opponent of the regime; then, on 22 December, after the tyrant had fled Bucharest, it was he and other dissenting artists who swelled the crowd occupying the TV headquarters, from which he proclaimed victory.

Since then, he has sometimes been asked if his life as an actor and director has changed between the fall of the Communist regime and thereafter:

> There have been huge differences, of course. I think after 1989 actors and directors have, paradoxically, lost a privilege. Before then, theatre was the only space in Romanian culture where you could buy a ticket and see forbidden things, freethinking ideas, political criticism. We'd invented a language that subtly directed the public to the truth; we couldn't talk plainly about dictatorship then, about freedom and power, about stupidity, but theatre addressed all these issues through the choices we made in constructing onstage characters and situations. These aesthetics, and our will to fight in our own way against what was going wrong in the country, gave us the privilege of being ourselves in times when it was forbidden to be. The public loved to come to the theatre and used those three hours to be themselves and learn to hope again.
>
> As for *Hamlet*, I'd like to quote the British director Deborah Warner, who was once asked which Romanian Shakespeare performance she liked best. Her reply was: "*Hamlet*." She explained: she loved the translation. Next question: How was she able to establish that without knowing the Romanian language at all? She replied: "the public's reactions. I know this play by heart, and they reacted in places I've never thought people could be

made to." This made me understand that translating a play and performing it insists on the freedom to exploit situations that are only slightly hinted at.

And translation meant more than just changing the words; we were translating the realities in a language at hand for the public. We had this amazing freedom. Today, we're bound to be rigid, and we perform only the original play – no more "interpretations" of it! But I do feel that little by little, we've been sliding back to the temptations of "re-interpreting", but the process hasn't the same high intensity, since there's no more censorship in the theatre. Political dictatorships give birth to cultural resistance – and to masterpieces.

Caramitru went on to play an active role as Minister of Culture for a four-year period in the 1990s.

Yes, I was directly responsible for cultural affairs. It was then that I started to approach all the Romanian artists and intellectuals living abroad, asking them to return home. Eugene Ionesco, for instance. Many promised to come back but never did: in June 1990 Bucharest was invaded by violent mine-workers, an event that raised serious concerns for those living in the West. But some did come back: director Andrei Serban's return to Romania served the theatre well and the rising interest in it that followed the fall of Communism. Liviu Ciulei also came back and directed, but he wasn't interested in running a theatre company. And Lucian Pintilie too, but he was more interested in making films than theatre.

Everything went smoothly until the economic crises hit. In six years Romania had seven to eight different Ministers of Culture. It was 1996 that I was asked to become the new one, and I agreed. I've tried to improve the lives of all Romanian artists, not only theatre people, and I've initiated pieces of legislation much needed for a healthy cultural environment.

In these early 1990s, arguing that the granting of diplomas and privileges had become an instrument of political corruption, Caramitru had already been instrumental in forming an outfit known as the Association of Non-Privileged Revolutionaries. But he very much disliked the bureaucracy of being a Minister – he had much of the charisma and identity of Václav Havel in Czechoslovakia – and he received an OBE from us for establishing cultural links. In 1997 the French made him a *Chevalier des Arts et des Lettres.*

Now his image (and name – though everybody knows it from his face) is on the 450 lei postage stamp. And this popularity is in spite of having made few films – how many other specialist theatre people (and I speak with feeling) can say as much? And now he's running the National in Bucharest, a theatre with nine playing spaces, from which he sends me impassioned reports of the extreme straitening of their grant as his country – like so many in Europe – swings inexorably to the right again. But how splendid it is to see that actors who play Hamlet twice can change their societies…

Hector in Troilus and Cressida,
with Meg Davies as Andromache (RSC, 1976).

RSC

1973–1981

All hid, all hid; an old infant play.
Like a demigod here sit I in the sky.
And wretched fools' secrets heedfully o'er-eye…
– Berowne, up a tree in *Love's Labour's Lost*

Richard Griffiths (with thirty-five years ahead of him), wandered on in 1978 looking about as scruffy as the King of Navarre in *Love's Labour's Lost* could possibly be, a ragamuffin schoolboy with his shirt out of his trousers, the owlish spectacles falling off his nose and, of course, his gorgeous girth. Ian Charleson, twelve years before his demise, as well as enduring as Longaville in that same *Love's Labour's*, made up for it by singing superbly in *Piaf* at the Other Place in the same season (this being all part of a Stratford repertoire that also included *The Tempest*, *Measure for Measure* and *Antony and Cleopatra*); he'd (I imagine) not yet come across Sam Shepard's *Fool for Love*, in which he was to have a big success later at the National Theatre and in the West End, directed by Peter Gill; or starred in the Hugh Hudson/David Puttnam *Chariots of Fire;* or been at the very last a fine Hamlet, before leaving us; a gorgeous Scotsman, rather puritannical in a Presbyterian way, but in the end succumbing to AIDS; the inventor, too, of the very best excuse I've ever heard from an actor for being late for rehearsals ("sorry, the wind was against me").

Alan Rickman, with three years longer to live than Richard, was also *en rout*e to what he would regard as better things than Boyet in our current show; the legendary Michael Hordern (seventeen years left to him) was the fantastical Spaniard Don Adriano de Armado; David Suchet, like me still alive and kicking now, sinking slowly down within his hobby-horse (a very early prototype for the NT's *War Horse*) to convince as the shy curate Sir Nathaniel trying to play the mighty Trojan Hector in the villagers' show of *The Nine Worthies* – easily a match as a Shakespearean comic *tour de force* for the Mechanicals' performance in *A Midsummer Night's Dream*. Jane Lapotaire was Rosaline, thinking it was all a bit beneath her after *Piaf,* in which like Ian she sang her heart out – unfortunately, however, she sang mine out as well, and I embarked towards the end of the run on the most doomed possible of liaisons with her, in which my main purpose became babysitting her adorable son Rowan and ministering to one of the few theatre egos that might be even larger than my own. Ruby Wax, arriving from Berkeley California via Glasgow, was the village wench Jaquenetta, eventually impregnated by Don Armado.

No, this is not Celebrity Walkdown, it's *Love's Labour's Lost* again, at the Royal Shakespeare Theatre in Stratford, and John Barton is telling me I must wear a wig as Berowne, because, he insists, the one thing the entire directorate at the Royal Shakespeare Company knows is that my hair is too fine for Shakespearean purpose. I wondered if this featured in the agenda and minutes of their Board Meetings, or whether he'd got his pills mixed up this morning (see below). John Barton, who had already cast me in his mind as the RSC's next Hamlet, and put his own job on the line for it; and who has been dead for forty months now. No, thirty-six.

> Time hath, my lord, a wallet at his back,
> Wherein he keeps alms for oblivion…
> (Looks at the walls of Troy)
> There they stand yet… The end crowns all,
> And that old common arbitrator, Time,

> Will one day end it.
> Shakespeare, *Troilus and Cressida*

John was obsessed by Time in Shakespeare – not just by its passage but its poetic presence, its looming sound and influence. So he was naturally obsessed with *Troilus and Cressida*, which evokes it most eloquently, as do some of the sonnets. John loved to encourage all RSC actors to use the word as if "Time" was a musical phrase of just the right length and pitch to suggest Time's inexorability, its function as shaper and controller of Shakespearean events. He himself kept Time at bay till he was eighty-nine in 2017, which I call not bad, and now I'm increasingly trying to do the same.

I must say this was boom-time for me. John championed me from the moment I arrived for my second chance in Stratford (1974) as Angelo in Keith Hack's *Measure for Measure* and Ferdinand in his *Tempest* – John, who had shown me the door in 1965 almost as peremptorily as had Peter Hall. He had pronounced then that my short spell as Berowne's understudy revealed only that I had none of the qualities for the part: he then politely wished me well in my future endeavours, and showed me to the door of his office.

Now, off the back of the Angelo (and less so because of the Ferdinand), and perhaps because of the Johnnie Hobnails I then did for Ron Daniels that autumn in David Rudkin's great *Afore Night Come* at the Other Place, John and Trevor Nunn would in short order, from 1976 to 1981, require of me not only Berowne in my own right at last, but Mercutio in *Romeo and Juliet,* Edgar to Donald Sinden's very good King Lear (in a production John started rehearsing but quit after a week as the play wasn't really to his liking), the title role in Euripides' *Hippolytus*, Sean O'Casey's *Shadow of a Gunman*, David Edgar's *Destiny*, Howard Brenton's *Thirteenth Night*, Hector in *Troilus*, the ubiquitous Duke in another *Measure for Measure*, Mirabell in *The Way of the World* opposite Judi Dench, the first of my four stage marriages to her over the next four decades, and also many one-off performances of *The Hollow Crown*. They also, as above, announced from the start to anybody who would listen both within the RSC and the world at large, that

I would be the next RSC Hamlet – they hadn't done the play in the main auditorium since Alan Howard undertook it in 1970. I came to know that John ultimately put his own future with the Company he had done so much to found onto the table as a bargaining counter: if any of his colleagues should disagree with this casting, they would lose both him and me for good. This struck me – and still does, perhaps even more so – as an astonishing act of loyalty to a favoured actor, since his own standards allowed him to offer no favours, and there were on the face of it plenty of alternatives. Once we'd done the production in 1980–1, I repaid him by turning him down quite often – never because of lack of trust, only because of disinclination for the part offered. For instance, it's always been pointless asking me for Bassanio in *The Merchant of Venice*; but John, normally so supportive, disapproved so much when I declined that he took a razor blade as we discussed it and absentmindedly started to shave his index finger, as careful not to draw blood as, it was said, he had been in olden days when he would chew just such a razor blade for recreation – or perhaps to keep awake, having just driven into Stratford car park after taking sleeping pills to see him through the day, just as he used to take amphetamines to go to sleep at night. This was not because he was a sophisticated addict trying something new, but merely out of carelessness.

His grizzled figure, bearded like the pard – he had had startling good looks as a young man comprised of the same basic ingredients, rather like a royal Plantagenet – is now at a corner table in a Newcastle restaurant next to the Theatre Royal, in 1979, during the RSC's annual springtime residency in the city, approving something I've just done because of its decency – not something on the stage, but some kind of encouragement I'd given a colleague, which validated me in his eyes not as an actor this time but as a considerate and kind enough human being, rather than his important but not necessarily obliging protégé. So was it some act of solidarity I'd shown with a small part player? Perhaps standing up for one such (against John, perhaps)? Or pastoral care – some thoughtfulness about someone's difficulty at home – or was it my attempt at humour in wearing a Newcastle United shirt (offstage) to encourage one of my colleagues who was born and bred locally – and who unfortunately then denounced me as a patronising cunt. Ironically John didn't like this, though he told me I was a cunt often enough himself when I turned him down, or didn't listen to his threat that if I didn't recant, he would block my potential inclusion on the RSC Associate Artists list; my stubbornness resisted his, and I only achieved this flattering but rather pointless title some twenty-five years later in the regime of Greg Doran.

This is all good fun to remember, especially on the occasions after John's death when his nearest and dearest from the RSC years fall to recalling his eccentricities; but it genuinely raises, for what it's worth, the question of how – certainly at that time – an actor fortunate enough to be largely formed by the RSC should conduct themselves. Should they show gratitude for what they've been given by occasionally playing a small part as a matter of team spirit – a sort of gratuity – or simply pursue the golden bough as ruthlessly as one might in the commercial theatre? Or something in between? Certainly Terry Hands (he never directed me, but I came to know him well when he ran the Company from 1978 to 1986 with Trevor and then alone till 1997) and I had an enjoyable row or two with him about this. I once complained to him that *Hamlet* had fewer performances scheduled in the Aldwych season that followed on from Stratford than any of the Company's other shows (all of them directed by Terry). His response was that the RSC had "made" me but I had never taken on the responsibility that entailed, such as playing a part I didn't want to touch rather than looking for more performances of my own. Both his and my tongues were I suspect in our cheeks as I defied this principle, though significantly, within five years of leaving the RSC I had formed the English Shakespeare Company with Michael Bogdanov, which in some ways functioned like the RSC in that ensemble was everything – so that I would accompany my Richard II or Henry V with the odd Mechanical in *Henry IV* or old dying Mortimer in *Henry VI*. I think it amused Terry to point out that just as he had been a producer as well as director, I was now an actor-manager running his own Company like a slightly more generous Donald Wolfit.

However, there *is* a responsibility if you take the best part – it's a phase that may not last anyway, particularly as age kicks in and cameos beckon – and it was pointed out not so much by John but more convincingly by Ron Daniels, a very important figure in the Company's work at the Other Place and the Warehouse, who, when we were engaged in *Hippolytus* – or was it *Destiny* – or was it *Afore Night Come*? – said I had a lot to learn not so much about acting but about nurturing the Company around me. He pointed me to the example of Alan Howard, who in many ways had dominated the Company for years but who, in every production he led, knew the names of his colleagues' children, their circumstances, their line of parts in the season. He said I should learn this knack fast, and I've tried to, in the knowledge that it won't last for ever and soon I'll be grateful to be offered anything at all.

I also insisted, especially to Ron, who was the director most likely to listen, on being a character actor – within myself I knew that since the transgressive Leach in *The Connection* at Cambridge I was ready for Johnny Hobnails, the slightly demented juggler of pears in the Worcestershire orchard proposed by David Rudkin in *Afore Night Come*; or the name part, all passionate prudishness coming to a sort of ecstatic grief in *Hippolytus*; or as a near-enough Enoch Powell figure, a rabid racist brought low by the loss of his beloved son in David Edgar's *Destiny*, a part I had to talk myself into as he was sixty-odd years old, like my father. In allowing me these self-casting surprises Ron used to warn me that I should be careful not to overplay my hand, but acknowledged that all the parts chosen were a lot more interesting than the standard student/youngish lover/angry man that was being routinely offered.

***

Thirty-five years later, at Richard Griffiths' funeral in April 2013, Holy Trinity Church in Stratford groaned at the seams – I'd never quite seen that before, certainly not at my wedding there. At the appointed moment, a presence made itself felt behind us and something like a great wooden liner started to process from the West door towards the altar, supported on the shoulders of six slightly buckling Atlases. Suddenly, in the rapt silence, a mobile phone started ringing. This was a thing Richard always detested, and in that way I'm glad he's not around to suffer it any more; he used to stop his own performances to rebuke any user from the stage. In Holy Trinity Church I swear the entire congregation, on left and right of the procession, swung to stare at the coffin and momentarily believed the lid would lift and Richard would emerge in eloquent reproof. And since Shaggy Dog Stories were, as it happens, a speciality of Richard's, they might have had to park him there, knowing that from now on, he could conduct proceedings from a supine position in the aisle.

It was a lot better than crying.

And most of all, I kept remembering how kindly Richard was. At the wake after the service Nick Hytner asked me how well I knew him; I said that having joined the RSC at the same time, I had swiftly become the resident romantic like Richard Burbage, and he was the star comedian, like Will Kempe. So we used to eye each other quite carefully at first, though I could always get Richard going by quoting the wonderful re-working by the 1950's Beat Generation stand-up comic Lord Buckley of Mark Antony's "Friends, Romans, Countrymen, Lend me your ears…" that I invariably used to do for Richard just before he went onstage, guaranteeing him good luck:

> Hipsters, flipsters and finger-popping daddys, knock
>   me your lobes;
> I come to lay Caesar down, not to hip you to him.
> The bad jazz a cat blows wails long after,
> The groovy is often stashed with the frame…

Nick said Yes, because, at some level, the tragedian and the clown always want to change places, yes, isn't that always a truth… He's right. It's always been the case since Pinero's invention of the very low and defeated comic actor Colpoys and the absurdly self-admiring romantic lead Ferdy Gadd in *Trelawny of the Wells*.

Talking of hipsters, I observed Richard for several seasons at the

Stratford Green Room poker table losing his wages to Jonathan Pryce, who was as quick as Richard was deliberate, in cards as in acting. And when in *Love's Labour's Lost*, for its one performance on Christmas Eve, I arranged the hire of Father Christmas outfits for the King and his court instead of romantic Muscovite costumes in Act V, Richard was the funniest and the quickest to make the idea work. Perhaps he was just humouring me. When Jane Lapotaire set about wrecking my peace soon after, while Richard and I were rehearsing Mikhail Bulgakov's *The White Guard* at the Aldwych, he would loan me his flat in Henrietta Street to go to, even for an hour or so's kip, during the working day. That was kindness indeed.

As you may have gathered, some considerable water had run under the Avon Bridge since Peter Hall had stood me down in 1966. Trevor Nunn's RSC had replaced Holm's, Dotrice's and Ashcroft's supremacy with, let's say, that of Alan Howard, Patrick Stewart, Helen Mirren and Janet Suzman. And in some ways (and I mean this affectionately) joining the RSC in the mid-1970s was a matter of deciding whether you liked the work of Alan Howard. Though also an expert comedian, he will of course be best remembered as Coriolanus and for the Histories, from *Richard II* to *Richard III*; in the gentlest way he dominated the Company. There were pert young actors who joined during that time who announced right away that they disliked the voice of this colossus of the stage, comparing him to a hectic trumpeter; most of them reconciled themselves to it, and I didn't have to.

So here is his King Hal in 1975, doing a sort of aggressive sidle down the steepish rake of the RSC stage to the very front of the apron, almost into my lap in the stalls: what with the slope and his rather haggard resolution he seems to be hurtling towards us. As Henry V, his voice, both rasping and melancholy, hits the back of the Stratford circle and bounces back to the stage. This is a form of projection that you might think would hurt, but Alan was smarter than that. As for me, I was watching *Henry V* because now that the RSC was showing an interest in me I wanted to observe how a master of that traditionally difficult old house at Stratford really operated. And that's how I know now.

How yet resolves the governor of the town?

Thus Henry V requires surrender following the successful English siege of Harfleur, and there are a number of ways of playing it. When I did the part some dozen years later I wondered about the historical dysentery that dogged King Henry during the French campaign. A suggestion of it, I hope not too pointed, gave me a desperate quality, though much more muted than Alan's, and I hope made you see King Henry not as a war machine but a man struggling with his own element of torment.

His influence reminds me of the fact that Alan has been one of the great co-ordinates of the classical theatre for the last forty years or so, an absolute hero in comedy or tragedy: his uniqueness lay in his simultaneous evocation of a great tradition of heroic acting and a form of lyrical intelligence which was entirely his own. He was his own masterpiece, and like all masterpieces somewhat inexplicable, having been working in this way for some fifteen years since he arrived at the RSC with Trevor in 1966, fresh from the Belgrade Theatre Coventry, in short order provoking a perfect storm as a thrillingly bisexual Achilles in John Barton's 1968 production of *Troilus*. As he was inclined to do under the direction of Terry Hands, Alan's tone as Henry V would shift up a notch with every line of his unfolding speech, like the *tirade* of a French actor (Terry had directed at the Comédie Francaise), or, an unkind critic might say, like a Victorian ham; but the fact is this was one of the greatest sounds of late twentieth-century theatre, a trumpet voluntary but more varied; it sat side by side with that of Paul Scofield, the supreme vocalist of my lifetime. It's only fortunate that Alan had run his Shakespearean course before amplified sound flooded the classical stage as it already has the musical theatre, neutralising the peculiar uniqueness of every actor's register: Alan's was processed on his own internal mixer board, and he didn't need another. He also, most amiably, broke all the pastoral rules: he liked a drink, he was a lifelong smoker (although a diabetic), as well as a colossus of the classical stage, but he was also extremely and deftly funny (*Wild Oats*) and as the most naturalistic portrayer of conscience (C.

P. Taylor's *Good*). Though he's left us now, he remains one of our enduring presences.

He and I never met on stage in the eight years we co-existed, but he reprised his Achilles in small measure in 1979, when the RSC improvised a workshop on Shakespeare entitled *Word of Mouth* compered by Trevor and John for Melvyn Bragg's *South Bank Show* on TV. Among other things Alan and I faced up to the cameras to demonstrate John Barton's reading of Hector and Achilles' long-awaited confrontation in *Troilus and Cressida*: before their two armies Hector stands still while Achilles prowls around him, eyeing up his prize:

> ACHILLES (AH): Tell me, you heavens, In what part of his body
> Shall I destroy him? Whether there, or there, or there?
> That I may give the local wound a name
> And make distinct the very breach whereout
> Hector's great spirit flew. Answer me, heavens!
>
> HECTOR (MP): Wert thou an oracle to tell me so
> I'd not believe thee. Henceforth guard thee well;
> For I'll not kill thee there, or there, or there,
> But by the forge that stithied Mars his helm,
> I'll kill thee everywhere, yea, o'er and o'er…

This unexpected showdown was one of the pleasures that perhaps only exists within a longstanding Shakespearean Company with a sense of continuity. People have been kind enough to say, Alan among them, how good it would have been to see us locking horns in an actual production – but the nearest we got was perhaps when Terry Hands suggested to me, slightly flirtatiously, that I should play Bolingbroke to Alan's Richard II so that Stratford audiences could witness Alan Howard taking off his crown in the Deposition Scene and surrendering it to Michael Pennington. This is the sort of thing directors occasionally feed your ego with and we ended up laughing, I asking Terry if this was an outcome he'd suggested to Alan. Naturally he hadn't, and I didn't play Bolingbroke. David Suchet did. And as for the flattery, I probably told bigger fibs when I ran the ESC.

But that wasn't all. Early the next year, 1980, while getting ready to go back up to Stratford to play Hamlet, I did Troilus again (thus finishing what I'd begun), on BBC radio, with Maureen O'Brien as Cressida. That was my third encounter with the play: having gone from Hamlet to Troilus in the Cambridge spring term of 1964, I had reversed the order by playing Hector in John Barton's 1976 production, on my longish path to the great Dane. I've an idea that my Hector then was a little reminiscent of Alan's 1968 Achilles, but without the shimmying, and we both owed something to Robert Stephens, so prehensile as Atahualpa in Peter Shaffer's *The Royal Hunt of the Sun*.

Shakespeare makes you think of Homer, *The Iliad* of *Troilus and Cressida*, Hector of Achilles and Achilles of Howard. Greek mythology and Elizabethan knowledge of it via the Roman tragedians is enough to keep these two great poets locked across time, however much their methods diverge. At twenty-four heroic books and over thirteen hours of audio performance, Homer's masterpiece – often deferred to rather than read – is no small undertaking in any medium; but recently I was impelled, by the demands of medical recuperation, to listen to the whole thing, duller bits and all. The actor entrusted with the *Iliad* recording I'd found was the terrific Anton Lesser, displaying the same magnetism and force that first sprung him into public attention in the RSC 1978 production of *Henry VI* (in whIch Alan Howard played the name part and Anton was his nemesis as Richard of Gloucester, soon to be Richard III). It was a magnificent debut engendering a brilliant career, in which the reading of Homer's masterpiece for home listening might seem a sidelight. In fact Anton's recording is no less heroic than the poem itself or perhaps than my resolute listening to it. For one thing I hadn't realised that Homer could no more resist a list of euphonious names, whether Trojan or Greek, for those either enlisting for or dying in battle, than could his successor Thomas Malory with his hundred and fifty Knights of the Round Table in *Morte d'Arthur*

(John Barton knew them all by heart and would list them at a moment's notice), or could Shakespeare (look at the roll-call of the French dead after Agincourt in *Henry V*). It's especially pleasant in the middle of one such cadenza in *The Iliad* to hear that one of Hector's victims in the battle was called Doris.

I also hadn't expected the identification by adjectival repetition – "his words had wings", "glorious Hector", "Diomedes, expert in war-cries", or the unsparing anatomical detail that causes the victims of savage spears and swords to "feel Death's black night slip over them"; or the precision with which the blind poet establishes Achilles as the tragic hero of the story and Hector as almost the juvenile lead; or indeed the emergence of a truly great love story between Achilles, whose spear is made from the ashwood of Mount Pelion, no less, and his beloved friend Patroclus, who when he imitates Achilles seems to "shine like a star". However, a mistimed impersonation of his friend costs Patroclus his life: he dresses in Achilles' armour and Hector, mistaking him, stabs him with his spear. Then Achilles, his hair shorn and covered with ash, circles his beloved's funeral pyre three times and piles it ever higher. He also organises a tournament of manly games, and prepares a sumptuous funeral feast for his friend: he covers the corpse with the fat of sacrificed animals and pitches horses onto the pyre as well as twelve Trojan prisoners of war. The fire burns till dawn: Achilles lies down to sleep, having doused the flames with wine and a suffocating double layer of fat.

Patroclus, ever confrontational, then visits him as a ghost:

> You're asleep… You've forgotten me… Give me your hand… we'll no more sit and make plans together… Don't lay your bones away from mine, but together as we always were… Let the same jar hold our bones, your mother's jar…

Next to this, even Shakespeare, who used so much of *The Iliad* for *Troilus and Cressida* (except the love story, which he got from Chaucer), looks cheap: he allows Patroclus only the status of a catamite or toy-boy rather than a truly heroic lover and friend. However, he does retain Patroclus' death at Hector's hands as being Achilles's decisive motive at long last for re-entering the War and revenging himself. He goes on a rampage, even taking on Scamander the river god, who waylays him with floods, roaring like a bull, hurling corpses onto the shore like a great dark wave, until Hephaestos, blacksmith of the gods (fire, metalworking, stone masonry, forges and the art of sculpture), son of Zeus and Hera and married to Aphrodite by Zeus to prevent a war between the gods fighting for her hand, intervenes to turn the very river into fire. None too soon: by now Achilles has turned it blood-red with his sword, taking a dozen stupefied Trojan figures "like fawns" as hostages in blood retribution.

After all this, Achilles is resolved "horse-taming Hector" will one day be "eaten by the dogs". When they finally come face to face, Achilles pursues him three times round the walls of Troy and its "windswept fig tree" (a nice if rather diminutive detail), in his blazing armour with his ashwood spear; they remain locked off at an unchanging distance from each other, so that Achilles cannot catch Hector but nor can Hector escape. The goddess Athena has intervened to arrange this – just as she does later, when Achilles throws his spear at Hector and Hector is inspired to duck so that it lands in the earth behind him; whereupon Athena, unobserved by Hector, returns the spear to Achilles to have another try. Nevertheless, Homer comments that anyone watching would agree that Achilles was like a mountain falcon swooping on a lone pigeon. Some pigeon.

Presumably, when the two heroes go hand-to-hand, the same cheery divine intervention by Athena causes Achilles narrowly to miss Hector's wind-pipe with his first sword-thrust, so that Hector has breath left to speak to his conqueror and bid farewell to the world. Zeus watches this reprieve from a distance like a sports fan. Incidentally, Athena is for some reason disguised throughout it all as Deiphobus, a Trojan, a name that Shakespeare borrowed for a tiny part in *Troilus*.

Mortally wounded, feeling his "fatal day slide down", Hector asks with his last breath that his body should suffer no indignity in death – a vain hope indeed since, as Achilles reminds him, a sheep can't bargain with a wolf. It is with an instinctive (and precise) theatricality that, as "death's long sorrow slides over Hector", Achilles celebrates his triumph with a night of utter grief as he reaches out for Patroclus, his comrade without equal. Homer identifies his state of mind unerringly:

> Achilles kept on weeping, remembering his dear companion … all-conquering sleep could not overcome him … as he tossed and turned, longing for manly, courageous, strong Patroclus, thinking of all he'd done with him, all the pain they'd suffered, as he kept remembering he cried heavy tears, sometimes lying on his side, sometimes on his back, sometimes on his face…

Then, as the sun comes up, he rides in distress along the shore in his chariot, first taking care to tie Hector's recently ruined body to its back – just in time, before Hector's wounds miraculously heal and he is finally left unblemished by death.

This is all superlative storytelling and highly theatrical: and indeed, if you read nothing else in *The Iliad*, look at the ending, which is both Homeric and Shakespearean, or even Chekhovian. Hector is dead, and Priam has come to Achilles to beg his son's body back and to shoot the breeze. He is surprised by the warmth and gallantry of his reception: and in fact what could be more beautifully and surprisingly done by Homer than this wisdom and respect, this acknowledgement of wrong and grace in the enemy, this devotion to the friends:

> Achilles: Vex me no longer; I am of myself minded to give up the body of Hector.

With these words Achilles springs like a lion through the door of his house, and bids Priam to be seated within. Together they lift Hector's body from its wagon, as well as two mantles and a "goodly shirt" that Achilles might wrap Hector in to be taken home to Troy. Achilles then calls to his servants and tells them to wash and anoint the body, but first takes it to a place where Priam cannot see it, "lest he should break out in the bitterness of his grief and enrage Achilles, who might then kill him."

Once the servants have done this, Achilles himself lifts it onto a bier, crying aloud as he does so, calling on the name of his own dear comrade:

> Achilles: Be not angry with me Patroclus, if you hear in the house of Hades that I have given Hector to his father for a ransom…

Then he goes back to the tent and takes his place with Priam, saying:

> Achilles: You shall look upon him at daybreak. For the present, let us have our supper.

Then he springs from his seat and kills a sheep of silvery whiteness, which his followers skin and make ready. By now Priam is marvelling at the strength and beauty of Achilles – he is as a god to see, and Achilles marvels at Priam as he listens to him and looks upon his noble presence. When they have gazed their fill Priam speaks:

> Priam: And now, O King, take me to my couch that we may lie down and enjoy the blessed boon of sleep. Never once have mine eyes been closed from the day your hands took the life of my son; I have grovelled without ceasing in the mire of my stable yard, making moan and brooding over my countless sorrows. But now I have eaten bread and drunk wine; hitherto I tasted nothing.

As Priam speaks, Achilles tells his men and women servants to set beds in the door of the gatehouse, to make them up with good red rugs, and to spread coverlets on top of them with woollen cloaks for Priam and his companion Idaeus to wear. The maids go out carrying torches and get the two beds ready in all haste. Then Achilles says laughingly to Priam:

> Achilles: Dear sir, you shall be outside, lest some counsellor

out of those who come to advise me should see you here in the darkness of the flying night, and tell King Agamemnon about it: that might cause delay in the delivery of the body. And now, tell me and tell me true: for how many days will you want to celebrate the funeral rites of noble Hector? Tell me, that I may hold aloof from war and restrain our host.

And Priam answers:

Priam: Since, then, you suffer me to bury my noble son with all due rites, do this, Achilles, and I shall be grateful. You know how we are pent up within our city; it is a long way for us to fetch wood from the mountain, and the people live in fear. For nine days, therefore, we will mourn Hector in my house; on the tenth day we will bury him and there shall be a public feast in his honour, on the eleventh we will build a mound over his ashes, and on the twelfth, if there be need, we will fight.

And Achilles answers:

All, King Priam, shall be as you have said; I will stay our fighting for as long a time as you have named.

As he speaks he lays his hand on the old man's right wrist, in token that he should have no fear. And so Priam and his attendant sleep in the forecourt, full of thought, while Achilles lies in an inner room of the house, with fair Briseis by his side.

***

Returning the compliment to Homer in *Troilus and Cressida*, Shakespeare does one thing Homer hasn't quite managed – an astonishing death for Hector, accomplished in a moment. Achilles's private army – his Myrmidons – swoop on the unarmed Trojan hero as he's resting from the fray, having himself just killed a character simply named "One in Sumptuous Armour" (and played when I was Hector in 1976 by the great, and greatly funny, Alfred Molina, who drew rich laughs from his panic as, having presumably stolen the armour, he turns a corner on the battlefield to come face to face with the Trojan Superstar himself).

Moments later, a harsh reality returns, as Achilles sees Hector and disposes of him. Then Shakespeare has the killer, flushed with his satisfied ambition, reflect:

> The dragon wing of night o'erspreads the earth
> And stickler-like the armies separates.
> Go tie his body to my horse's tail
> Along the field I will the Trojan trail.

What he's done is to allow his half a dozen Myrmidons to converge on Hector with their swords, and more importantly blood bags, only to disperse in a matter of split seconds, leaving me as gory as a pig's carcass hanging on a hook. So effectively in fact, that my ten-year-old Mark was propelled out of his seat at this moment in the dress circle at Stratford with a cry of "Daddy!" – an experience as gratifying as when he used to look into the back of the set if I was on radio or TV to check whether I was inside.

***

Alan Howard died at 77, on St Valentine's Day 2015: his own Valentine, Sally Beauman the writer, survived him by an inconsolable year and a half. This was two years after Richard Griffiths, a year after Donald Sinden and Richard Pasco and five months ahead of Roger Rees – it had been like an RSC cull. As if in prophetic memorial to Alan, there's a very ancient tomb painting in the Archaeological Museum of Naples of a local "attore" putting on his "maschera", and it looks exactly like him. By chance he lived opposite me in London for his last twenty years: I went to his funeral and read him a sonnet while – as I thought – his wicker coffin groaned a little.

Alan had looked boyish all his life despite his myopia and gradually diminishing health. By the time I met him in 1979, I already knew his best friend, the equally great Norman Rodway, with whom I'd just been in a TV production of Buchner's *Danton's Death*, in which Norman gave a truly definitive performance as Danton: it should be compulsory viewing for young actors. He'd used to play comparable parts at Stratford such as Richard III and Simon Gray's Butley, but they had dried up a bit. But in fact it was Norman, who beat Alan to the exit door on 13th March 2001 by 14 years, whom I'd come to know better. They'd been best friends ever since 1976, when they hilariously played together as Sir John Thunder and Rover in John O'Keefe's *Wild Oats* for the RSC, and had, quite simply, come to think of each other as affiliated.

As for me, in the theatre you sometimes catch up with your heroes. Norman's performance in a devised show taken from James Joyce's canon titled *Stephen D* had arrived with a bang from Dublin in 1963 and suggested an awesome buccaneer I never imagined would become my friend. In fact he had an Honours Degree in Classics – surely the course my father would have wished for me as he bowled to me in our garden; Norman's cricket-mad father likewise bowled to him, but would then listen to opera with his son all evening, which my father would never have done. I was to learn that my friend's red-blooded manner hid a spirit almost too delicate and fine – kind, anxious and always on your side. I think always of his high taste and his fearlessness, his mixture of boisterousness and extreme sensitivity, the bracing unexpectedness of his judgements. He was one of the very greatest radio performers (especially good in Evelyn Waugh's *The Sword of Honour*), a Shakespearean to the heart (he was Ulysses in our radio *Troilus*) and a first-class classical scholar, a pianist who could name every Köchel number in Mozart (but loved his Schubert even better); and he was completely unpredictable in his assessment of a performance.

Norman played Ulysses and Alan Thersites in the radio *Troilus* I've mentioned: it was indeed a cast to die for. Then (1980) I was almost immediately in Sean O'Casey's *Shadow of a Gunman* at the Other Place in Stratford as Donal Davoren with Norman as Seumas Shields, Dearbhla Molloy and Kilian McKenna, directed by Michael Bogdanov (of these only Dearbhla and I are still alive). This wonderful short play is set in 1921, towards the end of Ireland's War of Independence, written in 1923 as the first of a trilogy, before *Juno and the Paycock* and *The Plough and the Stars*. Seumas was perfect casting for Norman, forever quoting Shakespeare even when his room-mate Donal is desperate for a little sleep. As for the latter, I was put squarely and very welcomely off my patch as Donal Davoren, "poet and poltroon, poltroon and poet", an inadequate would-be Shelley caught in the crossfire, quite falsely rumoured to be an IRA assassin, and indirectly responsible for the murder by the Black and Tans of Minnie Powell, his tentative lover. It also marked my first proper meeting with Bogdanov, with whom I was to do so very much more. We'd been yoked together on *Gunman* by a bit of managerial *legerdemain* and were a little suspicious of each other: for one thing Michael knew Dublin inside out and was sceptical of what he thought were my posh credentials. I got there in the end, but I didn't imagine we'd work together again; but we sure as hell did, and formed a friendship that lasted till his death in 2017, raising a glass of good red wine to his lips on the island of Paros, before falling unmistakably dead on the ground.

When *Shadow of a Gunman* came to the Donmar in London, we were a short walk from the theatre to the Crown & Anchor, and there Norman, Michael and I would meet with Eileen O'Casey, Sean's widow and keeper of the flame, who, it turned out, thoroughly approved of us; I pinched myself to think I was shaking the hand that had held that of the great dramatist, much as I would one day feel about a close descendant of Anton Chekhov. The encounter probably boosted my confidence as I embarked, also in 1981 at the Warehouse, on Howard Brenton's fascinating *Thirteenth Night,* directed by Barry Kyle, about the corruption of socialism, based unashamedly on Neil Kinnock. It imagined a Macbeth-like assassination perpetrated by a Kinnock clone (me): a brave idea that acknowledged the porous boundary between socialism and Communism.

Shadow of a Gunman meanwhile consolidated my rest-of-life friendship with Norman. Over the twenty years following I would see him, unhappily on his third marriage and living in Banbury. He could drink all right but he couldn't cook at all: he once gave me as successive courses macaroni cheese and cauliflower cheese (both M and S) for supper. By now the dearest of friends, he used to tell me, with entire calmness and even warmth, how he would really prefer to be dead, his third marriage having been such a disastrous mistake, particularly in respect of his much-loved daughter Bianca from the second. Every time he stole down to London for supper with me I became used to dropping him back off at Marylebone Station, and his saying without the slightest melodrama that in view of this marital deadlock he was quite willing to expire that night. Eventually he had a stroke and lingered on in Banbury Hospital: I used to visit every few days, often together with Jane Morgan, a great radio director who also loved him (Norman was tremendous as Abthorpe in her equally tremendous version of *Sword of Honour*). Deathly ill and immobilised, his eyes locked onto his visitors and followed him or her around the room, undeceived at the end, like the Lear he should have played. I would sometimes go alone to read him James Joyce and Samuel Beckett, to what looked like his childish delight, until the final visit came, when he stopped me with a gentle gesture of his hand halfway through and then executed a small smiling wave of farewell instead. He died the next day, in 2001. Sadly, Alan Howard deeply disapproved of his last marriage; death caught Norman out before they made it up and Alan was distraught at the funeral – after all, they had completely thought of and addressed each other as siblings. And they remain the only RSC actors I've known who seemed to hold an all-night key to the Dirty Duck and have an inkling of imminent police raids. They would put the Shakespearean world to rights, go to bed at dawn, and be fit and buoyant for a matinée and evening that day.

I miss Norman almost more than any of my now quite numerous departed. His laughter, for one thing, came in two registers – a full-throated chuckle and a sort of incredulous whinny, or trill: both were somehow to do with his conviction that everything in life was a form of comedy, including tragedy; nothing was more serious than the first, nothing more foolish than the second. A great spirit gone. I hope he's laughing his laugh.

Michael Pennington

***

Thirty-five years after *Shadow of a Gunman* and *Thirteenth Night*, in the summer of 2017, I was playing at the Donmar again, as Dogsborough in Bertolt Brecht's *The Resistible Rise of Arturo Ui*. When kind young people on the theatre staff asked me if I'd perhaps played their theatre before, I was ready for them, and followed an instinct each time as to whether they were up for a full version of the answer or an abridged one, or even just for a twenty-first century soundbite to reinforce their sense of entitlement.

A short pause is worthwhile because The Donmar, once called the Donmar Warehouse, and before that simply The Warehouse, is, among London theatres, second only in evocativeness to the slightly less productive Roundhouse in Chalk Farm. Both began as what are called Found Spaces, and both have retained a little of their historic air (the Roundhouse was a railway turntable shed long before Arnold Wesker adapted it as a performing space for his Centre 42 project in 1964 – we had it for the London run of the Nicol Williamson *Hamlet* in 1969). Nearly a century before this, In the 1870s, the Donmar site was a hop storehouse belonging to the Covent Garden Brewery, until it began to be used as a film studio and then as a banana-ripening depot. It's been a theatre since 1961 but has passed from hand to hand, changing its name with some regularity, owned by impresarios such as Donald Albery, Nica Burns and the Ambassadors Theatre Group; it's been a Rehearsal Studio for London Festival Ballet; been led with great success by Sam Mendes, Michael Grandage, Josie Rourke, and now Michael Longhurst (this much my listeners do know); it's housed Cheek by Jowl, hosted stand-up comedy and Stephen Sondheim, and actors and audiences love it for its intimacy.

I pause to see how I'm doing with my speech: if time is short I refer my questioner only to David Greig's play *The Cosmonaut's Last Message to the Woman He Once Loved in the Former Soviet Union*, which I played there in 2005, by which time the theatre was autonomous, kept alive by a sage mix of West End ticket prices and sponsorship. Having taken another moment to assess my audience,

I tell them something much more important, which is that the show also featured my first and perhaps last nude scene (much to the disgust of the *Observer* critic, who said he didn't go to the theatre to see my 62-year-old backside – so he'd checked on Wikipedia). My thanks to Iain Glen, an old friend, who had advised me on the phone that if I was really to play in the buff, I should be sure to do some preparatory exercises in order to cut, shall we say, a good figure. He'd learned this from working with Nicole Kidman in *The Blue Room*. (Actually, you may also remember I'd likewise lost my TV virginity, with Penelope Wilton, in the Thirty Minute Theatre back in 1971, but the camera didn't linger long.)

Cosmonaut was a production remarkable for suspending two actors – Paul Higgins and Sean Campion – as spacemen above the action in harnesses for the whole evening; they twisted and swung parlously and in some considerable discomfort, giving their considerable all to David Greig's text.

If my interlocutor's eyes haven't glazed over with one emotion (shyness) or another (hilarity) by then, I hasten on to a bigger point, which is that between 1977 and 1981 I did half a dozen shows here with the RSC. Their eyebrows lift – the RSC at the Donmar? I explain that towards the end of 1976 Trevor Nunn called a meeting of his Stratford Company, of which I was part. He was hotfoot back from London where he'd found a solution to the Company's dilemma *du jour*: although we were ending our Stratford season with the usual expectation of bringing the classical repertoire from its main house into the Aldwych Theatre, the remarkable work that had been done in The Other Place (a great deal rougher and more temporary-looking than it is in its rebirth now) – had no London venue to move into because of its very much smaller scale. Trevor had been tipped off about the Warehouse, as it was then, and spoke luridly of its ongoing decomposition – perhaps on the basis that to be forewarned is to be pleasantly surprised. Broken windows, lousy acoustic, rats; but Donald Albery, its owner, had agreed to house our smaller-scale repertoire here, within shouting distance of the Aldwych (as were the two Stratford theatres to each other), so the idea of encamping gave a pleasing sense of familiarity: Covent

Garden was about to become as much the home of the RSC as of the opera, the ballet or the vegetables.

I wasn't in the first 1977 season at the Warehouse – *The Good Soldier Schweyk* featured Michael Williams, Edward Bond's *Bingo* Pat Stewart, and Charles Wood's *Dingo* prevailed; I was busy shouting at the Aldwych as Edgar in *King Lear* and in David Edgar's great play about the National Front, *Destiny* – in the latter case dodging the fights that regularly broke out on the pavement between enraged liberal audiences coming out after the show and Front members who, imagining the evening to be an advertisement for their cause, were hanging around trying to enlist the customers, like more toxic *Star Wars* fans. My own Warehouse debut came a couple of years later, when we transferred from Stratford David Rudkin's stripped-down translation of *Hippolytus*, Euripides' version of the Phaedra story, with Patrick Stewart and Natasha Parry as my father and step-mother. This was the second time I'd worked with Rudkin, the first having been the revival of his classic *Afore Night Come* in 1974 at the Stratford end, in which I played the village "idiot" tractor driver Johnny Hobnails, who cared only for the handsome young student working in the orchard and for juggling with the windfall pears (a particularly tricky juggle, may I say, because of the relative irregularity of their weight and curvature of their bases). Not transferring that had been particularly frustrating for Ian McDiarmid, who was playing the lead; for me too, it would have been a chance to demonstrate a character range rather than simply playing the eligible young man.

Three years later, however, *Hippolytus* offered me another chance. He is the proud but innerly catastrophic young man desired by Phaedra, not least perhaps because of his puritannical and misogynistic nature: he cares only for hunting. The pleasure of being with Rudkin again was to witness the Greek scholar in him: he was a proud and upright man, bearded and coiffed like Silenus, the patron saint of wine, but always shoeless in rehearsal, where he would produce magnificently complex unanswerable arguments to do with choral anapaests etc, to explain why not a single line could be cut. At those moments he looked like Aristotle, and though I'd got into university on my Classics, he left me standing. I much admired him, and I was grateful for a part that made me feel my own work had taken a step towards the dimensions of a full-blooded tragedian (just as well, as Hamlet was confirmed for the following year). I don't mean in the old-fashioned, Edmund Kean manner, but I did revel in the gradual charting of a brave soul declining from golden boy to embattled, pervasive desperado.

On the first night in London I unaccountably developed a slight tendency to yawn and therefore had to suppress what is technically an oxygen deficit. While being cross-examined by Pat Stewart as my father Theseus, I strode towards the audience (as we often do now in *Ui*), and asked frankly, truthfully and as openly as I could (no hiding when confiding): "Am I acting wrongly?", only to find myself looking straight into the eyes of the critic Michael Billington, who immediately looked down at his writing pad and jotted down a note. So that's the *Guardian* review fucked, I thought (in fact not).

I had yet another chance with Rudkin the scholar some thirty-five years later, when he wrote me a radio play (*Macedonia*) about the author of *Hippolytus*, in which Euripides himself was the central character; it imagined the playwright's withdrawal to Macedonia towards the end of his life and getting the idea for *The Bacchae*. The same David: upright, proud and inordinately imaginative, completely and wrongly out of fashion. This time he kept his shoes on.

Macedonia made wonderful radio, together for some reason with a slight sense of mission fulfilled: in 1978 I'd spotted in the Stratford ensemble, playing voiceless whores and nuns and all the rest in *Measure for Measure* (in which I was the Duke this time), an actress straight out of RADA called Juliet Stevenson: I instantly knew how good she was, or would be when she had a chance to speak, and I started banging on the doors of the resident directors – Barry Kyle, Ron Daniels and others – nagging them to give her something to do. The outcome had been *Hippolytus*, in which she played two goddesses – Artemis and Aphrodite, who represented the twin poles of hunting and sex between which the hero gyrated. We went on together into Bulgakov's *The White Guard*, which opened at the Aldwych soon afterwards. I can boast about this talent-spotting because of course if I hadn't noticed Juliet somebody else would have done pretty soon, though there was some prejudice in senior areas of the directorate, one of whom declared, offensively, that her face resembled a pudding – a nice pudding, of course. but still a pudding. Shame on him. Now, forty years later and by pure chance, she and I and, until he died, Alan Howard, have been half-a-dozen-doors-away neighbours in London. This feels like – I don't know why – a curiously redemptive outcome. She is of course one of the very best of our kind, and certainly needs no further praise from me.

In 2017, this lengthy folkloric account of my Donmar years has quaintly intrigued my new colleagues, but for me has had a more serious consequence. The problem increasingly is not so much that none of them remember Norman Rodway or Natasha Parry or Alan Howard, but that I myself keep turning a corner and seeing the three of them, and Patrick Stewart. Then the present-day Donmar suddenly fills up with the past: ghostly bricks and mortar replace the contemporary elegant plastic trim, and a cavernous sense of barn like spaciousness replaces the congestion brought about by such modern necessities as an entire, not-much-used overflow office for the production team, a Green Room that smells at all times of slightly burned Welsh Rarebit abutting on the cocktail bar front of house, a tricky spiral staircase and every variety of toilet. This has led, for me at least, to a time-slip about the entire building, like that of the two ladies of Versailles, or, if you like, the effect the Gardens at Glyndebourne can have, when a single evening dress or dicky spins anxiously round to assess your parking skills on arrival as if they'd never seen a car before. Like a demented archaeologist, I keep stopping in mid-corridor to assess where I am in relation to what, standing on the 1978 groundplan rather than today's; I often expect to turn a corner and be flipped back to some forty-year old conversation.

The one thing that ls almost exactly the same is the stage. The same runways pass from it through the audience along two diagonals; they have become open invitations to the public to stretch their legs stubbornly onto the runway even when an actor is signalling their immediate, surely unmistakeable intention to use one of them for an exit.

The dressing rooms are the shock. In those old days, to get from yours to the stage upstage right (by far the most common entrance), you would leave behind you a big open dressing-room space, square and light, with a partial partition down the middle dividing the men's quarters from the women's. Rather as at The Other Place in Stratford, you then entered a little antechamber (you could see it as an isolation chamber where you magically became someone else), turned briefly left then right, and there you were, on and in action. You could also enter (and exit) downstage right through the front of house, but I think the farther side, upstage left, formed one of the routes directly down to the street. Then, coming offstage, you could pass through the isolation chamber again, past the dressing-room partition into the far more tasteful women's area, where their company often seemed preferable (that hasn't changed) – and then, I remember vividly, down a long flight of stone steps to the street, which I can still identify as the one that now leads away from the vomitorium entrance downstage right, just at the limit of the audience's domain.

In these dressing rooms of old there were even windows and stretching space, as well as a slightly unfinished air: they were workmanlike and busy, but not overcrowded. In the men's area I used to sit two or three places along the outer wall, next to Norman Rodway one night or Patrick Stewart, depending on the repertoire, the next; and this is where Trevor Nunn came through one day in 1979 to sell us another initiative: his plan to do the *South Bank Show* that I mentioned on Shakespeare and Stratford for Melvyn Bragg. *Word of Mouth* ended up as a great success in its own right and was also the trigger for John Barton's longer series that is now studied by all the young US actors I have ever met.

All gone. The dressing rooms are now a fraction of the size and without mercy. I entertain myself by trying to work out, allowing for the slightly different architecture, who sat where I am now and who's where I used to be. I figure that Gloria Obianyo is now perched pretty much exactly where I was when Trevor Nunn made his announcement; but if she was to hear it now she'd have to prepare for it by unloading undreamed-of equipment – ipod, charger, etc. – that none of us then would have understood at all.

It strikes me sometimes that another reason to support gender-blind casting is that it could even up the unjust fact that at present the women, being often in the numerical minority, have far more elbow room in the same size of room than we do in ours – instead both could be 100 per cent shared. One consequence of the present arrangement is that the women's quarters are a haven of peace, its tenants going about their business with grace, gentle music and the scent of roses, whereas ours rapidly declines into a locker-room. The adorable hooligans I share the room with – individually kind and thoughtful people, loving husbands and fathers, intellectuals, artists, highly musical, highly aware – have quite rapidly declined into fetid adolescence: horsing about, watching old movies without earplugs including Tom and Jerry cartoons, singing soul music, doing full decibel impersonations of Bruce Forsyth and a great deal other clamour besides: this is what my beloved friends get their adrenaline up with for the show, generally sustained by infinite conversational variations on the theme of imagined, outlandish *fellatio*. I turn to Alan Howard sitting on my left and make a face across time. It's a pity that seven males are in a room with four mirrors only; if you bend over to pick something up from the floor you'll either crack your forehead or cause a major traffic jam in the room.

Well, I'm as gamesome as the next man, but to be candid, from ten past seven on (curtain up 7.30) all this clamour is almost unbearable to be in a room with. So I slip away from my hemmed-in place in the Stygian midden and sit quietly in the corridor between the water machine and a dominant staircase upwards – and, as it happens, next to the Ladies loo. Or sometimes, next to it, half inside a tiny paint shop (once it would have been Jane Lapotaire's place in *Piaf*). The fact is that different performers have different ways of getting their adrenaline up for the job: by ten past seven my own is already running like a steady underground canal, so if I see a bentwood chair in the corner of the corridor I grab it. I consider my lines, I think about Chicago (a city I know well, though not from 1930), and dig into Dogsborough, City Hall boss and Brecht's barely concealed portrait of von Hindenburg, if not a little deeper, then a lot more intently. I'm not meditating, just sitting quiet to consider what I might be able to do better tonight than I did last night. So, without denying my love for my colleagues, I get the hell away from them and sit outside these lavatories. I don't think they miss me, but by turns respect and take the piss out of me. In my Chicago businessman's double-breasted suit I do look like a well-to-do comfort-station attendant or perhaps a wealthy Peeping Tom; I find the girls are more larky about my presence so close to their private activities than the men, fraught as the latter suddenly are, sometimes after the beginners' call, by the urgent prospect of having to shut up and start the show. As I reflect sometimes a little on the story of my days, suddenly, making his way through for his own first entrance, Rodway laughs his whinnying laugh at the fastidiousness of our successors.

Justine Mitchell, whom I already regarded as a kind of genius – she was astonishing in the show, with access to her emotions like that of Vanessa Redgrave – writes to me as I write this (I promise):

> I often think very fondly of you sitting on your chair at the bottom of those stairs at the Donmar, escaping from the roiling banter of the boys' dressing room, so quiet and peaceful – and then boom! There you were descending those stairs, Lenny waiting for you, uncorruptible surely. Mesmeric? Definitely.

What my apparently awesome professional longevity (53 years on the game) means in practice that, though I'm still fit for purpose, I take precautions rather than depending on my former merry abandon; breathing in, straightening my back as Hippolytus or Donal Davoren without a second thought. Also I go over and over my lines each night, at speed until the moment of going on, which then becomes just the latest of my run-throughs, but this time with some acting added. I have my own map of the steeplechase ahead: between Scene 2 and Scene 4, I know I have time to go over Scene

4 two or two-and-a-half times, listening for the links between one thing and another, realising that one or two of them have become opaque or have never quite been resolved. I don't know if I need to do this, but I feel much better for it, in spite of the fact that when I very occasionally make a slip – no more often than anybody else – it clearly has nothing to do with not preparing, being just that involuntary little dip of concentration we all know – it's not the loss of memory in fact, but of the ability to stay on the moment, that needs sustaining as you get older. It also means, to my astonishment, that I still feel a following wind, or at least a current of air behind me at the last moment before entering, between incurable fear and sudden confidence, as if to say: This is where you're happiest, what you can do and you're still good at it. I recently realised that I do an exit along the left-hand vomitorium after Scene 2 of *Ui* gently playing with my Deed to the Shipyard Trust, and it is in fact the same exit I do after Dogsborough's agonised confession in Act Two. I realise this is what it means to Cast a Spell. That is, I can feel the collusion between me and the audience on that repeated walk, of them happy to believe (and keeping their feet out of the way) and me as a relatively familiar actor to some of them, the slide of trusting belief in them from the actor to the character that they've come here to find (as have I). It's the purest Make Believe, and utterly validating.

***

Even thirty-six years earlier, violence seemingly attended me at the Donmar. The Tommys shot out the tenement in *Shadow of a Gunman*, Hippolytus died at the hands of a great and improbable sea monster, my own Neil Kinnock hands were bloodstained in *Thirteenth Night*; now it is the routine savagery of Arturo Ui's gang. I've doubled my age, with two King Lears behind me and who knows what else, and now I'm in the company of Lenny Henry, who would have been twenty-one when I was reading Joyce to Norman Rodway. Most of the cast are still younger – Giles Terera (Ernesto Roma) was coming up to twenty-three, and several weren't yet born.

And today has been my 74th birthday, the cue for a generous cast celebration, and there's a certain amount of Grand-Old-Mannery in the air. The warmth of younger actors is one of the major gratifications of my life, though I pretend to believe that all of them have sat a special module in their final year of training called How to Be Nice to the Old Fellas: I can make this joke because I know it's not true. These young actors are in any case quite brilliant; they sing, they play, they dance, they juggle. And they're everywhere: after our show closed one of the first things I saw was at the Old Vic, where Conor McPherson's *Girl from the North Country* was blessed not only with Bob Dylan's songbook and encouragement but with a superb set of similar young talents; to hear 'Like a Rolling Stone' or 'Sign on the Window' sung for once not by the old corncrake himself, wonderful as that is, but by passionate young voices in duet, ensemble and solo, lifted you out of your seat.

I seem to be being viewed for the moment as a Living Legend. How is that? It's probably necessary from the start to have stories from the inconceivable era of studio television; a lifetime of Shakespeare helps a bit too; but neither competes with the fact that after finishing Hamlet at the RSC in 1981, I did three underpaid days on *Star Wars* for a buy-out sum of £300. It was an engagement I accepted rather as a response to pious though well-intentioned questions as to what was the next "mountain" I was thinking of climbing after Hamlet. Well, it was Moff Jerjerrod in *Return of the Jedi*.

All I really remember about it is the gentleness of the director Richard Marquand, who was to die soon after the end of shooting; the remoteness of George Lucas, the limpness of Harrison Ford's handshake on greeting, or my old friend Ian McDiarmid in the make-up chair at about 6am as the Emperor. I affected to pretend he looked just as he did at the RSC as Shylock or Don John; I now know how the words "Fuck off…" sound gently coming from an Emperor from behind several layers of latex. And Dave Prowse telling me about the money that could be made at the Conventions, and then breaking into an unholy sweat as he added "… and the *women*…" He also complained that at the end of our first take I had stepped on his cloak, even though we were out of shot. It was accidental but small recompense for the fact that he had long ago taken the position not to trouble with learning his lines but rather leaving me, who knew the text better, to assess roughly how long it would have taken him had he actually spoken them. This also serving as a subtle revenge for the fact that no inch of his own skin was visible, ever, as Darth Vader, and he was to be re-voiced in any case by James Earl Jones. And that, as an old hand, he had the satisfaction of ticking off a newcomer (how unlike Eric Porter).

This comical half-week resulted in the terrible birth of a *Star Wars* survivor pursued since 1981 by autograph hunters, many of them with no scruples of any kind, except that they don't want their signatures personalised. Well, I wonder why. Now I sell them at the odd Convention (and my goodness, they can be odd there), to make up for the original underpayment. There tend to be gasps of astonishment at this in dressing rooms when this news breaks – today's young actors are enormously generous in general – and I have even found myself in the *Arturo Ui* pre-show warm-ups finding that my new friends have re-staged my main scene in the film – the Storm Troopers in line, Darth Vader and me – and of course they know the lines far better than I do – well, I don't remember them at all. All I can do is give them a pre-show exercise of learning and delivering Richard Griffiths's favoured Lord Buckley riff on "Friends, Romans, Countrymen, Lend me your ears..." or sometimes a spirited rendition of Marie Lloyd's *The Boy I Love*:

> I'm a young girl, and have just come over,
> Over from the country where they do things big,
> And amongst the boys I've got a lover,
> And since I've got a lover, why I don't care a fig.
> The boy I love is up in the gallery,
> The boy I love is looking now at me,
> There he is, can't you see, waving his handkerchief,
> As merry as a robin that sings on a tree.
> The boy that I love, they call him a cobbler,
> But he's not a cobbler, allow me to state.

For Johnny is a tradesman and he works in the Boro
Where they sole and heel them, whilst you wait.
The boy I love is up in the gallery,
The boy I love is looking now at me,
There he is, can't you see, waving his handkerchief,
As merry as a robin that sings on a tree.
Now, If I were a Duchess and had a lot of money,
I'd give it to the boy that's going to marry me.
But I haven't got a penny, so we'll live on love
    and kisses,
And be just as happy as the birds on the tree.
The boy I love is up in the gallery,
The boy I love is looking now at me,
There he is, can't you see, waving his handkerchief,
As merry as a robin that sings on a tree.

– which has always seemed to me the key to any performer's anxiety about failing to reach out or even to be audible at the furthest point of the biggest imaginable theatre audience. But audibility is only marginally a matter of technique; it's primarily one of inordinate desire.

A meeting in Assisi Town Hall in 1981.

THE FREEDOM OF THE CITY

An Invitation from
Maria Teresa Biondi Minciotti

P laying Hamlet not only brings you a certain self-esteem, but if you do it twice it can win you the freedom of the city of Assisi. In theory you might have heard of someone who has played Romeo or Juliet gaining the freedom of Verona, or seen a biopic of Bernadette winning the liberty of Lourdes, but I haven't; and if you can boast of a week on *Star Wars* (making you more famous than a couple of hundred performances as Hamlet) you get the global password to all Comic Cons. Would I lie to you?

One day at Stratford, round about my hundredth Hamlet performance in 1981, I got a letter from Maria Teresa Biondi Minciotti, who sounded young. To my eternal sorrow I have now mislaid it, but I recall exactly the little crest on the top left hand corner with an ink-drawn vista of her house, Casa dei Pini, just outside Assisi. Her letter began "Caro Gran Maestro", and was deeply appreciative of the performance, though not particularly detailed about it. (Later in our friendship, she calmed down and wrote "Dear Great Master" – I'm not sure which I preferred.)

To cut a short story shorter, a correspondence ensued, in which Teresa was good enough to come clean by saying she was a widow of advancing age: whatever other fans were writing to me at that time, none was either so elderly or in a position to offer me the freedom of a city (with the enthusiastic endorsement of the Mayor) and a free holiday staying at the Hotel Subasio… Could I bring my fifteen-year-old son Mark in his summer holiday, I wondered? Yes, he would be welcome too.

Arriving at the Subasio, seemingly built into the city walls and presiding over the valley of Perugia, on an August Sunday, with him all ragged and be-travelled, we find Teresa in the lobby together with a young friend called Vicky, who will be in attendance throughout, and another who will not reappear, allegedly called Annunzia. I have an impression of bombazine black and lace moving at high speed towards us in greeting, waving aside our regrets at delaying her and then, without much further comment, darting away into the night. We are then shown three different rooms by the manager and opt for the third, a suite with a big balcony overlooking Santa Maria degli Angeli in the valley. Mark can't believe it. I am, as often in those days, poised on a critical edge with him all evening, wanting him to enjoy the humour in all this but not to take it too much for granted, or to embrace it opportunistically: in fact, he will now always associate luxury Italian hotel suites with the falsetto riffs of ravening Perugian mosquitoes.

10.40am Monday
Teresa and Vicky are there and ready; while Vicky gets the car, Teresa falls to establishing how much French or Italian we might be relied upon to speak. She fairly hums with energy: black and white dotted dress, her bouffon hair firmly in place. We're off to meet the Assistant Mayor, since the Mayor himself is in Spain, *molto dispiace*, he cannot meet us (I hear the first brick falling out of Teresa's wall), but Dottore the Assessore has worked with her on the invitations to celebrities for the summer festivities, he is a nice man, *molto bene, mio caro*, who has worked hard with her on the assembly of 'notables' for the occasion.

Now we are climbing a hill towards the Town Hall while Teresa offers:

"You know my very sad story, very very sad, I lost my husband and my son, and now I am all alone, but I have my faith, my faith, yes, and I travel whenever I feel sad. And my friends, for friendship is the greatest good, is it not, don't you agree?" – and a bird-like hand darts out from the back seat to grasp my arm – "and now we are friends, yes?"

A friend as well as a mere honoured guest. Teresa's cheekbones are smooth as if with weeping, especially in contrast to the rest of her face, which is creased like a map of the Appennines, and her eyes are clear and brown and alive. Now she is indeed weeping, or nearly, at her own confession, but in a moment she moves on to the excitement of our visit, and I reflect how good it must be to have this emotional tide so available to her, allowing her not so much to hide her sorrow as to move on from it in a trice.

She bustles out of the car and up the steps of the Town Hall. Halfway up she stops as if she'd made a sudden mistake and asks how we live – where is Mark's … mother, yes? A brother and a sister? I explain without embarrassing her with the actual D word, as I suspect she would not approve of Divorce. On the first floor we are augmented by two escorts: a seedy-enough looking journalist, and a large, assessing woman from Radio Subasio who, it turns out, has a list of questions for me and a cassette recorder. It seems they don't know my theatre work, but they have, she assures me, "seen me on the radio"…? We're in the Mayor's Office by now, arguing about the stage management of the interview. When the chubbily courteous Dr Assessore shows up to stand behind the Mayoral desk nobody talks to him, being too involved with the mechanics of the interview – who will interpret, etc? Teresa has decided to, though her English is no better than Vicky's, but perhaps this is a matter of honour. She listens a little shakily to my answers to the questions – luckily I have boned up a little on St Francis and can work into my answers the recent thunderstorm at the La Verna Franciscan Sanctuary and Mark's genuine enthusiasm for the saint. This piece of mutton-as-lambing is so great that if I catch Mark's eye we shall both be lost. Teresa's finger darts up in a cautionary gesture, a sign of her enthusiasm rather than disapproval, as she will do every time she reaches her maximum for translation.

Gifts start appearing from nowhere. A book of fresco prints for me, and a medal of Assisi. A book on St Francis for Mark appears by magic, and one from the absent Mayor proper to Teresa as well about Shakespeare (thank God for him). Cameras flash: I sign the register under a grand full page headed: "Visit from Michael Pennington, August 9th".

Then we are out and across the hall "– mind your feet, my dearest, all this pink marble is from our own Mount Subasio, very slippery". I genuinely admire the marble; and now we're off to see the Hall of Conciliazione with its heraldry and honoured citizens round the walls, and while everyone waits for a confirmation of how many are coming to lunch, the journalist, who is of the Right Wing (sharing with the Assessore a dislike of Communists), launches into an expatiation on the brotherhood of man, the uselessness of war, and St Francis – a speech which he says he makes whenever he sees a foreigner – presumably because only an Italian could have such thoughts, and perhaps putting us on notice that we are not the only ones to be honoured by it.

"I have an interesting thing to tell you too, here is the story, *mia carita*. The Russians – oh! Oooh – poor things, praise be to God."

Teresa's hands flap melodramatically in my face when I tell her that in my experience you can only spend one evening with a Soviet acquaintance before he gets into trouble. She is imperious only in her need to tell me, or agree with me, which she does so intensely that I initially think she is disagreeing. Sometimes she is camp, sometimes girlish, sometimes imperious from her breeding, and will not let you speak if you go to thank her or open your heart in return.

The talk moves to Italians who only gossip and never travel (I think, like Russians?), unlike the English, unlike me. She doesn't like to gossip, would rather talk to the nuns or a poor old lady in the town. She is all the things I guessed – eccentric rich widow and mother, but also a snob who nevertheless loves St Francis and the poor. Today she is in a mauve dress, her earrings pearl and diamond, her wedding finger bright with diamonds, her hairnet still in place, and as she goes to show me the cross next to her heart she almost exposes her shift and all. She tells the story of a sick Russian soldier in her town, a POW, who once prayed with her in silence, out of pure fear. By contrast, we also talk of banking, promissory notes, how her late husband used to pay cash down for a car, and the moment there is the hint of a pause or a thought of going, she is on her feet, waving us away with all her love. She can't bear, obviously, for things to fizzle out tamely,

Of course you learn more and more. We stayed a week and it turned out that Teresa wins international prizes for her delphiniums. She loves her Shakespeare too, without having seen very much, so I was able appositely to quote her the eloquent gardeners in *Richard II* on the subject of their apricots. Then she starts requesting that I perform the bit in *Julius Caesar* when Antony says (she says): "Listen to me, my fellow-citizens, my friends" and then from *Romeo and Juliet*: "Romeo, O Romeo, where are you, Romeo" (quite a familiar misreading, that one).

Mark and I had Christmas cards and pre-Christmas letters for a good dozen years from Teresa. Then came a year when we got neither, even after quite a bit of prompting. May she rest in peace.

Strider – The Story of a Horse *(National Theatre, 1984)*.

"ON, ON"

– Peter Hall, *passim*

> Into a thousand parts divide one man
> And make imaginary puissance…
> Carry them here and there, jumping o'er times,
> Turning the accomplishment of many years
> Into an hour-glass…
> – William Shakespeare, *Henry V*

By 1992 it seemed to me I'd barely seen Peter Hall for twenty-five years, though he always seemed to be just out of sight, inventing most of what we now (or till recently) have all taken for granted about British theatre. The idea of production previews, of long-term contracts for actors, of a permanent London home for the RSC: all his – not to mention the conviction that an artistic director (such as himself) could run the National Theatre and Glyndebourne at the same time. In truth though, I'd bumped into him on the backstage stairs of the Festival Hall one night in 1982, when Janet Suzman and I were providing narrations for Simon Rattle's version of Berlioz's *Beatrice and Benedict*, sung supremely by Philip Langridge and Maria Ewing, who at that time was married to Peter. After the show he looked like an eager schoolboy hoping for an autograph as he clambered up to Maria's dressing room. This is not altogether out of character; for all his sophistication, his musicality and his fine judgement of performers in all fields, he had several dollops of the youthful excitement of a lifelong fan who still couldn't quite believe his luck; and that, for that moment, included running into me.

And in reality, I had seen him from time to time during 1984 when I was at his National Theatre, not so much at his behest as that of his trusted associate directors Peter Gill (*Venice Preserv'd*), and Michael Bogdanov (Tolstoy's *Strider – The Story of a Horse*); he'd also given his blessing (sight unseen) to my having a forty-performance run in the Cottesloe of my brand new solo Chekhov show, of which more later. During this period he talked cheerily to me about what he and I should do next – Antony (Cleopatra's, for which I was surely too young)? Or Richard II (much better idea but we butterfingered it). He had a great gift for calling an actor that he wanted for a show at home at about 8am and singing the praises of Goldoni's *Mirandolina* or *The Servant of Two Masters*, say, before I for one dropped off to sleep again or made breakfast for my recently widowed mother. On the other hand, if refused in his efforts, he had a characteristic phrase, a resigned but friendly "On, On" – the equivalent of today's irritating "going forward..." but far more cheery, and exactly the same comment as, more assertively, he would utter when trying in rehearsals to persuade the actors to get on with it or to concentrate harder, or whatever.

We parted again at the end of that year, not least because I had declined the lead in *Yonadab* – the only Peter Shaffer play I disrespect: it turned out to be a considerable flop, despite the presence of Alan Bates in the central part. Michael Bogdanov and I formed the English Shakespeare Company immediately after that, and delightedly sustained it well into the 1990s, when we signed off and produced a rather good Memoir of those heady times, titled *The Story of the Wars of the Roses*, which without shame I recommend. From that time forward for several years, Peter seemed to offer me almost everything he was to direct – Shakespeare, a much better Shaffer, Harley Granville-Barker, Anton Chekhov, and, at my own instigation, Eduardo de Filippo – frequently opposite Judi Dench, to whom I have thus far been professionally married four times, like some monogamous bigamist. In other words he became a huge part of my life, far huger than his brief rejection had suggested in 1965.

Peter Shaffer's *Gift of the Gorgon* (originally titled *The Cap of Darkness*) was the first of these reunions, and long-term memories such as Fortinbras vanished as if they had never been. Peter had read a notice for a Macbeth I'd done with my ESC, which followed a review of a production of his own in the *Sunday Times*: I'm sure that was what gave him the idea. Judi and I would be thrown together for the first time since we had played Mirabell and Millamant in Congreve's *The Way of the World* at the RSC in 1978. The fact that *Gorgon*, which eventually moved into the West End after opening at the Barbican Pit, didn't then transfer to Broadway, has to do entirely with the fact that Peter wouldn't do it without me, though the New York producers were urging him to cast a more famous name. Shaffer's view was identical to Hall's, and he often said that he'd written the part with me in mind: he said he had purposely given my qualities to the character. This was all extremely flattering, and more than recompensed for my melancholy quitting, after several years on the road, my own Company. I repaid Shaffer his gift after his death by impersonating him (no easy matter) in a Celebration of his life at the National Theatre, in which I aimed to catch the timbre of his voice, part academic, part queenly, part bitchy, extremely generous, highly intelligent of course, and very sentimental. As for Hall, from this encounter on, his enthusiasm for working with me for the next several years was by any measure extremely unusual and obdurately loyal in a director.

Some years later I was jubilantly telling my friend, the brilliant Gerard Murphy, all this, and he did point out to me that in spite of such bracing examples, all us actors are in the end like working girls in a huge brothel, leaning in our doorways waiting for their regular gentleman or gentlewoman; if so, then Peter Hall was undoubtedly the Parisian client, the gent in the Toulouse-Lautrec painting with the cigar, loyal to you for a while and then wordlessly abandoning you for another; a serial monogamist for a time in the meat trade. At least the gifts Peter offered while it lasted were sweet – I've lost count of the plays we were going to do at one time or another. He also managed, in an entirely characteristic coup, to persuade Bill

Kenwright, potential West End producer of *The Gift of the Gorgon*, that Judi Dench was desperate to achieve a West End transfer for the show after its season at the Barbican Pit. But the truth was that brilliant as she was in it, Judi didn't really like the play – it was hesitant in its implied embrace of pacifism and forgiveness rather than the violent retribution my character represented – and she had declared that she didn't want to stay with it. But without her it was hard to imagine, however much Peter Hall wanted it for his, Peter Shaffer's and my sakes. Bill was convinced by him, and insisted on what turned out to be a happy three months at the Wyndham's, possibly London's loveliest West End theatre. Like the kids' parties my mother used to persuade me reluctantly to go to, Judi liked it once she got there, installed in the No 1 dressing room in which I'd blotted my copybook with Alec Guinness.

Peter's famous ruthlessness was part of the fun of all this, as was his pride in being an "iambic fundamentalist" when it came to Shakespeare: in the vocal disciplines of the great man's verse he was inclined sometimes to bully the defenceless towards "the right way", and he certainly preferred the self-confidence of a sophisticated veteran. Also, he may have believed utterly in his view of how to deliver Shakespearean verse, but if you were experienced enough to disobey him but remain effective he was still happy. The reason for his other quirks was that he understood exactly how the showbusiness system worked: it is indeed a meat market, and would be even if he wasn't part of it, so you might as well enjoy his idiosyncratic touch: for in fact, Peter Hall was a man of unswerving principles which could be abandoned at a moment's notice. He also used to declare that since we don't cut Mozart in performance we shouldn't cut Shakespeare; nevertheless he agreed to every strategic cut I suggested as Claudius and the Ghost in his hugely long *Hamlet* a few years later. His pragmatism I now approve of: he made changing his mind into a quality of virtue. Like Suffolk over Queen Margaret in *Henry VI*, Peter for a long time ruled like a wandering planet over me; on the rare occasions I quarreled with him, he would ignore it completely.

One day while we were rehearsing *Gorgon* in Clapham High Street my eye was caught by a tapas bar opposite the rehearsal rooms. A couple of days later, Judi, Peter and I had just been to the Memorial Service for the actress Janet Key, and we then went there for lunch before starting the day's work. At this meal, shadowed as we were by mortality, Peter told us that he thought of death every day. Judi confirmed that she did the same. I was puzzled: but then I was still in my forties. Peter had certainly spoken about Janet at the service (in St Paul's Church in Covent Garden) very beautifully, and it had left him as upset as a child – so much so that he stayed on in the restaurant, as I've known him to do more than once – ordering inadvisable desserts until we were resoundingly late for our afternoon's work and found Jeremy Northam, who had the third leading part, waiting for us, pretty much out of patience; but you somehow didn't complain with Peter – not because he was Peter, but because you might as well argue with the wind and rain. And at any given point, his most offhand achievements would always outstrip his foibles: his workaholic singlemindedness seemed to be the consequence of a knowledge that, although only in his early sixties, he was on a motorbike heading straight for a brick wall; in rare moments, he may have thought that like Steve McQueen in *The Great Escape*, he would somehow lift off and take flight over it. In a somewhat related way, he could watch a performance develop in rehearsal while clearly at some level of sleep – would he fall out of his chair? – and then give perfectly accurate notes on what he'd slept through.

Still, for the last dozen years of his life it became impossible for most of us to know what Peter was thinking – he was crouched under dementia's wing and may or may not have been contemplating death or anything else. (Now I too think about it more or less routinely – the how of it, what about Prue, Mark and my grand-kids Louis and Eve, what moment and how ready will I be?) And then he was gone, by coincidence as I was on a train coming back from Cardiff, where I'd been delivering a eulogy for Michael Bogdanov at the Sherman Theatre. Michael, another giant figure in my life, had after all narrowly beaten Peter to heaven's gate, passing on a Greek island in the very action of raising his first companionable glass of wine of the day to toast somebody's health; Peter meanwhile had capitulated to an Alzheimer's commensurate with his talent. I thought my address about Michael would be a straightforward thing to do – the gathering had been well prepared for by the family, the Sherman foyer walls were completely covered with pictures of him, both in rehearsal and out, and every single one of them had him characteristically laughing or smiling (or making actors in rehearsal laugh). It was a brilliant thing not to have a single note of solemnity or earnest purpose. I started what I'd prepared to say, carefully talking about my lifetime of memories, aware that the audience included many actors who had participated in our very first shows with the ESC thirty years before (*Henry IV Parts One* and *Two* and *Henry V*), and I made a reference to the fact that we sang a song at the outset of that trilogy that Michael and I had invented by way of a Prologue – absurdly called *The Ballad of Harry le Roi*. The whole Company, stage management and all, spilled nightly onto the stage to perform it. At this distance, I now said to everyone, I can remember the tune but not the words; I'd hardly finished this disclaimer when Charles Dale, one of our founder members, softly started singing perfectly from the depth of the audience, as he had in 1986. Within moments, the whole room was on a roar with a full-throated rendition by men and women three decades older, all of them dead-letter and -note perfect. We could have been at the Old Vic, or the Theatre Royal Hull, or at the Spoleto Festival in Melbourne, or any other of our myriad touring dates. I'll never forget it, and like Richard Griffiths at his funeral, I thought that Michael was about to rise from his grave to give us cheery corrective notes on our performance.

That wasn't all. A wheel of sorts came full circle for me, as for many others, with the Celebration for Peter Hall in 2018, first in Westminster Abbey and then in the Olivier at the National Theatre, which brought out, it seemed, almost the entire profession, and the best out of it. It was an imperishable event for all of us, whether we were speaking, acting or just attending. I found myself leaping onto the stage, egged on by Jimmy Laurenson, who had joined Peter's RSC in 1964 at the same moment that I did and was now waiting to do some of *Waiting for Godot* with Alan Dobie. I say egged on, because in fact all we could do for each other as we waited was to grip each other's hand for some quarter of an hour in the Olivier wings in sheer, uncharacteristic terror at the thought of fucking up:

> MICHAEL: Jimmy, do you remember, this is the 53rd anniversary of the opening night of *Love's Labour's* in Stratford, when we played the Longueville twins (we did – we looked exactly the same in those days)?
> JIMMY: (says nothing, but, better than words, grips my hand almost to breaking.)

It had been a brilliant suggestion from Peter's brilliant director son Edward Hall (not from me) that I should do for the occasion Hamlet's famous advice to the Players who come to Elsinore. "Speak the Speech" is a passage that has served everyone in different ways, including Peter in his teaching about verse-speaking: how should I handle it for a good purpose today? In the play of course, it represents a lot of possibly unwelcome advice from the Crown Prince to the Players as to how to do their job better, which as an actor himself Shakespeare would not have welcomed had it been Queen Bess or King James who interfered. There has always seemed to me to be something comic as well as dubious about Hamlet's use of royal privilege in this way, but it's only the beginning of several layers of meaning: in another sense Hamlet is Shakespeare himself, showing that he had all the instincts of a type of director of actors that in reality didn't arrive till the twentieth century, when the job finally received a name (and fame), and of which Peter was such a major exemplar. It was certainly the advice that he might have given me or any other of his actors:

> … use all gently, for in the very torrent, tempest, and, as I may say, whirlwind of your passion you must acquire and beget a temperance that may give it smoothness.

There's a further meaning as far as I was concerned; for the first time in my own couple of hundred performances as Hamlet, I had seen that this is what Hamlet himself needs to do to modulate his assumed zaniness and the unsimulated emotional whirlwind of the great soliloquy he has just given that starts:

O what a rogue and peasant slave am I...

– and of the next, which starts:

To be or not to be; that is the question.

Indeed these two great monologues – and the prose homily that follows the first – have something of the function of the ultraviolet light directed on a Leonardo drawing to make it fully clear and vivid at last. You have Hamlet reflecting on his own situation, Hamlet the expert critic, Shakespeare advising his colleagues (we are still his colleagues) and a few other besides. Who, I said to myself, am I to direct the speech to in this unique context on this melancholy day? In a packed house at the Olivier, many of the audience were contemporaries or senior to me. So I played it semi-humorously straight to them as Hamlet's acknowledgement of something we all knew and Peter best of all, and for the first time discovered the comedy in the paradoxes involved. At the party afterwards Peter Gill and Trevor Nunn rather untypically wept on my shoulder, muttering savage criticisms of the younger generation of actors who wouldn't know how to do such things; I was as proud as Punch and above all I like to think the whole event eased Peter's wonderful widow Nicola, Edward, and his whole clan.

For of course for much of the day, in Westminster Abbey and then on the Olivier stage, most of us were trying to work out what it felt like not to have Peter – not in the stalls, not in the wings, not in the rehearsal room, not in the world at all – an estrangement that had vexed most of us for a couple of years, and still does, with only a little sign of abatement. It was, as you will have imagined, a day for untypical preparatory nervousness – it's not a performance you want to dry or fluff in. I'm sure I saw him wink from the banks of the Lethe. I went home that evening and immediately out to supper with Prue, with half a century of memories and a bad case of verbal diarrhoea.

However, my best reminiscence for her that evening was that once, in rehearsals for *Hamlet*, Peter's mobile phone had rung as I was rehearsing the Ghost's big speech, and on the spur I turned the line I was on:

But soft! Methinks I scent the morning air

into

But soft! Methinks I scent the mobile phone

which got a good (and still metrical) laugh from the Company: Peter didn't notice but would presumably have approved of the precise iambic rhythm of it.

With Ion Caramitru.

THE DEAR ROMANIAN: ION CARAMITRU

> Mercutio: Van ca Regina Mab, azi-noapte, draga!
> [O then I see Queen Mab hath been with you]
> Romeo: Queen Mab? What's she?
> Mercutio: Te-a cercetat. In lume zanelor…
> – Shakespeare, *Romeo si Julieta*

Romania's greatest actor turns to me, his eyes bright, in the Upstairs Bar of London's National Theatre. He is breathless, apparently having been running.

"Is that Alan Howard over there?" he wants to know. "He is my hero."

Clearly he feels the same level of excitement as I did when I was going to meet him, Caramitru, in a hotel foyer at Craiova in Romania in 2010. Although I hadn't seen his legendary Hamlet I knew all about it and his fame and about its effect on Ceauşescu; I was going to do a seminar with him on the subject of Shakespeare's play convened by Craiova's Shakespeare Festival. An interpreter was waiting with me in the lobby of the cheap – which you really don't want in Romania – hotel, apparently in a state of some tension.

As I waited, I reminisced, largely to myself. I'd been to Romania a couple of times before, first in May 2008, when it was announced that "British actor Michael Pennington, one of the greatest to ever play Hamlet, gives the recital *Sweet William,* which he claims is a sort of a declaration of love for Shakespeare" (hardly a "recital", my quite lively solo show was translated elsewhere as *Nobile Shakespeare by William Pennington*). This was part of the sixth Shakespeare Festival in Craiova, founded in 1994, and I was sharing the bill at the city's National Theatre with Declan Donnellan's prize-winning production of *Trolius (sic) and Cressida*, Peter Brook's Bouffes du Nord *The Grand Inquisitor*, a *Macbeth* from Vilnius (directed by Eimuntas Nekrosius, together with *Othello* and *Hamlet*), Silviu Purcărete's *Measure for Measure*, Lev Dodin's *King Lear* from Petersburg, a Rustaveli *Twelfth Night*, Robert Wilson's *Threepenny Opera* from the Berliner Ensemble, who were also doing *Richard III*, a Bucharest *Edward III* (a newly-discovered Shakespeare play) and *The Two Gentlemen of Verona*, hedged in by an infinity of workshops and talks – all these shows getting an average of two performances (in my case three) in the ten-day period shared between Craiova and Bucharest.

Each of the first five Festivals (which always linked the two cities, 150 miles apart) having taken place three years after the last, it was intended, from 2006, that a Festival should now "manifest" itself every two. Its "crucial scientific dimension" was to be marked not only by performances but by "Shakespearology sessions", scientific seminars and theatre workshops.

Craiova was, throughout that time, I must say, a dismal town. In the Communist early 1960s, it had been a hub for the automotive and chemical industries; the welcome it offered now was as rusty and derelict as its streets. In 2010, as I waited for Caramitru, no one seemed to remember my 2008 visit; certainly nobody had turned up with any welcome. I'd been dropped unceremoniously the previous night at the hotel, which gave no sign of having expected me, but by then the taxi had vanished. At breakfast, I had recovered my strongest memory of 2008, that the level of tobacco smoke in the residents' dining-room was like a London pea-souper. Had you been able to see through the windows, you would have glimpsed a desolate Andrei Tarkovsky landscape much resembling the Zone in *Stalker*.

On the other hand Craiova always had a portentous National

Theatre of its own, of which the Romanian equivalent of *The Stage* writes rapturously: "You sometimes wonder if this company is not the best built since Brecht's Berliner Ensemble or maybe Peter Brook's Royal Shakespeare Company" (Brook, of course, never ran the RSC). The first evening of my first visit I had wandered down to it and gate-crashed a post-show party – I forget what of – and tried to locate someone – anyone – to discuss my next day's rehearsal and evening performance; instead I found myself regaled with several slices of glutinous cake by way of welcome, before being invited to participate in the Yerevan Shakespeare Festival and the Gdansk one as well (nothing came of either). In the event *Sweet William* had gone fine, and the following morning I bounced in a Romanian LADA all the way to Bucharest to do a second and third performance, which also went well apart from the surtitles getting out of synch – the text coming up either ahead of my speaking it, so that any laugh came before the delivery of the English punchline, or after, when the joke had run out of steam. There was also a pre-show showdown when I threatened not to perform unless I was paid first in euros as had been agreed instead of unexportable leis – which led to much signing of new contracts and a mad rush to the bank. This was less worrying than being again dumped by car later on, on the outskirts of Bucharest at midnight, at a hotel which like that in Craiova had no record of my booking. I paid.

The next day being free, after coughing and spluttering in congested Bucharest all day, manoeuvring through a gasping multitude of cars confidently parked on every pavement, but also after an excellent lunch with the Arts chief of the British Council, Nigel Townson, I went to see the National Theatre presentation of *King Lear* by the eminent Russian director Lev Dodin, a "professor of most of Saint Petersburg theatre directors", which had originated at that city's Maly Theatre. All I need to tell you is that Lear made his entrance for the first scene as if he had just completed a five-act tragedy rather than starting it and was thus utterly exhausted; that the Fool wore hobnailed boots, beach shorts and braces over his vest, a punk look that we had in the UK too at that time. It also had everyone in the Hovel scene stark naked, but skilful at taking up precisely rehearsed positions where darkness would scrupulously cover their privates, which I felt rather destroyed the point.

Returning now, two years later, I found the Festival dedicated to only one play, *Hamlet*, explained thus by the press release:

> The presentation of Shakespeare's masterpiece in different directorial visions and interpretations brings an opportunity for theatre professionals and audiences to compare, discuss, comment, and debate.

This – much more fun – would require Caramitru and me to be bundled onto a stage to discuss the play through an interpreter. So here I am in the same Craiova hotel, wondering if Caramitru will be a highly formal People's Artist, inclined to bow on greeting in a way that combined pride with due respect, fellowship and a little touch of hauteur, or at least a recognition of the great seriousness of our endeavours – particularly his, in view of the political engagement that has characterised his life.

***

That morning of first meeting, our interpreter, thoroughly briefed on the pattern of Questions and Answers for the event, stood ready to instruct us in turn. She seemed to me to have rather too many precise ideas about what we might say to each other, particularly in reply, and how, and was busy sharing them with me in the foyer when I was suddenly encased from behind in soft black leather: a Romanian bear in a biking jacket was embracing me. Ion is a little late but not much, and as merry as a cricket. It being our first encounter, we lean back on our heels to attach each other's face to their name more fully. It was a sort of Look at You, There You Are at Last look. All we had in common was Hamlet, but of course it was enough, and as anybody familiar with actors will understand, that precludes any other small talk. How did I play the Gravedigger Scene? What was Hamlet's attitude to his mother after the Play Scene? And you? Really? Did you? Oh really, *that's* good... What, you punched Ophelia? At the Royal Shakespeare Theatre? In fact, we were starting a lifelong friendship which would include ample appearances as a double-act at numerous Hamletfests and other events, some very satisfying workshops for me to run with Ion's National Theatre actors (he had taken over the directorship of the theatre in 2005), both in Bucharest and also in Iași in the beautiful north of the country; in between he would come to London for recitals with me, both at the Globe and at the Romanian Embassy; we had dinners to die for in both capital cities, our friendship even surviving the still-birth of a mad plan to do *The Winter's Tale* together in both capitals, which floundered because of a merry disagreement (or gentle war) as to which of us should play Leontes, and in which language.

Meanwhile the zealous interpreter hadn't worked it out that when two Hamlets meet, they do their best to swap languages and, where words fail, they resort to a certain amount of mime. It got to the point that Ion began to speak in English to me across her bows, whereupon she would turn to me earnestly and translate his words into fluent Romanian.

***

Since then, Romania and its star actor have regularly extended me the best welcome imaginable. The fact that the first of the acting workshops Ion had proposed was in Iași, a lovely university town on the north-eastern border with Moldavia, offered an opportunity for Prue (perhaps weary at that point of the ceaseless bulletins at home about the Hillary Clinton email scandal) to join me in Romania: beyond Iași's limits is a medieval landscape, where you can still watch horse-drawn carts bringing in the hay with old women guiding them. Or take long walks with Caramitru, trying to understand his almost obsessive admiration for the much-loved national poet Mihai Eminescu (who was born in Iași, and whose work he has sometimes dramatised).

The workshop was like summer camp for myself and the actors, who had been carefully chosen by Ion from all over the country, and who were pleasantly billeted in a series of dachas in the grounds of the arts complex we were working in. We concentrated on *Hamlet* intensively for a week, alternating enthusiastically if not always easily between Romanian and English, and indeed switching characters within the Company at will from one hour to the next. What I was unprepared for, delighted to find and eager to encourage was that the actors, all with different backgrounds and measures of experience, had an extraordinary innate inventiveness as they set up the circumstances of each scene, and from the get-go played with an inordinate passion similar to that of Russian actors, controlling it somehow with simultaneous wit, rapture, precision and aggression. I specially remember a Hamlet playing the Gravedigger Scene in Act Five and reflecting on the loss of his friend Yorick by staring not at the conventional skull but at a hard-boiled egg. It made perfect sense to me: the egg was now a skull.

On this visit Prue and I also broke off for a side trip first of all to Maramures, the county near the country's northern border with Hungary and the Ukraine, rightly renowned for its wooden medieval villages, many of which are now on Unesco's World Heritage List. The extraordinary ability of these structures, particularly of the churches that will seemingly last for ever, adorned with the beautiful and apparently imperishable work of local artists from the 18th and 19th centuries who decorated them with their unassuming folk motifs, was to make you want to call Andrew Graham-Dixon and get him to give Caravaggio a rest and dart out here to make a BBC programme.

By contrast, nearby Brasov and Bran and Sighisoara take you into the heart of Dracula country. Indeed you can visit the room where (also known as Vlad the Impaler) he was born (*visitate camera lui Dracula on Etaj 2*: the toothy one's birthplace, in other words, was the second-floor bedroom).

I went on to enhance my experience of Romanian acting workshops some years later in a less rustic setting with Ion's resident National Theatre Company in central Bucharest. This week became a lurch through the entire Shakespearean canon, in which all my latest actors preferred to do the text in halting English rather than highly eloquent Romanian (which suits it very well). And sadly, the truth was that almost all of them dreamed of coming to the UK or the US to work in films and TV. The painfully banal fact is that most Romanian actors who manage to come to the West disappointingly end up playing leather-clad dope dealers or small-time hitmen, controlled by a UK boss (I've played one of the latter, briefly, in the BBC's *Between the Lines*).

While I was working, Prue went over to look at Ceaușescu's People's Palace, from which he had chased all the people into poverty in order to convert it into the Romanian Parliament, complete with golden furniture and arches and floors like ice rinks. While she was licking her wounds one evening after that, I saw Mark Haddon's worldwide triumph *The Curious Incident of the Dog in the Night-Time* for the first time and was deeply impressed by the Romanian acting. Ion and his wife Micaela then took us to dinner on our last night in a trellised restaurant and ordered a giant fish – in fact I never saw such a fish, the size of the table, and didn't know for sure what it was called. It turned out it was a giant turbot, provoking in me a silly game of rhyming slang in my search for a good English Christian name. Yes, you've got it.

And strangely enough, at the precise moment of writing this (a few days before Christmas 2020), a huge smoked trout (which rather suggests a bomb attack from *Star Wars* fans I have failed to sign for) has arrived at my door from my cousin Martin. It'll last us till the New Year.

***

Ion is the dearest of men, and whenever I think of his name I also think of the Russian diminutive, Ionych, which seems to suit him, as well as providing the title for one of Chekhov's very best short stories.

I've in any case always been quite drawn and then close to other European actors and directors (as well, of course, as American); I've written elsewhere about my relations with Yuri Lyubimov, who arrived in London from his Taganka Theatre in Moscow in 1983 to re-present his legendary Moscow production of *Crime and Punishment*. Throughout, while I was haunted by the nightmare world of Raskolnikov, he was riddled with an understandable fear of KGB assassination in London – he daily imagined being pitched from one of the elevated balconies of the Lyric Theatre Hammersmith in a rehearsal break. I loved his gallantry, his extreme sensitivity, and his demonstrative brilliance with actors. Once the show was done, Yuri deferred facing the Moscow music and seized an opportunity to make a run from London in the other direction, moving to Milan to do a couple of operas before returning to the Soviet Union, where he had been stripped in his absence of his directorship of his own Taganka. I went to Leningrad to see him soon after and at his request attended the premiere of his *Brothers Karamazov*, in which he sat on the stage like a conductor for the entirety, and, at the first night party, as he was urging me to play Timon of Athens for him but not specifying in which language, his interpreter more or less cleared the banqueting table of all the canapés and vodka, thus speaking volumes about the struggles of her real life.

Lyubimov was a great enrichment to me – and so was Peter Stein, in many ways the German equivalent of Lyubimov. Having been in the latter's *Crime and Punishment*, I shirked his next project, *The Devils*. But I did do Stein's Edinburgh Festival *Seagull* in 2003, finding him a brilliant though contentious director whose brainwave was to import his Company in a group to rehearse on his estate in Umbria (tough, eh?); then, having often declared that British actors were tiresomely unemotional, he found himself struggling for sleep nightly while we sat on his balcony till sunrise for extended jam sessions: Iain Glen on lead guitar, Cillian Murphy on vocals, Eliot Cowan on rhythm guitar, as I urged the band to put aside Van Morrison from time to time in favour of the old masters – Tim Buckley, Fred Neil, Bob Dylan, Tim Hardin; this gave me credit as an old-time hipster, until Peter would stumble down to breakfast after another night of insomnia. On parting from us, he jubilantly declared that British actors, whom he'd always thought so reserved, were even wilder than his Russian colleagues (he'd done a lot of Chekhov). Back in the UK, I would commute between

Edinburgh and Leeds, from playing a nightly *Seagull* in the first to a daily rehearsal of Alan Bennett's version of King George III in the second, but being sure to be back for the next *Seagull* that night. The King's Madness thus involved, once we'd opened the Chekhov, a commuting madness of its own.

Ion Caramitru and I had continued to meet and do recitals in half Romanian and half English, both in Bucharest and London: Romeo and Mercutio and Queen Mab, and Richard III for Ion on his own. One of his later visits to London, as regular as mine to his country, coincided with the very agreeable annual Ian Charleson Award lunch at the National Theatre, when a guest list of older actors and directors give a cash prize to the UK performer under the age of thirty who is agreed to have given the best performance of a classical role in the preceding year. It is much the most congenial Award ceremony in the English theatre calendar, notable for goodwill between the generations, swelling with love of the job in both constituencies. (It was created by John Peter, once the *Sunday Times* critic, and funded by the paper.) The Award is a way of saying that our job is the oddest mixture of individuality and membership of a tradition, of novelty and nostalgia, of fraternity and originality, an acknowledgement that someone had designed the wheel generations before the motor car was invented.

On this occasion I had called Nick Hytner, then running the National, to see if it would be OK to bring Ion along, as he was in London and I thought he'd like to mill around with our community – he might even meet some more Hamlets. He would thus be the best of guests, and Nick agreed. On the day, I prepared to introduce Ion to everyone, imagining his gratitude. When we arrived at the NT I ushered him into the foyer as if he was a shy girl going into a party; but suddenly from behind us came an enormous voice: "Ion!... Ion!" – Michael Gambon at full Olivier Theatre volume. Ion and he ran at each other – they'd once been in a film together – and I stood discreetly back.

Still suffering a little from the delusion that it was only I who knew Ion, I then climb the stairs with him – and the first person he then meets is Simon Russell Beale, who reminds him that he once put his head round Simon's dressing-room door, I think in Bristol, when the NT were touring *Hamlet*, and complimented him as one Hamlet to another, and how he's never forgotten it. They rejoice in each other for a minute or two, while I continue to rejoice in my bright idea. Peter Gill passes by and so does Richard Griffiths – and of course I take a moment to do for Richard Lord Buckley's "Hipsters, flipsters and finger-poppin' daddys" that I invariably used to whisper to him to guarantee him good luck (and no bad jazz): as ever this reduces Richard to a jelly, though it's a little lost on Ion, who is by now playing the field very effectively on his own.

I lassoo Nick Hytner too – not for Lord Buckley but to encourage a handshake with Ion – but he is in a bit of a hurry as he has a rehearsal, and you'd need an appointment. Nevertheless, Ion doesn't quite understand why Nick hasn't automatically offered him such a meeting later in the day.

And that's the moment when Ion stops in his tracks and glimpses Alan Howard, no less, on the far side of the room. He weaves his way towards him. Alan's heroic status in his eyes began with his supreme Oberon in Peter Brook's *A Midsummer Night's Dream*; it turns out that Alan, though shyer and more tentative, feels the same about Ion as Hamlet. And, you know, so do I. So it has all been very satisfactory.

Filming Outside Edge *by Richard Harris for LWT (with Chris Humphreys, Jonathan Lynn, Paul Eddington and Gary Waldhorn) in 1982.*

VILE JELLIES

DEMETRIUS: These things seem small and undistinguishable
Like far-off mountains turned into clouds.
HERMIA: Methinks I see these things with parted eye
When everything seems double.
HELENA: So methinks;
And I have found Demetrius like a jewel,
Mine own and not mine own.
– William Shakespeare, *A Midsummer Night's Dream*

I've worn various kinds of contact lenses since 1963, when they were called "haptic" lenses (now they're "scleral", and used for particularly bad corneal conditions), and when I tell someone in the eye trade what a veteran I am, I am met with an immediate glow of nostalgia. Maybe this is because I'm sharing the pleasure that they feel when they remember that the bodies of WW2 fighter pilots were rarely injured by embedded plastic (as opposed to glass, which was traumatic), or that Monet repainted many of his works once he had had a lens transplant in order to see his subject properly. One has to salute the invention, the pioneers and the practitioners, even though I shall now be teasing them a little, in admiration of their craft. For the truth is I've always liked ophthalmologists.

My first pair of haptics were fitted by Mr James Hamilton Doggart, who was not only a leading specialist but a lecturer, writer and professional cricketer (as a Gentleman presumably, rather than a Player) and, rather unexpectedly, an ex-member of the Cambridge Apostles and the Bloomsbury Group. The initial fitting, during my last year at university, was unforgettable: Mr Doggart encased the entire front surface of each of my eyes in a pre-made mould, or template, except that it had a crucial little raised bit in the middle over the pupil, out of which a small perpendicular funnel or miniature smokestack stood erect. Down this funnel he poured a lightweight ocular cement which duly hardened around my eyes as might a sculptor's cast. I don't know about you, but for me this was a moment of the highest anxiety; but he was able to flick it off the eye with a practitioner's panache, before ordering lenses to match what he'd found would suit both corneas and pupils. Once in place, the lenses came to resemble tiny buckets to be filled each morning to the limit with some kind of long-forgotten liquid, like a minute cup of tea about to overflow. You then bent over the bucket, tucked its top edge under your upper eyelid and let it sort of slap over the pupil, having swiftly opened the lower lid as if to accommodate eye drops. In this way the lens generally arrived in place safely, but the central area sometimes became a small reservoir of solution that gave it a look as opaque as that of a blind person. Undeterred, you went about your business – if you were an actor, in the hope that this wasn't the day you were shooting any close-ups. For the problem was that the solution over the pupil was inclined to froth: it had a way of bubbling up more like soapsuds than champagne, giving a ruinous effect to a camera moving in for a closer look, or to anyone who looked you in the eye, friend or foe.

Looking back on the whole period, I suppose that the relatively unusual wearing of contact lenses led to a certain self-consciousness, or even a feeling of disadvantage. This was well enough compensated for by devising a special heroism of your own. In my case, I learned to spot someone's contact lens on the floor at twenty paces – especially a tiled floor with the light in front of me – and to restore it to its owner before it could ever be crunched by a passer-by or savaged by a dog. I'd go straight to it and scoop it up, to the amazement of all, and restore it: this party trick gave me considerable *éclat* in the haptic community.

Soon there were to be hard lenses, soft disposables, SynergEyes with their hard centre and soft skirt around it. I've tried them all, and even now a perceptive shiver of pleasure flips across the faces of most ophthalmologists when I confess to having been so promiscuous a user. For instance: some years ago, I went to an eye surgeon because I had a small blister on the white of my right eye. He had a good look and declared it would be a simple matter to remove it surgically. As he explained this my blood refrigerated. I said I'd think about it; but when I went home I didn't have to think about it at all because the blister had, in a miraculous gesture of sympathy, completely disappeared. However, the surgeon and I had got on well and since he seemed quite interested I had agreed to get him tickets for the show I was in at the time, *Filumena Marturano* by Eduardo de Filippo. He duly arrived at the theatre with his wife and came round to my dressing room afterwards for a drink, as we had arranged. It was pleasant; and as he left he said that he liked the fact that he and I had something in common: we both worked in theatres, and the thrilling thing about all theatres was that however well you know your business, you just can't be sure, each time you start a procedure, what is going to be the outcome this time.

I resolved never to have eye surgery, ever, if I could possibly avoid it.

***

The Old Vic has played such a big part in my life – the teenage years, the seasons I did there a generation later in the 1980s with my own English Shakespeare Company, Peter Hall's Company in 1996. In fact I've been lucky enough to work there so often in the sixty-odd years since Michael Benthall's Five Year Plan transfixed me that my biography in its programme for the Peter Hall season included a misprint declaring that I had first appeared at the Old Vic in 1897. That is, a year before its legendary first manager Lilian Baylis arrived, so maybe I have a prior claim to the place. At any rate, I heartily refused all embarrassed offers from the Marketing Department of an immediate face-saving reprint of several thousand programmes, as it seemed to me to be an error the public would be amused by.

And now, fifty-four professional years having gone by, I've just seen the negative effect of clawing at your own eyes in an unsanitary dressing room to get the lenses out. The Vic are putting on the first stage adaptation in the UK of Ingmar Bergman's final film masterpiece, *Fanny and Alexander*. As it starts, the Ekdahl family are gathering for Christmas lunch. Though a number of them are professional actors, there will be no play about American Indians performed in the afternoon; however, the eleven-year-old Alexander, a solitary child who dreams of going on the stage, has already introduced himself to anyone who will listen by standing on a chair and brandishing a wooden sword as if he were the Bastard Falconbridge in his garden:

> I am lord of seventeen lands: hear my command. I am the extraordinary King of Persia. I am the murdering brigand with teeth threaded round my neck. I'll have your scalp and all your bones.

This tirade is partly for the benefit of his grandmother, who is the leading player in the Uppsala Theatre Company imagined by Bergman to reflect his own origins. But she now has her own speech to make: as Sven Nykvist's camera and the Company's attention swing across to her, she rises and addresses them (an interruption that would never have been tolerated by my Falconbridge in my mother's garden):

> There comes a time in every actor's life when they must let go of the reins a little and seek some peace and quiet … walking away from the stage feels like a little death, but the passing of things is something we have to accept – even me… We actors are children aren't we?… but the time comes when we leave the nursery and the dressing-up box and allow ourselves to grow up.

So she's announcing her retirement just as Alexander is his arrival. Like so much of Bergman's meditation on acting, her and his two speeches are both confession and incentive.

Bergman's film has now been adapted brilliantly by Stephen Beresford, with a crack cast that includes some marvellous children, as intent on making their name as were Alexander or myself sixty years ago. Penelope Wilton is Mrs Ekdahl, and I am Isak Jacobi, her lover in private and the family friend and children's *de facto* uncle in public, who also becomes in a sense the play's unlikely hero.

And now, in this last week of the run, I've done something to my eyes. To be precise, scratched them as though I was re-booting my 1986 Oedipus. I had friends in for the show last night whom I was anxious to join afterwards, and was thus a little hasty in removing my hybrid lenses – the type that generally slide easily off the pupil. Worse, in the process I scratched first one cornea then the other. Had I known it, I was at that moment ringing up the curtain on a new show: it would run for fourteen months, making a profitable return for its stakeholders, the Royal College of Ophthalmologists.

I woke in the middle of the night after this to find that my bedside lamp had become photophobically bright. At dawn, blurred and aching, I blundered, hotfoot and Dracula-eyed, to see a specialist I know who has helped me in the past. At this appointment with Ms Valerie, who was kindly pausing *en route* to a jam-making holiday using the legendary Agen plums of Gascony, she provisionally diagnosed Myopia, Presbyopia, early cataract and a mild epiretinal membrane in one eye. She also concluded I had caught a form of optical herpes and prescribed antibiotics, which had no effect.

This being the case (to compress a couple of weeks) she referred me to Ms Melanie, who specialises in the cornea – particularly the infections that swiftly visit the whites of the eyes once they are damaged. I go and see her: she prescribes a solution for the reduction of corneal oedema. However, in her standard letter to my GP she sidesteps Valerie's diagnosis, thus:

> This could possibly be herpetic disease given the corneal changes… But he has no specific history of cold sores… Mr

> Pennington's eyes are still variably sore and watering… His vision also remains poor at counting fingers.

Then she sends me for an MRI, during which the highly capable technician lets out a buoyant whoop as if he has found a crock of gold. I congratulate him, and he confirms that this is an infection called *acanthamoeba* and will take a very long time to fix. On my return, Melanie prescribes hostile eye drops, seemingly more caustic than the infection itself: they feel like Dettol to be applied to your eyes four times a day. Ahead of me lay a further three months of treatment, at the end of which (despite the candour of one optometrist who always started proceedings by noting that I was seeing "much worse than last time", even though I was feeling quite a bit better), she prescribed me a drug which the pharmacist didn't seem to have heard of but eventually produced in the form of ointment rather than drops as she had requested, and so wasn't usable. By then Melanie too had gone on a well-deserved holiday and couldn't be reached for three weeks, having thus sadly left behind a prescription that the hospital pharmacy had been unable to fill.

For the remainder of the run of *Fanny and Alexander*, I had turned all but one of my dressing room lights off, such was the glare and my photophobia, and in the show itself I slightly re-staged myself from time to time to avoid the very bright profiling side lights in our plot (when did I ever avoid a spotlight before?). I also took certain special measures to achieve the long bedtime sequence in the play when Isak reads a complicated story to the children, Alexander and his sister, which now is not only written in Hebrew (right to left, remember) but also resembles a sort of giddy typographical landslide on the page as my wounded eyes try to contain it.

And now, after weeks of suspended animation, Prue and I sit in a waiting-room at Moorfields Eye Hospital to see another specialist. It is comfortable and cheerful, looking rather like a furniture store selling a random selection of armchairs and sofas, in rust, puce, some the colour of blackcurrant-flavoured yoghurt, others a bilious greeny blue. Mesdames Valerie and Melanie now behind us, we wait to see the highly recommended (and they all, rightly, are), Mr Mark

Wilkins. A busy tide of optometrists, receptionists and consultants bustle to and fro along a fast lane on this floor that runs from door to door along one side of the waiting-room – a runway broad enough to allow for enough speed for them to avoid the petitions of the pack of seated, patient patients. Their professional eyes are ruthlessly trained forward and down to the ground as if to avoid catching ours, reasonably enough: you wouldn't want an airline pilot to admire the passengers or the scenery while trying to get the plane into the air. Otherwise there seems no real urgency, even though we do have an expensive appointment with Mr Wilkins for 2.45pm and it's now nearly 5. The Consultants' Secretary pops her head round the door every so often: it turns out she works an eighteen-hour day and seems so impossibly good-natured that I suspect she may calmly blow the hospital up as she leaves one night, and no one will understand her need to do it.

Clearly we're not the only ones impatient for Godot to come, and the delay has induced a kind of misanthropic anomie among us all; so that when an elderly female patient stands up and approaches Prue and myself, seeing a likely audience for a shaggy dog story she wants to tell, it is tempting not to point out to her that a doctor has just miraculously appeared behind her, inviting her into his consulting room for her appointment at last. It may presumably be only a matter of seconds before he will abandon her and move on, but as far as she is concerned, he will now have to be the one who waits while she tells us her story, which is all about malfunctioning buses and inconvenient roadworks.

I wonder why she's chosen us, and – never one to shirk a flattering comparison – I conclude that I must bear some magnetic resemblance to Leo Tolstoy waiting to meet his Maker on the deserted railway station at Astapovo before the stationmaster takes him in and gives him succour till he gives up the ghost. Or perhaps just to some minor Tolstoyan disciple looking on, an elderly Russian peasant in a straggly beard but with an approachable air, sitting dully in the middle of nowhere. I certainly have the air of someone who has alighted from one train and is waiting for another that may or may not arrive some time in the next week or so. Next to me, in defiance of history, a very different character sits waiting – if I resemble Lev Nikolayevich, Prue is not so much his disillusioned Sophia as Emmeline Pankhurst. Enraged by the delays, she is half out of her chair in protest at a state of affairs that is causing all of us in here such an exhausting vigil.

However, by the day's end, I will have learned that the *acanthamoeba* parasite is a singularly nasty piece of work among eye infections, in which minuscule settlers find in the human cornea the perfect place to harvest and thrive: this is what has caused an increasing number of ophthalmologists, when asked for a prognosis, to shift uneasily from one foot to the other, making "erm" noises – a recovery in days? weeks? months? No? Not even months? Silence.

The villainous parasite I'm hosting is not only hard to pronounce but has the oddest derivation. Somebody must have thought fit to associate it with the acanthus, a herbaceous shrub of some popularity, albeit with bold flower spikes and spiny decorative leaves and found in warm regions of the Old World. Perhaps it was the spikes and spines that gave them the idea: my eyes already feel as if they'd been massaged with a cactus. However, I have been fortunate in having attracted the amoeba's attentions so late in the run. Equally that I haven't had much work scheduled for a bit thereafter. The silver lining is that I've worked fifty-five years with only one day off sick, never broken a limb or had a serious illness – so what did I expect? And now, after four months, I'm to meet a third expert, arriving at Moorfields, where I should have gone at the start – why anywhere else? I'm of course hoping with this new self-referral to find a specialist prepared to prescribe something more emollient before I run mad.

And yes, I've always liked ophthalmologists. Mark Wilkins, my latest Eye-to-Eye, reminds me irresistibly of Philip Franks, my actor and director friend. Philip and I have done three happy productions together – Ronald Harwood's *Collaboration* and *Taking Sides* at Chichester and in the West End, and *The Master Builder* at Chichester; we were going to tour *King Lear* in 2016 but he fell ill and I found Max Webster to replace him, who oddly enough went on to direct the *Fanny and Alexander* that I've just survived. Now

Philip's lookalike is peering into my grievous eyes and forming the view – in between making passing comments about my "terrible cataracts" (by which he really means advanced enough to deserve his attention), and observing that *bullae* have appeared (big *bullae* that he is, or should it be *bullaeshitter*?). He also opens a whole new line of enquiry by insisting that the *acanthamoeba* especially attacks contact lens wearers. I retaliate with some pride that the little buggers have tracked down almost a founder member of whatever club it is – a veteran who even remembers the haptic lens. He puts me onto less lethal drops, saying that Melanie has made my eyes too toxic, then writes to my GP, one of those letters that may or may not get read:

> Mr Pennington has really quite marked signs of epithemial toxicity in both eyes with very irregular corneal epithelium and small areas of epithelial defect… Underlying the epithelium were bullae but underlying them there was no significant stromal capacity and no evidence of corneal vascularisation. After dilating him I could see that he really has quite significant cataracts in both eyes… I think we should try and reduce the toxicity by stopping the Brolene and continuing with chlorhexidine … a lot of the changes in Mr Pennington's eyes are due to drop toxicity.

You'd think it was a measured description of some performance I was giving in something, and I feel rather flattered.

Back home after the first of this series of diagnoses, I quickly see that the immediate future lies in audiobooks. Actually some of the immediate future lay in my having that very thought – had I known it, I was about to be asked to read an audio version of Freud Lectures and also Peter Brook's new book *The Quality of Mercy* at his specific request, which is just about as large a compliment as the likes of me can imagine. Meanwhile Dinah Wood, Editorial Director of Drama at Faber, ally and friend, has grabbed down an office copy of Milan Kundera's *Laughable Loves* and *The Festival of Insignificance* to alternate in my private reading with *The Iliad*, which I immediately started gloating over.

The whole thing eventually ends in surgery of course, both cataracts and even after that a new retinal problem, all beautifully performed to my entire satisfaction. The only glitch was when Mark Wilkins proposed to me the idea of a corneal graft as well. After much merry badinage – apparently the graft material comes from the States, and I had asked a couple of times if Fedex was reliable, and what was the standard price – we agreed that he loved eye surgery, I loved Shakespeare and Prue loved ballet, so let's leave matters at that.

Before the first cataract op I am in a sort of ante-room, separated from the surgical engine-room (the theatre) by a pair of sliding plastic sheets in the duck-egg blue typical of a hospital. The *mise-en-scène* is exerting a magnetic force on my imagination, I who have had only a hernia op in 2000 and my tonsils out when I was eight. I was interested to note the insertion of a canola in the top of my right hand with a tentative drip attached to it, the whole unit held together by I think the thinnest and most translucent tape I have ever seen. There are three of us out here: me trying to think of the gurney I'm lying on as a bed, Matthew the gentle young anaesthetist, and an equally gentle and maternal nurse adjusting my neck and sticking a bolster under my leg, and me with arms clasped on my chest thinking of every breathing exercise I know that eases the nerves before a first night. I may not be able to touch my toes or to sing a scale but I can draw and exhale my breath (though without vocalising it), to "find my centre, prepare to send my sound up to the ceiling", though aware that I won't be needing to do that. Still, it feels as if the RSC's Cis Berry should be my companion as the minutes begin to tick down. Or Bettina Jonic, a forgotten but brilliant voice teacher. I think there is distant music. Actually I most resemble Sir John Falstaff at the point of death, as described by Mistress Quickly. As fear closes in:

> A' made a finer end and went away an it had been any christom child, a' parted even just between twelve and one… I saw him fumble with the sheets and play with flowers and smile upon his fingers' ends, I knew there was but one way, for his nose was as

sharp as a pen and a' babbled of green fields… A' bade me lay more clothes on his feet; I put my hand in the bed and felt them, and they were as cold as any stone, and so upward and toward, and all was as cold as any stone.

It sounded like a good obit for me in *The Guardian*, I thought. And then suddenly, with an old-fashioned whoosh, the curtains separate with some of the urgency of a fast scene change, and I am propelled sideways to take my place in, literally, the centre of operations. I also feel a bit like a crematorium coffin sliding askance into the oven. And as the brief op went on, it was like watching some psychedelic light show – Pink Floyd maybe. Nothing else.

In the event, a surgical assistant was unlucky enough to drop a bit of cataract back into the eye, where it settled happily in the vitreous cavity and seemed likely either to dissolve in time or become nasty. There is an operation that can remove it but it is unpredictable and expensive. And in fact, like the blister I took to the stage-struck specialist a few pages back, the remnant, as if in shock, disappeared that night.

Directing Twelfth Night *for Haiyuza Company Tokyo with Sen Yano (Toby Belch) and Yosio Kato (Andrew Aguecheek) 1993.*

RUNNING THE RSC

In April 2002 Adrian Noble suddenly resigned as Artistic Director of the Royal Shakespeare Company. I decided to be his successor.

He's had a fair bit of stick for his timing insofar as he had waited to make his decision known until his (non-RSC) production of *Chitty Chitty Bang Bang* had opened in the West End and immediately been hailed by the press. It was as if in one gesture he'd skimmed through the first reviews and then picked up the phone to call his Chairman to say he was standing down with more or less immediate effect, but I've no doubt he'd been thinking of it for a long time: which raises the whole question of how long one person can or should, for their own good as well as everyone else's, run this extraordinary but highly complex organisation. Peter Hall, its founder, had done eight years, Trevor Nunn eighteen, Terry Hands nineteen (including eight shared with Trevor); after his eleven years Adrian was now, adduced his critics, looking for the break into musical theatre and big money Trevor Nunn had achieved with *Les Misérables*.

I understood the RSC, and in fact have worked under each of its Artistic Directors since Peter founded it. And I'd just gone back and done *Timon of Athens* for Adrian's (and Michael Boyd's) ultimate successor Greg Doran. Adrian's decision seemed natural and fine to me. I was rehearsing *The Front Page* at Chichester that sunny morning. My then girlfriend, who was a director and in the know, had heard the news before the radio got it, so I was able to go in to rehearsal and break the news to one and all before we started the day's work. This made me the centre of fascination: I left out the bit about my own intentions, which of course existed in my own mind only, but the very fact of being so *au fait* with these high events dropped a distant hint, I suppose. Walter Burns, the Chicago newspaper editor whom I was playing, was much given to boasting "You heard it in *The Examiner* first", so that line went well too that morning. BBC *Newsnight* were immediately onto me for an interview, but as it turned out to be five fatuous questions set by a Southampton news team on the back of an envelope, I ducked it: Sam West did it instead, very well. I wondered if he was going to apply too; as for me, I told myself I was keeping my powder dry.

A few days later I ran into Richard Pasco and Barbara Leigh-Hunt at a do. I admitted that I was thinking of applying, to their greatly excited approval. They had both always been biased towards me: praise for my work, dismissal of unsatisfactory girlfriends and all the rest of friendship. In fact, Bar had already thought I should apply for the vacancy, and she now urged me to write to Lord (Bob) Alexander of Weedon, the RSC's Chairman. So I did, safe in the knowledge that I could back out at any moment if the going got too tough. Then Stephen Unwin called and urged me to apply in league with a director or a producer (Stephen is a director and producer).

The reason for this general confidence was my English Shakespeare Company, the bright idea of Michael Bogdanov and myself, which had, between 1986 and 1991, become a mammoth maverick, something of a challenge to the RSC, likewise funded by both business and by the State, and had even made a small profit from televising its work. So I had management credentials alongside an acting record, and could bandy cashflow, amortisation and what would later become known as blue-sky thinking with the best, as well as playing Richard II, Coriolanus and such with the ESC rather than at Stratford. The fact that Terry Hands, on behalf of the RSC, offered me both of the two parts I've quoted at the very moment I was about to go into rehearsal with them at the ESC, attests his daring talent as a provocateur and makes me happy to mourn him the more now that he's (recently) gone.

I got a charming reply from Alexander: he had taken good note and advised me to send in a formal CV when the post was advertised, more or less for form's sake. I sensed he was winking at me. I dispatched the CV with indecent haste, emphasising my managerial experience and also the fact that I had worked as an actor in each RSC regime. But – equally important – that I'd spent more multiples of time not working for the Company at all but observing it – with concern, but also with some detachment.

Then came a coincidence so steep it seemed hardly a coincidence at all. I found myself at a dinner at Middle Temple Hall sitting next to Alexander and Kim Evans from the Arts Council. I should say that I don't often dine in the Middle Temple, and I nearly hadn't gone this time: but I had, in those days at least, a fan called Sir Charles McCullough, one of the legal gentlemen who could invite any guest from the arts world whom they would like to meet to their Annual Dinner. Sir Charles had asked me twice before, so in the nature of things this was probably going to be the last time, and I went along. At dinner Alexander and I acknowledged the social coincidence but skirted around the subject – in some style; but I saw that he rather liked my general demeanour and the hints I dropped. By a further coincidence, Judi Dench was sitting opposite us as someone else's guest: being the actor she is, she was able to radiate the conviction that I was the man for the job without saying a word or even appearing to eavesdrop: she created a warm vision of myself in the post that I hoped was enveloping Bob Alexander.

***

The only thing that gave me pause was a brief mental review of the cost borne by previous bosses: a certain amount of marital chaos, though the tendency on the part of some of them to produce new children in the later part of their lives who were younger than their grandchildren gave them a pleasing aura of masculine vitality in their private as well as public lives, even if you could never quite work out at parties which of these kids was whose and from when. And a related image which had struck me was that while the RSC had simultaneously demanded performance homes in London and Stratford, the acting Company at each end could often feel a bit disgruntled that the Artistic Director wasn't in town with them – which suggested the image of a man in a car driving round and round a roundabout on the Oxford bypass, say, uncertain whether to keep going forward to one set of needy children or turning back to attend to the other.

The Middle Temple dinner happened in mid-June 2002, the 18th to be exact. A few days later I got a phone message from Bob Alexander to say his Selection Committee had now boiled down their shortlist to four candidates – two from within the current RSC (who turned out to be Michael Boyd and Greg Doran), and two external, being myself and a homogenised double-act of John Caird and Simon Russell Beale, counting as one. Bob wanted me, in the next week or so, to arrange one-to-one preparatory meetings for myself with Chris Foy, the Managing Director of the RSC, with David Fletcher, their Finance Director and a History PhD student at Warwick University, and with Jonathan Pope, who was responsible for Capital Redevelopment – pleasantly literary-sounding names, though Chris's surname sounds more like an Elizabethan expostulation. The Agenda in each case would be to discuss the general finances of the RSC: they were opening the books to me. I was pleased but wary; in discussing money as an Artistic Director you have to have just enough fiscal insight to be interesting but not so much that they think you're less than an artist.

Pope's Capital Redevelopment Plan looked like the toughest topic an incoming AD would need to face. Already the cat among pigeons, it included the idea of pulling down the current Royal Shakespeare Theatre and building a modernised one in its place. This was linked to the idea of creating a "Shakespeare Village", a sort of tourist-participation carry-on just across the river, like a permanent version of the Richard Buckle Exhibition which I had encountered as soon as I arrived in town in 1964. Most people with a relationship with the Company deplored the idea of the Village as being extremely naff; the idea of a practical new playhouse was more divisive. The current theatre had been there since 1932, having been swiftly built after the 1926 fire had destroyed the Memorial Theatre next door (later re-equipped as a rehearsal room); although laughed at as "The Jam Factory" it was a perfectly serviceable proscenium arch theatre but was increasingly unpopular because of not being fashionably in the round. In the midst of this controversy I had already weighed in with a full-page article in *The Guardian* entitled "My Beautiful Carbuncle" in which I had stood up for the Jam Factory and repudiated the idea of demolishing it at a vast cost in favour of what was clearly being planned as an identical but bigger version of the three-sided Swan. This would result in the RSC having no proscenium arch theatre at its disposal at all – not even for an Ibsen or a Shaw or a Noël Coward. In other words, nobody born that year would ever in their lifetime see a play in Stratford that didn't have an audience on at least three sides of the stage. It seemed to me folly to abandon prosceniums altogether: what about a play that starts with a long scene in which sedentary people sit around and talk inconsequentially, given the energy and technique it takes to act for an audience on three sides of you?

However, at the same moment Chris Foy was denying in the *Daily Telegraph* that there was any plan at all to demolish the building, though some tentative conclusions were being drawn and put in the cupboard (as he put it), with six further months being allowed for more of them to arrive prior to a thoroughly informed review. This seemed to me a sentence in which a half-truth developed into an obfuscation. His views were now being echoed by Jonathan Pope, who was continuing to declare that the RSC needed to look at a whole series of major changes, one of which might or might not be the demolition of the RST; but he warned sternly that assumptions about that were premature (weak word, premature).

All these meetings, Bob said, would be in preparation for the next step, my formal Interview – a term, he hastened to say, which he disdained – in a month's time, on July 18th or 22nd. However, even before I met these gentlemen, he wanted me to come and talk to Lady Sainsbury of Turville (and perhaps Bob) at his house on Regent's Canal, just round the corner from where I grew up. Further good fortune – it turned out that Bob used to know our next-to-next-door neighbours. I happened to mention how long my parents had been married and it turned out Bob had been born on the very day of their wedding. He was also President of the MCC, of which I'm a member, so would have known Lord's Cricket Ground as well, and perhaps even Jack Robertson.

I knew Susie Sainsbury a little, initially when she was in publishing with the Oxford University Press, then as Director of Jackdaw Publications at Jonathan Cape and editorial advisor on education for Walker Books; she had been a benefactor for the RSC for over 30 years, and had also worked with the Bristol Old Vic, Donmar Warehouse, the Bush, Tricycle, Soho, Royal Court and Rose Theatres. She became a Governor of the RSC in 1990 and for the last couple of years had been Deputy Chair of the Board: her generosity has been instrumental in the transformation of the RSC's theatres in Stratford-upon-Avon. Together with her husband David she has made an astounding financial contribution to the RSC alone, currently standing at over £26 million and placing her in the ranks of the UK's greatest cultural philanthropists. However, what the beneficiaries of Susie's philanthropy have been eager to point out is the modesty and lack of self-interest in her giving: although prominent at the RSC, much of her work happens under the radar. Not only does Susie's input help drive the success of all these institutions in the UK, but it also makes significant impact in the USA, where she is Chair of the RSC America Inc. Beyond the RSC, she is also Deputy Chair and Honorary Fellow of the Royal Academy of Music, a Fellow of the Royal Society of Arts and Honorary Fellow of the Royal Institute of British Architects.

This is a shoo-in, I pretended to myself. Susie was well up to date with me, and I felt a whole blanket of graft being woven in my favour. When we did meet though, both she and Bob seemed a bit distracted, and I felt simultaneously like their initiated favourite and an interloper. Also that they were doing something unorthodox by meeting me in advance like this. Then things took a surprising turn; Bob asked me if I thought the list of questions he'd prepared for the forthcoming big interview covered the ground; in other words, I was to approve my own cross-examination. It's important, he said, that I read them to the end and tell him if anything important was missing.

This spotting of what's not there – such as weapons of mass destruction – is like a form of Pelmanism. The nominated questions I was to face were mostly in current RSC jargon. Is the role of the Artistic Director mainly as a catalyst or as a Pied Piper? Is the US connection they've developed simply for financial advantage (Susie being in the Chair); if so, will it compromise the RSC's artistic independence? I found myself wondering how much actual influence, despite their formal roles, these two pleasant and attentive people were about to exert: perhaps this was not so much a subtle test of me as a sincere attempt to make a road map for themselves on the advice of a forty-year associate (small "a") of the Company; they sounded a little as if they were learning an unfamiliar language. Then they asked me if I thought the final Selection Committee had been judiciously put together: I was so startled I hardly took in who they were to be, except that they included Zoe Waites, then a fine young actor working at the RSC. Did I think that was right to do? Should John Barton, the Company magus, though no longer directing for it, be involved in the selection process? Bob and Susie had a tendency to talk at the same time, but then abruptly to fall silent and look at me, unified in a question mark. At other times one of them spoke while the other's eyes were trained on me from a different angle, as if they needed editing choices – one from a close-up lens and the other doing the mid-shot – as they asked the questions, my expression while fielding them perhaps registering as an implicit answer. I kept going, feigning decisiveness about everything, while computing privately. Their eyes continued to swivel towards each other's.

A burning question was: How could the Stratford theatre, whatever it turned out to be like, become more user-friendly given the demotics – by which they seemed to mean that it is sustained largely by visitors rather than local residents. There seems to me a non-sequitur holding this question together, so I ducked it. I also realised that though aphorisms were in order, I might be giving too much away, and that I was gabbling a bit too. I gently mocked

Michael Attenborough's recent remark that artistic decisions are really "the same" as financial decisions; I also queried Sam Mendes's declaration that the new RSC AD would be inheriting a gift since things are surely bound to look up, whoever gets the job. I called this a little mean-spirited.

Throughout, I persisted in implying that I had ideas held to my chest which I'd hatch at the final interview only. But they did want an answer to one knotty matter: did I agree that the RSC was absolutely right to leave the Barbican – an initiative of Adrian Noble's that I didn't agree with at all, even though there will have been factors influencing him that I don't know about. Rebuffing the idea, I realised I was now outstaying my welcome, no longer sure that I was cutting that good a figure. As we summed up, the unspoken whammy came across the table, as unexpected as a hurricane, in the form of fury with Adrian (but was it real or assumed?) for his wilful defection, for his "bullying", mainly because it caused the two of them to miss the first night of *Antony and Cleopatra* (though they pretended afterwards they'd been there), because they were having to find an urgent way overnight to announce his sudden resignation to the press. We were well beyond discretion here, and I wasn't sure I sympathised: even if I agreed, I felt instinctively protective of him as a colleague. I then quizzed them about the RSC's financial constraints, which they admitted, to which I quoted, probably annoyingly, *As You Like It* – "Sweet are the uses of adversity" – and emphasised the great opportunities ahead as if I was the Panglossian Banished Duke in that play rather than the wicked Duke Elect.

On 27th June, with relief, I had dinner with my dearest of friends, John Shrapnel. Since keeping secrets is fun, I enjoyed his categorical view that Greg Doran would get the RSC job, there was no alternative. I nodded, both wisely and dishonestly. The next morning, however, I broke the rule and told all the above to Annie Firbank, an equally old friend, on the phone. She was knocked out, declaring that I lived "on a different planet from everyone else", and saw excitedly that it might even happen. I think she had picked up in me what Chekhov calls "incomprehensible daring ardour" as he sets off on his near-suicidal journey to Sakhalin penal colony four thousand miles away without any resources to fall back on.

She and I mused a bit about actor-managers and why on the whole they went out of business. Well, not entirely. Anthony Quayle ran Stratford before Peter Hall, and elsewhere there's been Olivier, Ken Branagh and indeed myself at the ESC. Olivier exercised his prerogatives all right and was a little wary of casting some of his acting rivals; in this respect Quayle strikes me as having struck an exemplary deal – very judicious, neither greedy nor over-modest about his acting reputation. Ken Branagh is a special case, the closest to Olivier but without the same *amour-propre*, generous while well aware of the value of his own charisma. We agree that Quayle is the best model for me if I need one.

Back in rehearsal for *The Front Page* Richard Cordery twinkles at me and asks "how it's going". I think he suspects something (is he an RSC Associate?). Then on July 1st I get a call from Chris Foy's office to say that Susie and the Selection Committee have determined that I should have my planned meetings with Foy, Pope and David all together, not one by one as originally envisaged. Apart from saving time, I don't see sense (or much meaning) in this but note that they pretend that it's for me to decide, though I know it's not. I say that's fine: whoever I'm speaking to at Chris's office adds incongruously that the three of them are "a very strong team" as if I was going into the ring. Susie's motive in this idea is that she wants to forewarn me, she says.

I then receive a cloak-and-dagger instruction about the venue: it's to be that low red-brick Hilton at Exit 15 off the M40, now a standard Welcome Break with an unapologetic Starbucks and plastic furnishing installed, but then a dark and dingy place morosely awash with muzak, all dim lighting and failed mood-setting. I wonder why we're not meeting at the theatre but the message comes back that that would set too many tongues wagging.

They must be planning to do this four times over: I hope the other candidates got a better lunch. We can't secure a table at all even though the restaurant is empty (thank God), and sit waiting an hour in the gloom for a sandwich to toast, discussing the future of the RSC with the noise of traffic and piped Engelbert Humperdinck as cover. In the end Foy has to gobble his snack on his way to another meeting (ah-ha, with whom?) and I picture him rushing around with four sandwiches on the go. However, he chairs our meeting as to the manner born, tightening and loosening the bridle with skill. He knows recent events have not made him popular – he is now routinely thought of as the Philistine from Unilever – but he has had to implement a list of notorious redundancies on Adrian Noble's behalf, and to achieve this clear-out the moment his feet were under the desk – and so he applied the skills he knew to that uncongenial job. I immediately see that, though I deplore the redundancies, he's just the man for Adrian, whose nature is oblique and informal, as a literate, dapper, articulate fixer.

Foy's main theme today at the M40 Hilton is the US link, whereby a well-chosen East Coast theatre will bring their mainhouse work here, in return for an RSC season there – an ongoing partnership which would lighten the burden of constantly seeking corporate sponsorship here each time. I say it's OK, depending on how well chosen for like-mindedness the partner is, as we can't be always planning to please them any more than we can to please a corporation here. He also acknowledges that people feel that the RSC need a permanent London home. I underline this – scouting around for available West End theatres for temporary residencies long enough to house full Stratford seasons of transfers and new work as well is no substitute for the long-term relationship we'd had with the Aldwych and then the Barbican. Currently the public is having to scout about to find which West End theatre is presenting which RSC production. And repertoire requires endless expensive change-overs, so in the West End you have to be looking at straight runs for each. And we need to be site-specific; it's supposed to be a home, like the Royal Court or the National, not a series of halls-for-hire. I've noticed that this slightly nostalgic talk of the very popular Aldwych goes down well, even though it's before my interlocutor's time: the Company's record there was legendary and the Barbican never inspired the same affection.

Jonathan Pope is the most guileless, and easiest to contact – he speaks with passion about the redevelopment, says it was never primarily going to be about demolition but conversion. It seems that the RSC Board met a Commons Select Committee last week openly to discuss demolishing the "Jam Factory". Depending on which report you read, the Board was either reproached for seeking £100m for such an "elitist" plan or urged to go ahead with it and destroy the "hideous carbuncle" for its own good. Well, it can hardly do one without the other. The MP who led the attack had visited the theatre only once in his life and then sat in the gods. Across the floor, the Tory Member for Bromsgrove, while agreeing, improbably thought there were people in Stratford who didn't know the theatre existed.

We shrug mutual shoulders, and I say (as I will say again) that it has been a queasy business watching this great Company, in their half-acknowledged desire for new premises, having to make common cause with those with no particular interest in the matter. As for the old theatre, many of us have gone back time and again to a stage on which we feel we have done our best work. After all, there's something wrong with most theatres: at the Criterion in London you can hear the tube trains from the back of the stalls; up the road at the Aldwych it is hard to see the height of the stage, as the lip of the Dress Circle is low. (Very difficult for Juliet's balcony and Romeo on the floor beneath it.) The Upper Circle at the RST in Stratford is a bit high, and thus a challenge, but it was always something to aspire to.

As for the money, David Fletcher has been the most remote witness, reluctant to put a figure on the average main house budget, but I come away with lots of other candid figures, which was the point of the exercise. I've allowed myself to forget many of them, though I'll never forget the atmosphere, and the restrained farce of the venue. All this Jonathan accepts graciously, and I come back to London talking madly to myself, perhaps feeling for the first time that I do have something to offer to this. Everything around me seems rather approximate, rather sloppily thought out.

***

On July 14th, just before Groundhog Day, a message comes through from Susie saying she wants to discuss "the programme following the selection process" as if I already had the job and were planning the next season. I call her back and we have a long and amiable chat, in which I gain the impression that she is more kindly disposed than before, and I attribute this to Judi Dench who, it seems, has definitely recommended me to both Susie and Bob Alexander. Susie now explains the very tight and precise schedule for next week which will lead to a decision and notification on the following Tuesday, before a week of celebratory interviews, lunches etc (for which one is assumed to be free — what if I'd been abroad these past weeks?). I go back to my eremite's cell, spending the first three days of the week in seclusion, going over and over my speech, which I've now written down; considering what to wear and how to stay cool in every sense, calling up Carol Malcolmson (now an expert on the history of the Swan, but in my time an in-house ally who used to slip me the drafts of the schedules for the shows I was in before publishing them), and Fletcher and Pope too (who explain that thinking is now more flexible about Development, very much into what I'd like to see). I lie down for long periods and wait for some new thought to strike me. The last people I speak to are son Mark and Michael Bogdanov, who is wonderfully supportive and rather excited, advising me to have a couple of glasses of wine and forget about it — all the information and ideas are in there and I should follow my "redoubtable instincts".

The day of the decisive Interview arrives, at Bob Alexander's Little Venice house. I sleep badly and turn up a quarter of an hour early, even though there's a tube strike. Another problem I'm told on arrival is that "one of our number" has to go back to Spain this afternoon, so time is short (after all that). I look round the room to decide who that quitter might be. Will my partisans on the Selection Committee turn up?

We sit in a circle in Bob's front room. The staging is quite good, as I feel that I am at its crown, rather as a director might be, confronting a cast on the first day — or perhaps like the stalk of an apple. The impression has some basis, because on either side of me are Susie and Bob, but a little behind me, no doubt so that they can catch each other's eye and make signs without my seeing. I prefer to think of them as the President's friend and possible enemy behind him at the State of the Union address.

Down left of me are two Assessors, one of whom, it soon transpires, will play good cop and the other the tough, if not bad. The soft presence is Kim Evans from the Arts Council and the tougher is Richard Eyre, whom I've known since our first year at university forty years back (he was a wonderful Herbert Rudge in *Expresso Bongo* and also my brother Happy in *Death of a Salesman*), and whom I like and admire but have never had more than a nodding acquaintance with since. My relationship with him completely gives the lie to the idea that the Oxbridge lot always stick together; we are mostly mildly embarrassed by each other when it comes to the serious business of working, as if afraid that such a university contemporary is a sort of spy who once saw you wetting your pants at school. Additionally, Richard is fairly reticent until you know him, and I'm glad to say that since this momentous morning when I'm applying to run the RSC and he already runs the National, we've become much warmer with each other. Down right sits the redoubtable Shakespeare scholar Stanley Wells, presumably there to guard his patron's interests, and the actress Sinead Cusack, an old friend who giggles; down right is Michael Hoffman (from the Board) whom I don't know but seems warm. I raise my first laugh when I make my joke about the circle we're in being a magic one, like Prospero's. Richard stares intently at me; Stanley glares at his notes, and Sinead gives me a wink.

***

I start by reminding (or perhaps informing) the Panel of the three sections of my life with the RSC. Bear with me, dear Reader, but I should probably repeat it in brief here. Repetitiously, I explain that 1964, the four hundredth anniversary of Shakespeare's birth, marked the third year only of the RSC under that name and also the beginning of my own career, which, by the way, is shortly to become longer than Shakespeare's own mortal life. That I was a supernumerary in Peter Hall's RSC in *The Wars of the Roses*, and was thus a very small minnow in his pond. Though the RSC was only three years old, I had been a bride of Shakespeare for ten; my version of a misspent youth had been to see almost all of Shakespeare's plays, at Stratford or at the Old Vic in London, and had worked up all the best parts too; by the end of adolescence I had my Leontes, Hamlet and even Falstaff at the ready, waiting for the call.

As a beginner in 1964, I said, I marvelled to see Peggy Ashcroft and Ian Holm (among others), working with a subtlety you would associate with film but sending the meaning flying to the back of the theatre: this is it, I thought; perhaps I can do the same one day. Back I went in the mid-1970s, when Alan Howard was taking the RST by storm in Shakespeare's Histories, and I cautiously thought I might be one of his successors. On the other hand, in a natural development, the intimate work done in The Other Place was beginning to affect the way we dealt with the classics in the main house. When I left five years later, after playing Hamlet in repertoire for two years, I knew that this theatre was the ideal place for an actor to develop the mixture of delicacy and muscle, speed and weight, that audiences need from the plays.

Since then, I said yet again, I had worked under every Artistic Director the RSC had had – and even under Peter I had had my own ideas about his job. In those days he was holding his most important actors (of which I certainly wasn't one) under a three-year contract, retaining and paying them even when they weren't playing: it was a gallant imitation of the ensembles of the German and Russian State Theatres. But I did notice, as did others, that when it came to the need to cast a Macbeth, a Timon or a Lear, Peter had a way of sidestepping the ensemble and Paul Scofield's phone would ring, much to the infuriation of ensemble candidates such as Eric Porter. I would pipe up about the rights and wrongs of this to whoever would listen in Dressing Room 16, though it had nothing to do with me. I told the interviewers about my successful retrospective audition for Peter and also about his sacking of me for not having fulfilled my early promise: I joked that a Fortinbras of such measured deliberation must have maddened the exhausted dead bodies lying still – but then Peter had assured me that Fortinbras was the most important character in the play, so what did he expect? In *The Jew of Malta* I had managed to wound a three-year-contract artist in the sword fight, though I also helped Eric Porter, that tremendous actor who was having a little difficulty, out of many a jam. Never mind. I'd begun a lifelong attachment to the idea, and often the reality of the RSC, its peculiar nature, its balance of priorities and occasional contradictions.

A second snapshot forms in the tray, I said, when I joined Trevor Nunn's Company in 1974. I had known and acted for Trevor since my first year at Cambridge and his last, and knew it was only a matter of time: in fact I thought he'd been a little slow on the uptake, but then I'd been quite busy on TV in the intervening ten years. That what developed in my time was an outstanding group of individuals, mixing established stars – Sinden, Howard, McKellen, Dench, Mirren – with some emerging in larval form – myself, Suchet, Annis, Rees, McDiarmid, Griffiths, many brought into the Company as guests by other directors.

In those days, I reminded them, the season would start rehearsing in January, the cast having been assembled before Christmas. We all signed up for sixty weeks at a time, and the received wisdom was that in the absence of attractive film jobs the actors would agree to continue indefinitely. Actually there were more rather than less inducements to stay freelance, like the profusion of TV, mostly studio produced, that was the glory in that decade in that you didn't have to go through fire and water for executives in order to secure a job from them. Still, we all signed up for sixty, so good did the RSC feel. I was frustrated that it didn't last longer, which was why I was soon to form the English Shakespeare Company, which in some ways challenged the RSC.

I told them how I had also worked under Terry Hands and piecemeal under Adrian Noble on a couple of projects. Now vilified for the manner of his leaving his post, I recalled the Adrian of 1980, when he was the assistant to John Barton on my *Hamlet*. A somewhat shambolic figure, like a younger version of John himself, physically driven this way and that by the pressure of his idiosyncratic ideas, he'd now become a world-class director, and if I were to get this job, one of the first things I'd do was get him back to do a show. Too much talent to waste. Once the journalistic delirium had abated and the individual pain receded, he'd be recognised for what he did for the RSC: his own productions had restored some financial viability, he had a taste for bringing less familiar plays back into the repertoire, and now his upending of the system has had the effect of making everyone inside and outside the building ask themselves anew what they expect of the RSC; 1960s innovation had become received wisdom by the 70s and 80s, and sclerosis by the 90s.

My point in this elaborate introduction was that everything you associate with the RSC is intact or recoverable; with all the building blocks lying around on the floor, waiting to be put together again. So the incomer was holding not a poisoned chalice but a lovely gift. The first thing it had to do, I said, drawing breath, was to present itself more honestly. I sounded off a bit about the crassness of the RSC's current marketing style, which continues to insist that the RSC is a guarantee of excellence (a thing that can by no means be guaranteed for each of some two dozen productions a year); in the 1970s the RSC, with a far more tactical modesty, merely expressed the hope that the audience would enjoy themselves. This spills over into an obsession with alliteration: nattily describing each show, ("innovative and inspirational … hilarious and harrowing" – all that stuff), and the reduction of the image of each play to the size of a computer icon almost impossible to read, and illiterate blurb.

Every great organisation, I continue, generates its own paradoxes. If you look at the RSC you see an international concern of enormous prestige, operating from a unique centre of study, performance and research: doors open worldwide. It's, in current phrasing, a brand name, but that doesn't justify boasting about its infallibility or its guarantee of quality. Walk to the other end of the telescope and you see something different: a local theatre in the middle of a large and loyal catchment area, like a manufacturing town with its factory at the centre. People have devoted their working lives to the firm, creating a producing base of specialised expertise – hatters, armourers, cutters – these are the people who in the recent shocking round of redundancies, or rather culls, burst into tears in the street as they describe to you how they themselves have been sent packing.

Fault lines snake across most of these models. The moment you see the RSC as an international corporation, you remember the more intimate fact of the place, that the plays are being done within walking distance of the great author's grave. If you walk to the west you find a mulberry tree in New Place which might be a descendant of Shakespeare's own, looked out on as he invents Timon's tree that "grows here in my orchard", on which all Athenians should hang themselves. If you go to the southwest you tramp the fields alongside the old Honeybourne railway, now the Greenway, among the knapweed and rank fumitory Cordelia invokes in *King Lear*; further west are Shallow's orchards. There had been a little bit of bleating from a handful of actors who said it's impossible to act truthfully in such a big theatre. This is nonsense, and I use the word bleating advisedly, since the complainers are notable for not being particularly powerful vocally.

Of course it's all very well for me to rhapsodise about coming back to the Company after twenty years, delighted to find the same make-up artists that in 1976 used a particular combination of Leichner's No 19 and Fuller's earth for me as Edgar (or the fact the Pearce's Grocery still used old-fashioned scales in 1965) – it's not enough of the point in 2002, when the need is for efficiency, leanness, competitiveness and training.

The same paradox lurks inside the building. Ideally where the RSC is supposed to do several things at once if they have the means. They have to be R for Royal and R for Radical too, both inclusive and specialised. They must be idealistic and cost-effective, allowing their actors to develop and nabbing new ones too. That's what the RSC does best and audiences love to watch: you don't sense quite that idealism at the NT or the ROH. However, large sums of public money are involved and despite having a duty of care, taxpayers may not be interested in that. The RSC must be competitive, taking its opportunities to make money, generating its own, exploiting its successes and burying its failures fast, on good terms with producers and theatre owners. I have positions on all these questions, about the fourteen-acre Stratford Estate, the redevelopment, about the Barbican, the West End and why an actor-manager rather than a star director might be able to help.

And when I went back in 1999 for *Timon of Athens*, only three years ago, the relationship between the stage and the house was very good, thanks to regular modifications. These have continued, at some cost. But now the building is under threat, and at this point the argument overheats. A scandalised spokesman has complained somewhere that the stage has to be tilted so that everyone can see. Doh, yes: it's called a rake, and theatres have always been built with one, as a means of creating better visibility. It is also said that only a third of the seats have good sightlines. Not at all – if that were so, audiences would have voted with their feet long ago, and the Company would be out of business.

The truth is trite: if the work is good enough to engage a new audience, the bricks and mortar hardly matter; what's necessary are feasible ticket prices and a competent press campaign. If Romeo and Juliet fail to touch the heart, no amount of backstage visits to the Village to see a model of the flying system and watch the armour being hammered (all of which can now be done in the workshops) is going to make people interested. Are the tickets in the Village going to be cheap? Why is the work bound to be better for its existence? The current building has served this great Company for seventy years, I say. Think of the numbers that have flowed into the despised place, and the performances that have ignited them. I happen to believe there is nothing wrong with the theatre that matters: it is a Grade II listed building with, I have always thought, a welcoming atmosphere.

I have to acknowledge that lately the rhetoric on both sides has been developing a meretricious edge, and we need some decisions, I say. Not much has been heard from the profession, while objectors are generally described, rudely, as "a minority of conservationists and local people". Not so. I know for a fact there is a large groundswell of opinion on both sides that for some reason is not being heard. Let's be having them.

Prue Skene at the launch of *Capital Gain*s, her book about chairing the Arts Council Lottery Panel.

MP, Mark Pennington, Louis Pennington and Eve Pennington, Brooklyn Bridge 2014 (*King Lear* rehearsals).

Peter Andreas Kjeldsberg, Marit Østbye, Prue Skene, Ola B Johannessen, Oslo.

As Macbeth (ESC 1992).

As Coriolanus (ESC 1991).

As Richard II (ESC 1987–1989).

As John Gabriel Borkman (National Tour 2003).

Above right: As Oscar Wilde in *Gross Indecency* (West End 1999).

As the Captain in Strindberg's *The Dance of Death* (Bush Theatre 2013).

As Robert Maxwell in *The Bargain* (National Tour 2007).

As King George III in *The Madness of King George* (National Tour 2003).

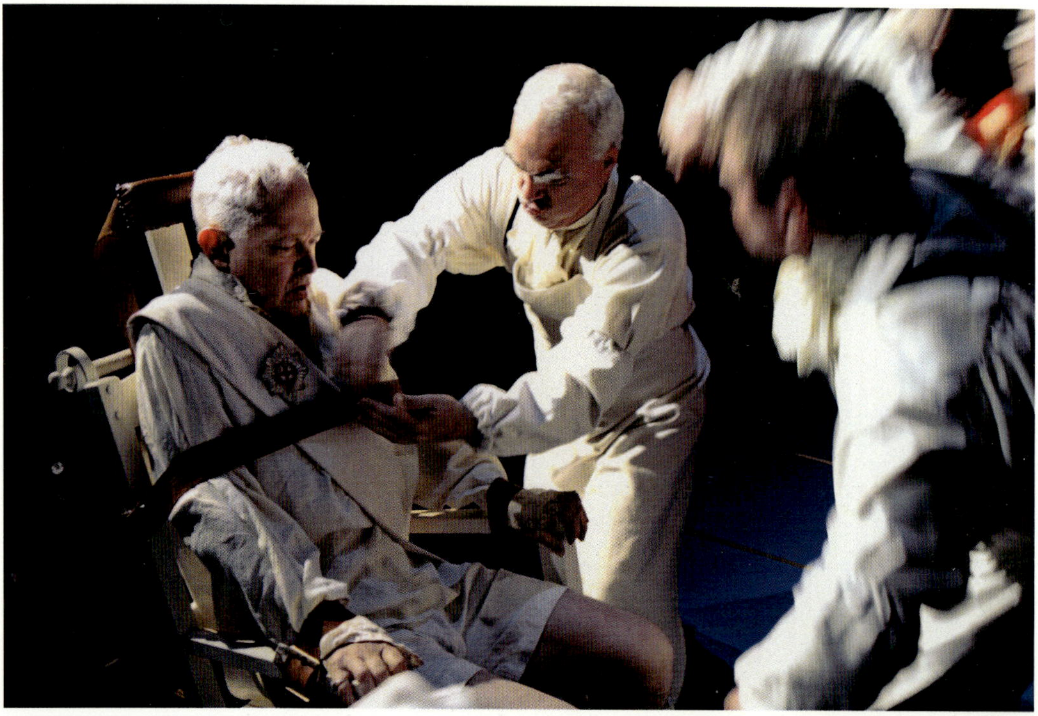

As Sir John Brute in *The Provok'd Wife,* with (L) Clare Swinburne and (R) Victoria Hamilton (Old Vic 1997).

As Walter Burns in *The Front Page* (Chichester 2002).

With John Gielgud (Tiresias) televising *Oedipus the King* (1986).

As Henry Trebell in *Waste*, with Felicity Kendal (Old Vic 1997).

As Lafarge in *Callan* (ITV 1972).

As Dr Fabio in *The Syndicate* (Chichester and tour 2011).

As King Lear in New York (2014), with Edgar (Jacob Fishel).

With Cordelia (Lilly Englert).

As Prospero in *The Tempest*, above with Kirsty Bushell as Miranda (Jermyn Street Theatre 2020).

I've noticed that the current RSC management also regrets that on Sundays the town is full of visitors but its doors are locked. I have the solution – open them. A repertory theatre is perfect for establishing seven-days-a-week playing (as Peter Hall did at the Old Vic in 1997), if only because not all the actors are in every play, so everybody gets a night off sometime. I know about the salary costs, but my guess is it would be rewarded. The rest is fixable detail, I insist: it's regrettable that customers sometimes have to queue for the loos for most of the interval – though at least that brings the RST into line with most West End theatres. But since there is a limit to how much should be spent on shortening the queue, why not simply build some more facilities?

I acknowledge that the RSC is currently declaring, with a degree of surprise, that it wants to be ideas-led, not buildings-led. But the work of Adrian Noble, his colleagues and predecessors, has always been ideas-led: how would it have succeeded otherwise? Nothing could be more dangerous than to imagine that pulling down a proven theatre and building a new one will cause certain magical properties to flow forth: a new demotic, new accessibility, a new forum for questions of race, gender and class. Gerald Kaufman, who chaired the Commons Select Committee, thinks the RSC already demonstrates those things, so where does that leave the argument?

So what would I do if I got the job?

OK, I'm for The Other Place (TOP) re-opening and for a London base. OK, so I would plan to find that London base to move into in the autumn of 2003, when it can be as autonomous as possible rather than at the nod of commercial producers and theatre owners who aren't always comfortable with the repertoire system, with all its change-overs. This summer in London has only been a qualified success, and we must feature properly next year. I would also talk to all Heads of Department, there's some fence-mending to do and I don't think it's even been started yet.

I propose a group of five or six associate directors with clearly defined jobs to do – there's no question of cleaning out the Augean stables, and I'd like two or three of them to stay on from Adrian's time, if I could persuade them under the circumstances. I say it is necessary that the long honourable list of Artistic Associates, most of whom haven't appeared at the RSC for years and some of whom are dead, needs to be cleaned up and given some role to play if it's to mean anything.

I propose a shorter Stratford season of thirty weeks – April to October – prior to a residency in Newcastle of four plays, five being too expensive and three too apologetic. Of them, three should be familiar to the box office and one could be a shot in the dark. Having looked at the figures I think we could reduce the figure of approximately £200,000-£250,000 per main house production; with good housekeeping this first season we (I'm now using the proprietorial we) could expect to save £100,000–£150,000 plus the whole cost of a fifth production before we start, and so achieve a financially sustainable season. I would run the RST season with a Senior Associate.

Meanwhile the Swan season should be run by Associate No 2, perhaps with its own Company, looking at another part of the repertoire – this year it hasn't gone very far into the very rich Jacobean period – and when did the RSC last do *Women Beware Women* or *The Atheist's Tragedy* or *The Changeling*? One day I'd like to see big-scale new work like Edgar's *Destiny* or Hare's *Trilogy* invited there as well.

The Other Place is a much-loved space currently stuck in a web of difficulties: at the moment it costs us £60 a seat before anyone sits in it. Its box office has reduced by 50 per cent since 1991, and with the RSC's finances under pressure the building is pretty much decommissioned. But like the Cottesloe and the Theatre Upstairs at the Royal Court, the TOP is one of the glories of the last quarter-century and I worry for its existence and its style – it's our main line to young audiences, as well as to young writers who currently see the RSC as a posh monolith and would rather get their work on at the Court or a found space or even outdoors. Zinnie Harris is attached to the RSC now, but we also need Abi Morgan, Jez Butterworth, Roy Williams, Bryony Lavery. I'd put in a third associate such as Vicky Featherstone from Paines Plough and directors like Erica Whyman, Rufus Norris, Andrew Hilton, Marianne Elliott.

We're scouting not only for actors to cast but for directors and designers.

The small-scale regional tour is one of the RSC's historic successes; it should be directed and run by Associate 3.

In the USA we should do main-house work such as *Midnight's Children*.

The work of Associates 4 and 5 has to be financially self-sufficient. A fifteen-week season at the Young Vic or the Lyric, say, of three shows in a row. A commercial tour directed by No 6. A carefully monitored co-production, not a commercial one with the RSC logo stuck on to it for quality. Directed by an RSC associate or a former one like Howard Davies, its star preferably associated in some way. The London end has to be financially neutral.

***

Then come the questions. The only ones that are difficult to answer are the ones that make no sense. Like "reconciling the vision…" Some are two or three questions disguised as one. Richard (Eyre) agrees there is a fault line in the RSC (nicking my choice of words), and asks how one person can reverse its decline (unanswerable); he wonders how I'll get stars to work there again (I say, ring them up and lunch them). He has some sympathy with my point that to be the AD of the theatre and also the star director is a big burden (and he should know) but he says creating a world in the rehearsal room is good practice for running an organisation. This seems rather whimsical to me, and I pull a face.

He talks of Olivier's famous selfishness and asks how would I behave as an actor in control of an organisation. I cite Strindberg, who built his own theatre just for himself. I get the feeling again that Richard's here as bad cop. He talks humorously about the Company's gravitational pull towards acronyms: he's only just learned what TOP stands for, and wonders why the Company has to be called the *Royal* Shakespeare Company. Got him: I mention that he has been the AD of the NT who added the Royal to make it grovel as the "Royal National Theatre". The air briefly crackles: for the first time I get a hint of genuine affection between us, which has turned out to be the case.

Stanley Wells asks whether my newly-engaged associates would be under contract or whether they could take freelance work? Yes, says I, but they might not want to. What about the verse speaking? Sinead doesn't understand why actors don't stay longer. She also asks how I'll get McKellen; call him, I say, and see what he wants to do and if that would suit us. On another hand Terry Hands did too much schmoozing and made too many unfulfillable promises. She thinks the press is permanently against the RSC.

Susie asks me a baroque question about delegation and admin. I have a feeling she has a personal interest in it, and choose to think she is referring to a Chief Executive. I say it's vital that this should be the Artistic Director as it always used to be.

***

In my growing fever after the interview, I've made a date with John Barton, my old friend and to some degree Svengali, in London, though I know he is reluctant to see me – my idea was supper and self-promotion – and there is much talk of confidentiality. The fact is, I am to learn that Greg Doran has been lobbying him for years, and Greg is John's man. He can't understand, he says, why I would want the job: I remind him about the ESC, of which he has only the haziest idea, not realising at all that I co-ran it, rather than just acting in the shows. On the other hand he's very unconfidential himself about other, absent figures among the theatre's associate directors – Barry Kyle, Ron Daniels, Bill Alexander. John clearly believes appointing someone from inside is right. He thinks I underestimate the complex personality of an Artistic Director, citing Trevor mercilessly doing *Les Misérables* despite 100 per cent Board opposition. His opinions of the Company's current work (Michael Boyd he is rather negative about) are as good as any advice – I agree with him about most things. I close the meeting, feeling like his protégé all over again. No matter.

Rather hurt today by a piece in *The Observer* about the "three contenders", whereas I'm a fourth, excluded. I read it in a doleful gas station, just as I did about Alan Howard's CBE – I loved Alan, but I wanted one too. Greg Doran probably hated *The Observer* more, as he is credited there with applying with his partner Tony Sher, whereas he has been careful not to, for rather obvious and sensible tactical and tactful reasons. As for me, I decide it is good to be a dark horse amidst all these delirious approximations. Meanwhile the *Evening Standard* credits me as "an ex-RSC director".

My claim now seems to me quite distinct from anyone else's. I try to neutralise the part of myself that wants the attention, even among *The Front Page* cast. I'm not even sure I want the job. How would I get any acting done, being instead obliged to take small managerial supporting roles?

***

Monday morning. Home from an evening Event dedicated to John Clare where I've found Richard Pasco furious with everybody at the RSC, who he thinks should just get on with it and give me the job: he says he prays every night with Bar for me. I'm surprised. Stanley Wells is standing with us (Richard clearly doesn't know he is one of the "they"), so I have to improvise a little: you could cut the atmosphere of intrigue like a knife. I brace myself for disappointment, which is the only sensible choice a brain could make. I've thought of a million reasons why I wouldn't get hired, and another million why I should be. This is my Second Chance at Artistic Directorship. Every time the phone rings, I jump.

Then Dearbhla Molloy calls me just as I'm driving somewhere, or rather, when I've just pulled in for a tentative cappuccino at a service station. I remember it was in such a setting that I heard about Alan Howard's CBE. Now Dearbhla's heard a newsflash announcing that the RSC has a "new Artistic Director". A voice now announces: "He is Michael… (breath-length pause in which Dearbhla drops her coffee cup) … Boyd."

She's miserable, but I'd got the news on the phone two days before, and I find myself comforting her.

Eduardo de Filippo, Toto and Anton Chekhov.

EDUARDO AND ANTONIO

Hanging on my study wall is a big photograph of an actor/director/playwright greeting his friend, fellow-actor and business partner, whom I happen to know he calls Toto. You can almost hear their excited voices suddenly raised in greeting – it looks as if they've just finished a performance, perhaps a first night: they'll want a drink in a minute. Beside them on my wall is an equally large image of another good playwright, executed by an artist called Osip Braz in 1898: his subject complained that after three weeks of sittings, and despite his dedicated consumption of twenty cherries at a time, it still makes him look as if he'd been sniffing grated horseradish.

This man, whom we'll call Number 2, initially distrusted the theatre and actors (though he enjoyed their company, "if only they wouldn't all *act* so much … the stage is a scaffold on which the playwright is executed"); and he was in two minds about the new trade of "directors". The first, by contrast, might as well have been born in a costume trunk, which is why I'm calling him Number 1. He was born in 1900 – the year in which No. 2, many miles away, was struggling to complete his last play – and made his professional debut at the age of four, the year in which No. 2 premiered his completed work, which he no longer thought much of, and died. The four-year-old's debut was in a Japanese operetta called *Geisha*, and he was trained up in it by his father, himself an actor-manager and playwright, and perhaps by his mother, a theatre seamstress and costumier who was his father's wife's niece, so the boy was well outside the marital blanket, a circumstance he never became resigned to despite considerable fame, even though he did take her name.

After a stretch acting with his half-brother, who had his own Company, followed by military service, No. 1 married an American woman called Dorothy Pennington, I'm glad to say, but I also regret to report that the marriage lasted about five minutes; he then formed his own group and soon became a fully-fledged actor-manager, disillusioned by his family's more old-fashioned acting habits. He was immediately successful with his own Christmas play, *Natale in Casa Cupiello*, which, as another Pennington, I have been fighting to get the rights of for a number of years; apart from the acting parts, it beautifully brings onto the stage examples of the Neapolitan practice of Presepio, the modelling of miniature nativity scenes.

Both my writers achieved a close relationship with the Establishment as well as with a new audience – No. 1's plays were seen by a Pope, No. 2's by what we would call a President. In 1974, as I went up to Stratford to play Angelo, No. 1 had major heart surgery but shortly afterwards married for the third time; in 1980, as I approached my first night as Hamlet, he gave his last live performance, picked up the equivalent of a knighthood and prepared his own version of *The Tempest*, which he eventually recorded, playing all the parts except Miranda. A few days after he completed this, he died, in the same year as my father, 1984, and lay in state, where he was seen by 60,000 people: the ceremony was screened live on television. By contrast, eighty years earlier, No. 2 had been carted to his resting-place in a refrigerated railway car marked "For Oysters" because there had been a mistake in the repatriating of his body. Indeed, some of the thousands of his mourners mistakenly followed the simultaneous funeral procession through the streets of a certain General Keller, to the accompaniment of a military band.

No. 2 is only No. 2 because his plays are slightly better known, though far fewer. He often attended rehearsals but could never have been tempted onto the stage; he had very mixed feelings about how his work was presented, complaining it was invariably made too "realistic" by the use of twittering birds and a whole lot of other technical devices.

Both writers had a genius for detail, for gravity lightly worn. No. 2 said that there was no point in trying to solve great questions like God and pessimism because for the most part people had dinner, just had dinner, but during this time their happiness was established or their lives were falling apart. Of No. 1, Thornton Wilder said that to appreciate him one must love "not the well-shaped play, not the picture of relatively superficial customs and manners, not the heated unfoldment of patterns of idealised heroism and villainy, but the show of the people, by the people for the people – absurd, extravagant, often preposterous but close to life and the stage. He is an incomparable dramatist, an incomparable *metteur en scene* and an incomparable actor. How sad his plays are – the weight of humanity. How controlled his acting has become – that powerful *quiet*."

All right, that's enough. No. 1 is Eduardo de Filippo, who was born, lived and died in Naples, whose son he will always be; everyone there seems to have heard of him apart from the newborn. Moreover his plays – maybe fifty of them – are written in Neapolitan dialect, not classic Italian; when his Company first did a classic play by Luigi Pirandello, the author died in mid-rehearsals. Eduardo's Company always worked in dialect, and they toured everywhere. As for himself, he was described by Harold Acton as resembling the last mask surviving from the commedia dell'arte, a Pulcinello grown older, sadder and wiser.

So when does a dialect become a separate language? Neapolitan is a badge of pride to its speakers, setting them above the rest of Italy in matters great and small. The pronunciation is not all that different, but its tonalities are more guttural, sometimes seeming more lazy, as if they had been baked in the southern sun. Exactly: anything could happen in these plays, any time. What comes through to us, at a safe distance, is the wonderful southern Italian pride in the making of a perfect cup of coffee or of perfect ice-cream or a perfect firework or pastry. All the unimportant things, you might say, the pleasurable accompaniments to life, Neapolitans are absolutely expert in; nothing could be worse than a bad cup of coffee. It doesn't matter about your marriage or what other tragedies might be happening as long as the coffee's all right.

There's always a displacement of love and creativity, generally very touching and funny. In de Filippo's *Filumena Marturano* I played Domenico, who at various points of the play is accused of bad faith of one kind or another by his wife. He at last draws himself up to his full height and defends himself: "Do you really think that Domenico Soriano, son of Raimondo Soriano, one of the most famous and respected [*pause*] pastrycooks in Naples, would do such a thing?" Wonderful, because he isn't one of the most respected of lawyers, judges or doctors, but of pastrycooks. And the Neapolitan characters talk, talk, talk as they think – not like the English, who so often seem to think a thought, decide how to express it, then half-express it. In Naples, they talk on their feet, the words tumbling as they interrupt each other, and the body language is different: Neapolitan has a huge repertoire of gestures, specially hand gestures, very specific – you've only to walk down the Via Benedetto Croce and you get the full flavour of it. In fact, an actor should (as I have) travel with a tape recorder to capture something, musically, physically, so that, back in England, he or she can trick the audience at a de Filippo play into thinking that they're listening to Italian and not English. Otherwise, some director (like me) will say no, that sounds too *English*, too ironic, too modulated. The peril for an English Company is to stick an accent on like a beard – it's got to come from inside: then it should lead to being able to portray a certain speciality of foreign character even though all the words are English.

No. 2 is Anton Chekhov, that enrichment of all our lives. And the final play he's labouring with is *The Cherry Orchard*. To declare an interest: I've been in *The Seagull* three times, with good directors – as Dorn for Peter Stein at the Edinburgh Festival and as Trigorin for Peter Hall in London, and once on radio long ago as Konstantin, with Angela Baddeley as Arkadina. I've been in *Three Sisters* twice, on a long UK tour as Andrei directed by Richard Cottrell, and later as Vershinin at the Gate Theatre Dublin under the eye of Adrian Noble. In some ways perhaps more significant than these, I have written and imagined, devised and performed an evening in the company of Anton Chekhov himself which I've played periodically since opening it at the National Theatre in 1984. It involved a complete transformation into the character of Chekhov – his sound, look, his sensibility (helped by having played him in 1982 on Granada TV in an interesting play titled *A Wife Like the Moon* – which was how Chekhov explained what he wanted of a partner and why he waited so relatively long to marry).

As we begin, Chekhov – my solitary Chekhov – enters the room, seeming to come out of the pitch darkness way upstage, and since he is wearing a long black overcoat and the light is initially low, only his face can be seen clearly, disembodied and approaching his audience like a ghostly visitation. Later on in the show, after many revelations and interactions – and jokes – with his audience, Chekhov goes to stay at a hotel in Yalta and rests for a night after his travels. He describes how

> A light wind blew in from the sea, sending my papers to the floor.

At the first performance in 1984, and at that precise moment in the Cottesloe, into which no breeze comes, a random gust blew my papers off my desk. I somehow took it as a judgement, or maybe a gesture of approval. I should mention in this connection that just before my scheduled first performance a few weeks previously at a drama school, my father had suddenly died and I had postponed the opening; this first night at the Cottesloe was when ghosts might be walking more peacefully. Towards the climax, Chekhov offers a little advice to his audience; on that night he addressed himself as a sick man might to the bereft, as if I was among them:

> Why do we never try to stand again when once we've fallen? If we lose one thing why don't we look for another? I want our lives to be holy, sublime and solemn as the vault of heaven: Let us live! The thief on the cross had hope even though he had less than an hour left to him, and the sun only rises once a day, so take hold of what's left of your life and save it… My holy of holies is the human body, health, intelligence, talent, inspiration, love, and the most absolute freedom imaginable – freedom from violence

and lying, whatever form they may take. That's the programme I would follow if I were a great artist…

***

As for Eduardo de Filippo, long before I got started on him he had been championed in this country by Laurence Olivier and Richard Eyre at the NT in particular. I've done my bit in this respect by reading most of his fifty-odd plays written over seventy years and working to get them on if ever I saw an opening. I was also familiar with the author's UK history: in 1972, Eduardo brought his own Company's production of *Napoli Milionaria* to London; then, in a 1991 English revival, Ian McKellen played the lead at the NT. *La Grande Magia* with Alan Howard followed, then *Saturday, Sunday, Monday* (with Joan Plowright cooking a real ragù every night), and *Inner Voices*.

When I was in *Filumena Marturano* in the West End of London in 1998 in Eduardo's old part of Domenico, Judi Dench was Filumena, and we were directed by Peter Hall. In fact I more or less engineered the occasion: I'd seen Joan Plowright play it in London with Colin Blakely in 1977, and I also knew that in 1946, after opening as Filumena (a part he had written for her), Eduardo's sister collapsed and died; soon afterwards he freely adapted the play to make the movie *Marriage Italian Style* for Sophia Loren and Marcello Mastroianni. (There's also, it occurs to me, a link with *Mamma Mia*, also about paternity.) I managed to persuade Peter, who'd also seen that production, that it would now suit the three of us very well; in the end we all agreed it was one of our most enjoyable experiences, ever. Though I failed to persuade Peter to study my DVD of Visconti's *Rocco and his Brothers* to understand fully about northern and migrant southern Italy (from the latter's point of view), I supplied a multitude of folk songs recorded by Roberto Murolo, the Grand Master of Neapolitan Song, who was still composing and singing when he was ninety-one. Timberlake Wertenbaker did the version; as for the dialect, once translated into English it became, as ever, a matter of catching rhythm and velocity

– and abbreviation. A Neapolitan pulls the Italian names around, sometimes swallows or only half-speaks them, compressing them rather as Russians do; so Rafelluccio becomes Raf', just as Russians don't say Anton Pavlovich Chekhov, they say Paltch: if you listen a lot, it becomes quite clear. I should have said, by the way, that the relationship between Neapolitan and Italian has little to do with class, more with the embattled independence of the former: English productions that use English regional accents so that the Neapolitans sound working-class while any posh characters do RP, tend to miss the point. All Neapolitans speak Neapolitan, except when they choose Italian – which might not be often. The main point to make is that they're as different from northern Italians as is everyone in Sardinia and Sicily and Calabria. (Pirandello, by the way, wrote in Sicilian and Dario Fo in Lombard vernacular.)

Fortune smiled on us, so did the press. Here, shamelessly, is Nicholas de Jongh in *The Evening Standard*:

> As for Peter Hall's matchless lead performers, Judi Dench and Michael Pennington: Pennington's moustachioed, bow-tied Domenico sinks delightfully into furious self-pity, voice a-tremble and hands haphazardly flapping like an electrified scarecrow, while Dame Judi's Filumena is a fusion of England and Italy: a rich, ripe, hip-swaying sensuality runs in train with a grim English introversion. Mr Pennington has done nothing better, or more delicate, than his slow thawing from rigid paterfamilias to loving Dad; and Dame Judi, skittish as the breeze, matronly as a mother hen and finally, like Niobe, all tears, gives one of her classic performances of rich comic domination.

The problem of the identity of Domenico's son ensures the play's tantalising hold; the self-interested decision of all the sons to claim Domenico as their father becomes the convincing stroke of liberation for Filumena to achieve her marriage. As Dame Judi manages the climax of this bitter-sweet comedy, the happy sight of Filumena, allowing herself to succumb to the liberation of tears, is, like the production itself, the source of high theatrical joy.

(I might add that in order not to swell our heads *too* much, I managed briefly to persuade Judi that the "lead" in the opening sentence "matchless lead performers" was meant to be pronounced as in "leaden" rather than "leading".)

As well as this very moving finale, the play has a fantastic opening, like all Eduardo's plays, all twists and turns, and you have to concentrate. It starts with two people yelling at each other and the audience baffled for about ten minutes before realising that she's a prostitute who's got Domenico to marry her as her last wish by feigning a mortal illness. Then she's jumped out of bed and cried "fooled you". She goes on to tell him she's got three sons – how he didn't know this I don't know – only one of whom is his and she's not going to tell him which, because then he would favour one over the other two, whereas he must, on pain of losing her altogether, treat them all the same now that he's married her.

***

If you look for Eduardo's home theatre, the San Ferdinando, rebuilt since the War, it's right in the depths of Naples – in the Piazza Eduardo de Filippo, no less. And I've played there, not so long ago, in a Shakespeare sonnet programme assembled and directed by Peter Brook. What a privilege, what a pleasure, in all sorts of ways. You go under the stage, amongst all the very old-fashioned trap doors and machinery (no computers); and suddenly, beyond the gloom, you detect the ghost of a man turned to look directly at you, the white figure of Eduardo de Filippo himself. It's a cut-out, very theatrically lit, and you jump out of your skin. Then you go front of house where they keep a lot of display cabinets with all his old sticks of Leichner make-up, his nose putty, his false beard for Macbeth. So that's pretty funny too. And in the stage left wing of the theatre there's a plaque on the wall, a very solemn plaque, which looks like a memorial in a church, a big message carved into it in Neapolitan, written by Eduardo. I had it translated, thinking it would be, you know, to the spirit of Dante or of Goldoni, or express thanks to some sponsor. But Eduardo boasted in *The Art of Comedy* that, as a director, all he ever needed was six metres of wooden stage, that he could do all of Shakespeare and all of Molière on those few planks, so in fact the plaque features a huge hymn of adoration to his Stage Carpenter.

> This is the man who took the hammer and the nail and banged the nail into the plank and joined that plank to another plank and made our stage.

A fantastic tribute, and I was very proud to have played there. I was dealing with a very unusual fellow, someone whom everybody in Naples refers to still by his first name. And beyond Naples most people have never heard of him.

There is, if you're interested, quite a deal of Eduardo the actor on DVD, both in his own productions and in other producers' screenplays, so one can testify that "his presence on stage was so compelling that it brought about a magic lightheadedness." (Worth noting: if you look at the available DVDs of his productions, they're subtitled in Italian, so there's obviously been a need for some translation into the mother tongue.) Dario Fo opens a small window on Eduardo's acting style, insisting (and he means it as a compliment) that he had a way of thinking what he would say before he said it – "Oh, Eduardo's pauses…" And Harold Acton again: "who else can mesmerise an audience with half a word, a pregnant pause or a gesture with the immobility of those features which express anguish and defeat more often than joy or success…"

I've also noted – with much amusement – that if you look at his plays of the 1930s, say, you find that on about page five it'll likely say "Enter a very handsome, eloquent, articulate and charming man". By the time you get to the 1940s, you reach your page five and it says "Enter a middle-aged but still charming, eloquent man with his youth still part of him"; in the 1950s you meet "a man of late middle age who somehow retains his youthful eloquence and charm". It's the same towards the end with *The Syndicate* – "a man who's bronzed, wiry and lithe, belying his years". You can see what's going on: Eduardo knew his audience needed him on terms with them after about five minutes and he shamelessly wrote timely entrance moments for himself: he was an enormously popular star. And he directed himself as well.

***

The Syndicate's full title is *Il Sindaco del Rione Sanita*, which translates as 'The Mayor of Rione Sanita' (the Sanita district is the Neapolitan pits), written and premiered in 1960, and it contains a marvellous central study of a more innocent Don Corleone, the kind of Mafia godfather who actually does some good as well as plenty of ill. Eduardo gave the performance of his life in it, but it has a big cast and isn't well known. I'd often proposed a UK premiere to anyone who'd listen, but I saw that nobody was going to put this on with only my name attached to it, so I sent it to Ian McKellen, offering to play his close friend in the play, Dr Fabio, if he would care to be the Don. He agreed, Sean Mathias directed, we called the play *The Syndicate* and we did it at Chichester with the greatest pleasure before touring it – a terrific experience. It's a play with, obviously, one dominant part, but I'd say that as a Company we got at least as far in terms of characterisation and psychological insight as, judging from the recording, Eduardo's original troupe did.

The play's main idea is that someone we think of as a gangster may be an idealist as well. As a young man Don Antonio killed a watchman, was tried, jumped bail, went to America where he spent twenty years, presumably learning the ways of gangsterdom, before coming back to demand a re-trial in the knowledge that he had the whole thing stitched up by a corrupt lawyer. The re-trial went so smoothly that he was immediately assumed to be a sort of Don, and people started looking to him for help. He spent money on property, because he'd come back from America with lots. So you see the two things going side by side: there's a Mafia background – or to be more precise, a Camorra background – but also a sort of idealism which he shares with Dr Fabio, my part: to help poor people settle their disputes so that they don't get exploited and abused by the system. Dr Fabio is himself dependent on him, but is also in the process of trying to escape to America: a thing he's tried twice before, and Don Antonio's made it impossible, one way and another. This time when Fabio tries to escape, Antonio promises him he'll have "a reception committee on the harbour in New York". It's very clear what he's saying – don't even think about it.

Dr Fabio Della Ragione is a middle-class man, a professional, and his father was professor of medicine at Naples University. So he's an honourable person. In some ways, having perhaps wasted his entire life amongst gangsters and crooks, his dilemma is as painful as it would inevitably be for somebody who could hardly afford to do otherwise. There's something here of the drunken doctor in Chekhov's *Three Sisters*, sentimentally attached to a family but with an accompanying self-hatred. However, Fabio does the job, gets the work done, as you see in the play; his problem is that he still can't get away, even in his late sixties. He now wants to finish his life with a certain amount of dignity, see his brother in the US, have a normal time, instead of spending all his working day pulling bullets out of people's legs, stitching up stomachs, repairing broken skulls. Indeed, the play has an astonishing opening sequence in which what looks like a welcoming country house in the hills outside Naples slowly stirs to life – maids, cooks, etc – and you realise that the furniture being wheeled on is mostly hospital beds, breathing apparatus, shining new cases of glistening instruments, drips and all the rest of it, surgical equipment accompanying them into what is now in fact a private field hospital. Antonio's various disciples and henchmen can be brought here when they've been wounded in street fighting; the first thing I did as the resident doctor was to dig a huge bullet out of a young man's leg and brandish it aloft – but in a routine way.

So – Naples as it was and is. The play is not simply about the Mafia, but the possibility of someone running an amoral empire outside the system, for good or bad, and what that might mean. It could be anywhere, but this is a city where you have to pay protection money to get your garbage removed, and nothing much works because someone's creamed off the money. It's a situation where it's very difficult to bring up a family. I know a couple with small children there: the schools are unsanitary, the rats are all over the classrooms and the intelligent thing would be to move to Rome or Milan, but Neapolitans can be extremely bound to their own city and their own culture. It's a tragic place whose vibrancy is very easy to like as a visitor but not so easy to enjoy if you have to survive in it.

***

I don't want to go on the record as saying Eduardo is like Chekhov in any crass way – he works in a hot climate, unlike that of the Russian landscape – but he certainly has something of the psychological depth: his characters have an unexpected, unpredictable element and his technique and dramaturgy are constantly surprising once you start working on them. What after all is the difference between Uncle Vanya bursting into the room with his gun to kill the Professor, then firing at him but missing; and on the other hand Domenico in *Filumena*, opening the action by impotently exploding onto the stage, livid that he could have been so "Pazzo! Pazzo!" as to allow himself to be tricked into marriage, not by his own desire but by a very much smarter woman, an ex-prostitute with three sons who's been simulating her imminent "death" to bring him to heel. All he lacks is Vanya's gun, and so he ends up being pacified.

Eduardo, like Chekhov, is always ahead of his audience; the suspense is masterly, but you trust him, the writer, he's always ahead. It's not like Ibsen, where someone will come on at the start and say "Oh you're the fellow who mistreated our little son fifteen years ago"; exposition like that doesn't arise with the Italian master. As Chekhov would have approved, people do things, have a row, cook a meal, then you have to work out why, without that old-fashioned narrative. The structure of the plays is very sophisticated, with vivid showmanship. Another example: what is the difference between the character known as Waffles in the same *Vanya*, who sits around playing the guitar but feels he should explain to the company that he has that nickname because he has such a terrible complexion, and also as a punishment for the fact that his wife ran away on their wedding night with another man, with whom she has now had children that he, Waffles, willingly supports; and, on the other hand, Domenico struggling to establish by a series of laughable tests his paternity of one and one only of Filumena's three sons; impotent and desperate, he checks them for his own foibles – a taste for women, a preference for a certain cut of jacket, a talent for singing – and so on. In both cases, the men have been thoroughly emasculated; Waffles accepts stoically and Domenico rages, but it might just as well be the other way round, equally painful and comic.

Both writers know their characters so well that they can wind them up and let them run: they're in the blood, especially that of Eduardo, the son of an actor and a child prodigy. The same geography in all the plays, the same few streets, which the audience right away recognises. In *The Syndicate*, there's one difference, because Don Antonio's time is spent in his country retreat in the surrounding hills and he only goes back into Naples towards the end: there's a moment where someone asserts "Don Antonio can't be in Naples now, he never goes back until October". Nevertheless they all talk affectionately about the local bakery shop – as if the speaker were constantly referring, from the distant countryside, to Notting Hill Gate, Kensington Church Street, Bayswater Road.

I've seen two film versions of Eduardo's productions of *The Syndicate*, one of which was shot in 1965, soon after it opened in the theatre, and the other fifteen years later. The actors knew each other so well by 1980 that they have a very interesting style, difficult to describe but very good, very real, entirely convincing. In fact the work is fine all the way through, but I think there's something that could equally be said: just now in this country we too have an extraordinary standard of Company work, so we have much in common with them. In any case, I can't imagine any good actor wanting to turn down a play by Eduardo de Filippo, especially if he likes Chekhov.

***

It was while I was playing in *Filumena* that my granddaughter Eve was born. Her brother Louis had arrived a year and a half earlier, while I'd been rehearsing *The Seagull* at the Old Vic – which only goes to show that my grandchildren have an instinct for the link between these two favourite authors. And Louis, equally sagaciously, was born on the last day of Conservative government in the UK in the twentieth century, April 30th 1997. I had finagled some time off from rehearsing with Peter Hall and Felicity Kendal to go and welcome him, coming back into rehearsal the next day with a passable impersonation of a chest-beating gorilla taking the credit for the reproductive event: Hall, a great breeder himself, particularly enjoyed it. Elsewhere the general response at the theatre was rather restrained – though dear Alan Dobie congratulated me heartily on keeping "the name" alive, as if I'd actually contributed something to the event, which as I pointed out I hadn't for at least a generation. As he did this, Alan sounded much like a character in a play – by Harley Granville-Barker, for instance – in which Victorian gentlemen flip their tailcoats and roast their bottoms in front of log fires while addressing their sons and heirs about their responsibilities or their finances.

On the other hand, the general backstage reaction to Evie's arrival was of a stampede from all the parts of the building where women were at work – dressing rooms, wig room and wardrobe – all of them careering down the stairs and spilling into my dressing room to find out Did she have any hair, Whom does she resemble, Did she cry a lot, How long was the confinement?

Which is why on the whole I like women the best in all creation.

Even though Louis and Evie used to look behind the TV if I was on to see if I was hiding there, Evie has never shown any inclination to become an actor, despite the evidence of her remarkable sang-froid, natural judgement and instinct in a succession of school plays. Instead she's about to graduate from the Royal College of Fashion and could become Mary Quant. Likewise Louis's declared interest – he's a sound designer and engineer by calling but can turn his hand to a variety of routine jobs, for instance to gardens and picture-framing. In the theatre he is thus far a spectator only, even though I've often surmised that he could have been an actor if he'd wished: at twenty-three he is idiosyncratic but stylish, immediately attractive and humorous, with a great deal of presence. But he's never wanted that, though I do remind him regularly of that moment in my Chapter One when he yelled out "Sheep", and leaped into the air at the prospect.

**

Out of the blue this year, soon after my Prospero at the Jermyn Street Theatre had to be abandoned, Ion Caramitru has sent me a link so that I can watch his *Tempest – Furtuna,* dupa William Shakespeare, directed by Alexander Morfov and lit by Chris Jaeger – which premiered at the National Theatre in Bucharest (named after the playwright I. L. Caragiale) while I was doing *King Lear* in New York in 2014, or possibly during its UK touring version in 2016, I'm not sure. He of course features as Prospero, and the show is now being streamed for two nights as Romania too struggles with Lockdown – he's also sent me an Apology for Poetry he's written and an address he's given to the public on behalf of Uniter (the Romanian Equity), about how theatre can possibly survive a pandemic; so one touch of nature makes the whole world kin.

Ion said to me once that he based his Prospero on Albert Einstein; at any rate the performance is humane, marvellously gentle and natural, almost pastoral. I've seen so little of Ion's work at first hand, despite quite a number of workshops he's brought me to Bucharest and to Moldavia to do with his National Theatre Company, that I wasn't prepared for this informal figure in baggy chinos and cardigan and scruffy loafers – no magic spells for this Prospero and not a very tyrannical father, but fully preoccupied, with a persistent characteristic gesture of emphasis when he jabs his index fingers rather floppily at the ground, deeply grieved at having to relinquish Miranda in the end but modest in his suffering, truly divided between sorrow and joy as he finally breaks his staff. Ion has a tempestuous side to his acting when he chooses to use it, but like me, he wants his Prospero to be both human and humane; I was probably a bit more neurotic, unreasonable when crossed. But I suppose I'd always wanted the character to have been partly written by Chekhov or de Filippo. Or like Oscar Wilde. As unpredictably as possible, in fact.

Certainly not like Ibsen, of whom, now I think of it, I've done most of the more tryingly obstinate characters, uneasy companions, hard to learn and quite hard to like. They feel like a Scandinavian speciality: and so does the Captain in Strindberg's *Dance of Death*, with his famous stamping dance; and closer to home, the dreadful Nicolas in Pinter's *One for the Road*, even Deeley in his *Old Times*, and both Major Arnold and Wilhelm Furtwängler in Ronald Harwood's great *Taking Sides*, in which I'm delighted to think that by playing both parts I have represented both sides of the argument about collaboration with Hitler, albeit in two separate productions with thirteen years between them – both in Chichester followed by the West End. So on both occasions, I've learned or re-learned the entire script of this complex play: it's perhaps something to be proud of, or at least relieved about as time goes mercilessly by, challenging even a retentive memory at every opportunity.

I have the same feeling of professional virtue when I recall that I was once able to learn an acting steeplechase created by Harley Granville-Barker in Act Two of *Waste* for his leading character, the Independent politician Henry Trebell. Trebell is running for office and in this long scene his diary dictates that he has one important interview after another with various VIPs and potential supporters, each succeeding the other at fifteen-minute intervals. Suddenly, he is visited (unscheduled) by his new mistress who tells him she is pregnant by him and that he must help her to get an abortion. In an exact reversal of what you might expect, she desperately wants the termination and he refuses to help, rather urging her for her own sake to have the child, even though there is no prospect of them sharing their lives: the play is set in 1906. It is a marvellous exercise for both actors, perhaps especially for Trebell, who then has to wipe all memory of the encounter without turning a hair and get on with his political lobbying interviews without coming to seem like a complete pig – in fact he is rather a decent man and by his own lights terribly torn. Barker, an actor as well as director and writer, has raised the bar very high for his successors, and of course it was a wonderful and testing scene for Felicity Kendal and me to play.

I'm also proud that I was able to survive (with delight) playing other notorious handfuls such as Molière's *Misanthrope*. And Coriolanus. And Jaffier in Otway's extraordinary *Venice Preserv'd*, Carl Gustav Jung to David Suchet's *Freud* on television, Henry in Tom Stoppard's virtuosic *The Real Thing*, and the torment of Raskolnikov in *Crime and Punishment*. And run the ESC, if not the RSC. And (proudest boast of all), get on top of Archie Rice in John Osborne's *The Entertainer* and being judged by Sheridan Morley as being better than Olivier in the part. I can only comment: most actors have shied away from even trying to follow Olivier in this great virtuoso role.

***

Oh yes, and I've played King Lear twice: once in 2014 in a theatre of 350 seats in New York and then, in an entirely new production, in 2016, in a succession of UK opera houses (Manchester, York) on a ten-week, eight performances a week (two matinées) schedule. I suppose that will be the last time I do the part, unless I'm spared to have one last shot at it in a very small room, which in fact I would like. The nearest I've been to that last ideal is to play Prospero in the Jermyn Street Theatre, and, as I reported at the outset, that was cut short by the Coronavirus.

In the UK tour of *Lear*, our Company would pitch camp on every Monday, shove the show on, settle a bit during the week, and usually be good by Saturday. My efforts to revive or re-mount the play after the success it had enjoyed in New York had been rewarded by what would have been a punishing (had I not enjoyed it so much) playing schedule, which by rights should have brought me to my knees. In a literal sense it did – I came home with a torn knee cartilage from kneeling so much, but my head ringing with an unusual species of compliment from my cousin Martin (remember the Christmas Day shows?) who marvelled at my ability at "our age" to leap up and hurl myself down to my knees like a mere fifty-year-old, or so he said.

But I'm fit for this purpose, if unfit for others – I could fall asleep doing the washing-up but barely ever when doing my job, which I find fascinates me more than ever. And I've been a touring beast ever since my English Shakespeare Company days in the 80s and 90s.

Halfway through this latest tour, we arrived in Cambridge, redolent of so many remembrances and forgotten patterns. I realised I'd never walked the town much until now, though I'd played professionally at the Arts Theatre a handful of times. The Arts was an exception in the *Lear* weekly pattern in that it was close enough to London to let me nip up one morning to attend the Ian Charleson Award, which I've already described to be by general consent the most enjoyable of all our Award ceremonies, insofar as it involves a lunch at the National Theatre for those up for the Award, and all generations are in attendance, a tremendous current of affectionate energy running between the old-timers and the recently graduated, already alight with their early recognition.

On this occasion it was slightly marred for me by having gone pleasantly to sleep the previous night with Nigel Farage peering out of the hotel TV more or less admitting defeat on Brexit. But by the morning David Cameron had resigned and the Monstrous Farage was hideously cock-a-hoop, spouting triumphalist nonsense about Independence Day. (The same jump-cut in consciousness was of course to be repeated in the US election not long after.) He was senselessly burbling about "getting our country back", and Boris Johnson was busy cooking the figures. So who did vote for them? I asked myself as I lay pole-axed in bed and gaped at the screen. Understandably enough, most of my colleagues at the Awards had felt the same shock; but it had also seemed to have affected the Cambridge hotel staff, so that the breakfast crockery smelled of washing-up liquid, and the simplest cup of coffee was not to be had. The muzak was on a loop: the Walker Brothers' *Make It Easy On Yourself*, over and over.

For the rest of the week, when I had no matinée I would walk through the town by varying routes, much of the time exchanging text messages with John Shrapnel and Guy Slater. I simply needed to consult on life in general with John, and I was reminding myself to check with Guy whether he lived in Thompsons Lane or Portugal Place – for it was he who, on the corner of one of them, told me I was certain to fail my English degree because I hadn't read F. R. Leavis on *Othello*.

Another day I walked over to the ADC Theatre, which I'd heard had fallen into steep decay since the Sixties, but which I found bursting into duck-egg blue slickness from a recent overhaul which at last gave it an efficient box office and a spacious foyer, and a feeling of fresh air. (Typically enough, the overhaul stopped as you entered the stalls.) The stage used to have a safety curtain which, unusually, sank into the ground rather than flying (like at the Barbican now); the wing-to-wing channel in which it did so was a little too shallow for it, and although apparently flush with the stage when in place, it had a tendency to wobble around and was thus something of a hazard to an ambulatory actor (let alone a duellist). This fault has been preserved in the renovation – allegedly at the behest of Trevor Nunn, who has helped the theatre financially, and who pointed out that nothing could be more helpful to a tyro director than having to cope with such a hazard in his or her staging, ensuring that this bit of no man's land was always stepped over rather than onto, for fear of unseemly comedy wobbles.

Each day in Cambridge felt to me like spotting an earlier layer of a picture beneath new brushwork – the "work of art" being, absurdly or not, the life I live. I would peel the sometimes flimsy skin momentarily off the original, then stick it back on again. Meanwhile, up at the station, the thick blob of white paint providing the 4 on Platform 4 has I suspect been there since 1961 and my trips to Derby to see Gillian, but most things have been re-done, and she died last year. Also – as an undergraduate, did I travel round Cambridge on the bus? I can't remember. Maybe I did in order to visit my newly-married supervisor in the boondocks every week and tease him for looking quite so maritally exhausted. Did I walk all the way to the quite distant station? How did I get back into college or my digs in the night?

And I doubt that this is the same pale grey brickwork on the house at No 7 Green Street where I tried to seduce a girl called

Chantal, especially as the ground floor has been taken over by a Patisserie Valerie and a jewellery shop. Perhaps because of the fruitless effort involved in such speculations I then find myself staring out of – that first floor window, was it? – the night before my Finals Modern Poetry exam, grimly looking out at the darkened nocturnal scene while opening a copy of Tennyson for the very first time – a matter of hours before I was going to have to write my leading essay about him.

***

The fact of Second Chances – particularly in the theatre – is more of a determinant than you might think: you mustn't mind walking in your own footsteps. For one thing Jack Gelber's *Connection* at the ADC started a whole sequence of American offspring for me: *Captain Jack's Revenge*, through David Mamet's *The Shawl*, MacArthur and Hecht's *The Front Page* and many other American plays beyond. So I see that life doesn't change you much: the same things please you, early doubts stay for good, whether they're about some lump in the personality or the wrongly shaped backside, and you could spend a lifetime processing the inheritance in your genes into something more useful. With luck, the moments you come to realise you may be some good at your job will recur throughout a lifetime to counterbalance the chronic expectation of failure.

So, in returning to *Lear*, what did I change – did I change anything – the second time round? I came to realise that there is a choice every single moment you cut into Lear's layer-cake of conflicting feelings: the part may seem straightforward enough but has infinite variety. In fact I don't know of another that gives you such a choice of possibilities from moment to moment, even in the Storm Scene – which will probably be loud, but doesn't have to be, not all the time. The Reconciliation with Cordelia could be sweet but also involve anger at his own confusion and uncertainty. How much of each? It could change from night to night. The only certainty is that there is a fanatical narcissism in the man – but, untypically, no soliloquies, and in the play no working men, such as the gardeners in

Richard II who talk more sensibly (and poetically) about the nation's political dilemmas than the principals. Lear has a mindset of rock, and a maniacal temper; and in my case a Fool wearing a dress with lipstick and rouge. I protested mildly at this – the misogynist Lear wouldn't have liked it – but it wasn't a battle worth fighting, let alone the fishnet stockings and high heels. They reminded me a bit of *The Ballad of the False Barman*, and eventually evaporated in favour of something simpler.

As for advice, I would say there are weapons for playing Lear that no one can take from you. You know from living your own life how quickly a mood can change, so you can permit it on the stage. One feeling will either grow out of another, gradually loosening its attachment; or sometimes it snaps free but continues to bump against its predecessor without apparent logic. Catching that true dysfunction rather than just digging up a technical trick from one night to the next is the real achievement.

Likewise you don't need to tell us what you're thinking all the time: an audience immediately senses (and tenses) when they're being informed rather than prompted to feel. Assuming they're in front of you, the only reason for looking at them is if you're looking at the fourth wall of the room you're supposed to be in, or out of its window – or, at the other extreme, if you really are speaking to them directly – which happens a lot in Shakespeare, though not so much in this play. Don't be afraid to let the character contradict itself. As far as possible let the audience eavesdrop on you as you try to work out why Goneril has come into a hovel, sat down and turned herself into a joint-stool, or why your long-lost Cordelia has appeared out of the muddled blue. The viewer really does want to see a life lived, however formal the play.

As an example, I now have two versions of *King Lear*'s opening scene. In New York I was all purple velvet and riding boots and everyone abased themselves; in the UK, we could have been in Ceaușescu's Palace after a good dinner with the *nomenclatura*, and Lear has ushered everyone into the next room to reveal his marvellous idea for a post-prandial game – not charades (or perhaps super-charades) but a contest between the girls, with a gold or silver medal as the prize. When Lear listens to praise from Goneril and Regan he's happy but also afflicted that it hasn't been Cordelia speaking – Cordelia, that unsmiling presence in the corner of the room, that space of cloud on the edge of all the sunlight. If only the truest devotion could come from the best-loved: if only Lear's own love could be requited rather than lightly fluffed up.

So, more advice: prime the canvas, set the key and rhythm and keep it constant. In Lear's case choose eleven keys for his eleven scenes, but be prepared to abandon some of them in the light of experience. The perfect Lear makes the craft invisible, and the outcome, seemingly, simplicity itself. The result may not win the critical prize, since often an award for Being Best is secured by a demonstration of skill and showmanship, a bravado that sits up and begs, or demands, to be rewarded. On the other hand, after a few years it may be hailed in retrospect as the best of its time, and its portrait painted for the Garrick Club. If you have the technical ability but also the transparency, and if you don't ask for admiration of the vocal range, the physical presence or the originality of the thinking, you will be, every inch, the thing itself, like Cleopatra or John Proctor or Hedda Gabler. And then you have indeed, like Al Pacino or Annette Bening or Paul Scofield, truly "consulted somewhere else". Beyond a certain level of ability, we're all part of the same organism in the eyes of the public, though they may pleasantly argue at dinner parties about who's best. When I played in New York, I received a particularly rapturous London review – in *The Spectator*, I think it was – accompanied by a photograph of Simon Russell Beale in the part: when I did it in the UK, the *Guardian* sent their notorious second-string critic, who duly mashed it (Michael Billington had promised me he'd come but then didn't, even though he lived opposite the theatre): she said that because the production seemed fascinated with the younger generation, Lear himself was rather sidelined. Well, I would happily award a cash prize to any audience member on the twelve-week tour who felt that Lear had been sidelined.

I digress. With such a part, there may in the UK alone be up to five contestants generally agreed to be the year's champions: *King*

Lear is like Celebrity MasterChef. If you're feeling the heat in the kitchen, here are some snappy self-correcting signposts you might like to mutter to yourself at 7.29 each evening, if only for a laugh:

1. The Skill Test. Try not to show off your technique, however long assembled. *Ars est celare artem*, etc. If you didn't have the goods, you wouldn't have been asked to play the part. And do you want to be remembered as a "skilful" King Lear? I see that throughout the play there's a danger of blowing your top. Laurence Olivier used to advise that at such a moment you should be sure to hold something back. (I for one could always see when he was doing that, so even he didn't entirely celare the artem.)

2. The Passion Test. A real challenge, comparable to going to five sets in the baking Wimbledon sunshine. Or keeping up the pace for the twenty-fourth mile as you're finally entering the stadium. Three and a half hours of suffering eight times a week? Including two matinées? Go figure: be kind to yourself in every way you can.

3. The Ingredients Test. You won't be much good as Lear if you don't make it clear – from the first scene, when everyone is together – that you have a relationship with each of your three daughters which, however distorted, however genuine, however unorthodox, is at all times complicated. Once you've discovered the anger, you could include the wish not to be angry. And the subsequent sorrow. This won't be done with a single gesture or whisper: you start the play by loving all three in your own way, but a very few minutes later you hate one and are deeply wary of the other two. Every time you look at any of them we should feel ourselves mentally slicing through that layer-cake: express through the lines, without breaking up the verse or too many silences. One way and another, we have to recognise the father, our father, someone's father, every moment.

4. The Pressure Test. You will inevitably be compared, often stupidly, to other contestants. To hell with it.

5. The Palate Test. Test and Taste in other words. How subtle are you? How affronting? How delicate? Keep checking.

6. The Choice Test. Antony Sher has just published a book called *Year of the Mad King* about the play. With all respect to a highly esteemed colleague, that's a misnomer – though I can see it chimes conveniently with his book called *Year of the Fat Knight* about Falstaff. It's really important that you, reader or imminent player of Lear, don't think of him as mad: the places he goes are where we could all of us go, given his temperament; there are a minute number of really barmy moments and they could be no more daft than talking to yourself as you do the washing-up. That's why Lear is accompanied so often by the counterpointing and truly nutty dialogue of Edgar and the Fool, both of whom obligingly assume madness for him – or at least absurdity.

***

As I mentioned, at each theatre the get-in time was barely enough before the Monday opening night generally insisted on by a host theatre on the road. I'd been used to this for the best part of thirty years, since inventing the ESC in 1986, and I believe in it in spite of all. As Monday races by, quick-change tents are hastily constructed in the wings out of spare flats and bits of masking, which make you feel like the poor condemned English in *Henry V*, awaiting their day of reckoning. But we probably look more like underground workers or a slow-motion rush-hour. Strips of luminous ballet-floor material form helpful guides for feasible routes through the wings. Heavy-duty tape attaches LX cables to the floor so they're harder to trip over. A wheelchair waits there (for Lear when he wakes up from his madness in Act Four), and there's a table of maps for Edmund, lanterns, bottles, Gloucester's bleeding bandage for when he's blinded, suitcases of every shape and size, decanters and trays, soundcases; twelve flying lines are in use (maximum load 230kg per single bar and 409kg per alternate bar), removal men's low trolleys (for wardrobe), flags, racks for guns and swords. White tape indicates sightlines – or rather warns the actors not to take one step further into the audience's line of vision, especially from its side seats. These tapes are visible in the dark, especially along rostrum edges, to save you from falling. Hundreds of power sockets. Property boxes. Little patches of worn red carpet with, for some reason, *fleur de lys* designs. The wings, like the set, resemble a warehouse.

Oh yes, and we travel with a wind-up gramophone.

In this schedule, 6pm on Monday is a rush hour, as we hasten this way and that in the dim light, rapt in our own thoughts, swerving through the dark to avoid each other, murmuring apologies if we cause someone to slacken their pace or change gear. We all have inner voices to listen to and are used to it.

Everyone in a Company, especially on the road, casts themselves in a part, apart from their part onstage. There's one who's always late. Most fearsomely, there's also one who emerges as a mimic, whose impressions of their colleagues you enjoy until it occurs to you to wonder how their impression of you will come out. There's one who's always suggesting a Company meal, as if we didn't see enough of each other; like a short-lived insect or plant, this idea usually withers and dies after about six weeks. In this anthropology of touring there's usually a mother hen and the one with a hangover at every matinée. There isn't much flirting … usually (that's over-reported). During the show, if I look from the darkness of one wing across the lighted stage to the other dark wing beyond it, a figure might be silhouetted on the edge of the light – Cordelia waiting to return from France to reinstate her father as King, for instance. The difference is her back is turned to me – not unlike a Hammershøi painting but more dramatically lit, perhaps more like the luminous figure of a Degas dancer, in fact. So all I can see is her outline lit from a source beyond her. The set is like a continuation of the wings in its grunginess. Beyond the opposite wing, towards the outside wall of the theatre, the universal blackness of the paint creates an illusion of deep perspective. Blackness is everywhere, on walls, floors, equipment. The Company bustles about its business, each checking his or her pre-set routes through the show, moment to moment, criss-crossing, never quite bumping, deferring to each other, weaving thoughtfully along; they seem from above like those little animated figures that illustrate a graph of population numbers on the move in a rostrum camera sequence.

Here's the reward, and it comes most nights. A standing cheering reception from a small audience is less exciting but more moving than from a packed house. And as for 'Whatsonstage', you might get this:

EVERY INCH A KING: The Lear of the Year

> He draws a clear line through betrayal and familial disloyalty to complete disintegration, undercut by a stunning return to realisation in his final scene. His versatile voice is a joy to listen to, his range all-encompassing, and there are some truly heart-rending moments along the way.
>
> This is not the flashiest Lear you'll see, and it's so much the better for that. Instead, his is a well-defined, poignant rendition of this mighty role in a production that consistently relies on a clear and intelligible narrative. In the 400th year since Shakespeare's death, it's a welcome addition to the anniversary tributes…

More importantly, Fergal Keane tweets that he loved it.

The *Lear* cast was quite a remarkable group of actors and human beings, as the New Yorkers had been. One more thing: I'd been in the play once before that, at the RSC in 1976, in the enigmatic but deeply rewarding part of Edgar to Donald Sinden's Lear (I remember Donald was immensely helpful to me). Forty years later I was much exercised as to who we would be able to get to play this very important part of the legitimate son, especially on a tour. Through no doing of my own I had a winner; a young actor with a tremendous drive in the classics, and also a continuer of what I think of as an honourable tradition in the trade: get locked out of your digs at least once a week, and have to climb in through the skylight; take one drink more than advisable after the show, especially before a matinée the next day, so there is a minor hangover to be absorbed into that performance.

He fitted every aspect of the bill perfectly, and I would love to be with him many times again. Nowadays he introduces me – as he did on the first night of *The Tempest* – "Michael was my Lear…" – a nice inversion. In fact I had also worked with him a few years before *Lear* – he'd just graduated from RADA and every day he had Oliver Cotton, Ian McKellen and myself enthralled throughout rehearsals of *The Syndicate* from the first day to the last of the run – a young actor who felt and expressed himself from the last hair of his head to his very toes.

His name is Gavin Fowler. And that first collaboration was at Chichester when he was *The Syndicate*'s love interest – Rafelluccio, written by the gentleman hanging on my wall next to Chekhov, Eduardo. One lunchtime before a Chichester matinée of *The Syndicate* I was summoned across the crowded restaurant by an extremely nice actor I'd known very slightly for many years, Frederick (Ricky) Pyne. He amiably demanded an explanation from me as to why I have no decoration, not a knighthood, not even an MBE. It was a huge oversight, he said. I managed to hint (I hope in a fine piece of Chekhovian acting) that maybe I'd turned down a knighthood, like Michael Frayn or Albert Finney. I think he was satisfied, and I ribbed him for wanting not just one knight of the realm but two in the forthcoming performance he'd travelled such a distance to see. Ricky's a terrific fellow; a veteran from *Dixon of Dock Green* and indeed the legendary *Talking to a Stranger* by John Hopkins; he also spent a long while on *Emmerdale Farm*, where my dear ex, Kate, who did the same, remembers him well; he served on the Equity Council for many years, and was its President from 1994 until 2002. He is also a trustee of no fewer than five actors' charities. And he specially lives on in my memory because he was in the acting Company at Derby Rep with Gillian Goodman in 1962 (no, not the character man); he was always particularly kind to a wet-behind-the-ears student from Cambridge making his regular doleful crusades to Derby to flog a dead horse.

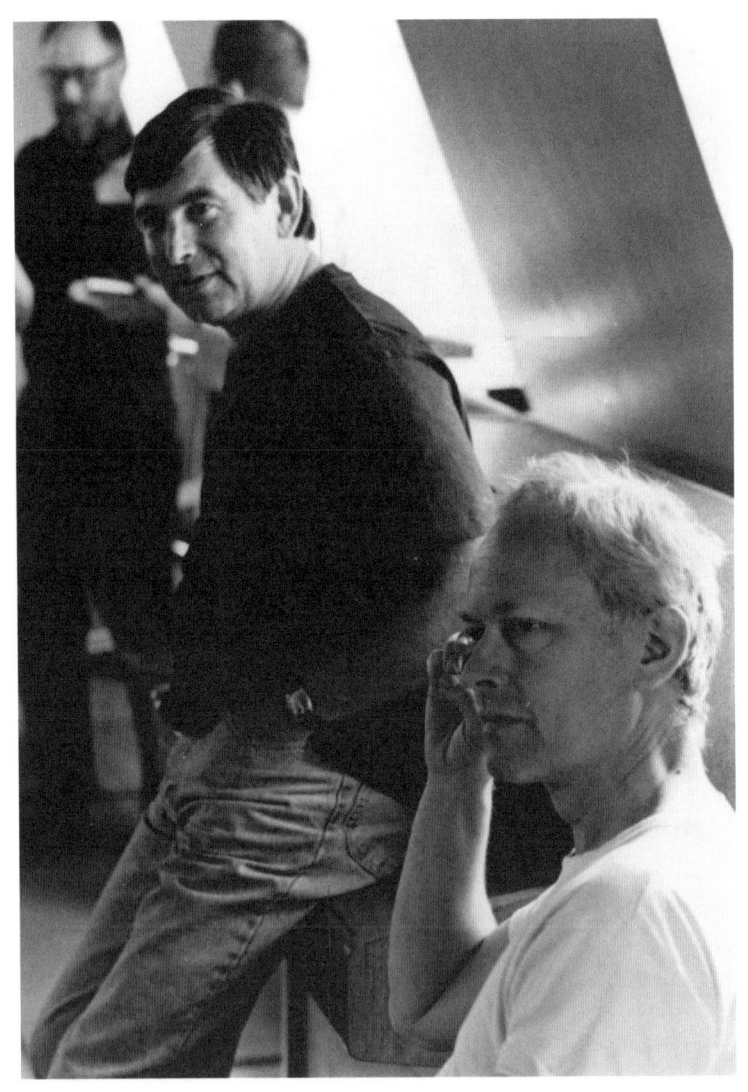

*With Michael Bogdanov rehearsing
The Wars of the Roses (1987).*

CONCLUSION

A RHAPSODY IN BLUE SUITS

> When I am prostrate at the feet of doom
> My hope of life torn up by the root,
> Take care to use my clay only for a goblet; the smell of wine
> Might restore me life for a moment…
> When you're in convivial company
> You must remember ardently your friend.
> When you're drinking mellow wine together and my turn comes
> Invert the glass.
> – *Rubaiyyat of Omar Khayyam*

My ghostly father (ghostly as in deceased, rather than in holiness like Friar Laurence) leaves his upstairs window after all these years and comes gently downstairs to have a word with me. He confesses, twinkling from beneath his much-loved beetling brows, that in the unnerving period of his only son's early theatrical fantasies, he felt the best thing he could do was to keep bowling at me, rather hoping that I would eventually stop dressing up in my mother's clothes and resume my older role as a passable Jack Robertson lookalike. After all, I'd got to the point that I could play a good cover drive, which he'd encouraged by installing a rough and ready cricket practice net down there in the garden – even though my wilder hitting, specially my semi-hooked drive through midwicket, always threatened to send the blossom from his beloved white magnolia fluttering to the ground in such heaps that it eventually needed protective armour, as if against slug infestation.

"Blossom, fare thee well – isn't that Perdita in *The Winter's Tale?*" – how much Shakespeare he's learned! I hug him with gratitude.

But that was also the moment, he says, that he saw that he was, in the nicest way, beaten, so he built me my model theatre in which to indulge myself (and to abandon my instinct for blatant cross-dressing). From then on, my gratitude caused me to drop my tendency to stand rigidly on our staircase in my plastic helmet, flexing one leg, and instead to start shoving little figures around on wires while accompanying them, as a soundtrack, with my own rendition of my chosen script, usually a Shakespeare.

All these conflicting images had continued to swirl around my father's considerable brain; and in fact he gradually came to enjoy the plays he took me to, all except for *Twelfth Night*, for which he had contempt. *Measure for Measure* and *All's Well That Ends Well* also presented a problem, and he drew the line against going to them because of their sexual bartering – my father himself was a shrewd mixture of personal warmth and sexual formality, and I had to discover the brilliance of those problematic plays by myself.

My dear Dad was to live another thirty satisfactory years. Was he proud of me in the end? I'm not sure that Hamlet at Stratford particularly captivated him, oddly enough (three bad father-figures perhaps, and one of them a ghost) but he liked Mercutio (opposite Ian McKellen's Romeo), and specially the Enoch Powell turn I did in Edgar's *Destiny*. In other words, the unexpected character parts. Later, at the National Theatre, he and my mother were seen clinging to each other's hands as my Strider – the old horse in Tolstoy's wonderful allegorical story, now dramatised – was beaten and gelded at close quarters in the Cottesloe (in my view probably the best work I've done). He was also charmed in the Lyttelton by the elegant Restoration tragedy/political satire of Thomas Otway's *Venice Preserv'd*, also with Ian McKellen – London hadn't seen it since Paul Scofield (Ian) and John Gielgud (me) did it for Peter Brook in 1953.

This was in 1984, just a few days before he suddenly died, at the wheel of his car but not in an accident, just while I was getting ready to become Anton Chekhov for the NT for the very first time.

1984 was also the fated, good-for-nothing year that claimed Eduardo de Filippo. The heroic Jack Robertson, however, lived on till 1996, aged seventy-nine, apparently after years of ill health – did he end up hitting the bottle, I wonder, or unsuccessfully investing in a sports shop, or any of the other melancholy strategies of the retired sportsman? When I heard the news I was again playing my solo Chekhov, in King's Lynn, after a day of proof-reading my first publication, *Hamlet – A User's Guide*. Would Jack Robertson have liked it?

Thinking of Robertson J. D. reminds me that in the 1950s I'd always needed a replacement icon to worship in the non-cricketing winter months: in fact his place in my imagination had been taken by degrees by Ron Reynolds, Tottenham Hotspur's reserve goalkeeper (and eventually their No 1: initially he was understudy to Ted Ditchburn). Reynolds was so brilliant in the air that I, a tyro goalie, never saw him punch a ball away (he could always catch it): he thus indirectly obliged my baffled mother to sacrifice her pair of white kitchen gloves that most nearly resembled Ron's divine ones, so that I might madly emulate him at school on the days when we all had to trudge, as part of the timetable, out to Canons Park to play. Unfortunately I see not a trace of such kitchen gloves in the extant pictures of the real Ron in action, just a series of dizzying horizontal dives four feet in the air, his sleeves rolled purposefully above his baggy shorts. Had I but known it, he was living through a ghastly period in which professional footballers were cruelly exploited by their clubs – so much so that it was later and famously described as "soccer slavery" by Jimmy Hill. It was also the time of the *maximum* wage: players couldn't leave their club without the express say-so of bosses with a serfs-and-masters mentality, and they themselves had no repeal from their employers' plans for them. So after a hundred-odd games Spurs routinely sold Reynolds to Southampton for £10,000, willy-nilly; having moved his family there, he crucially helped the club win the Division Three championship in

1960. Players also had to find their own way to away matches, and if injured, even to the point of concussion, they were still required to drive themselves home or to hospital afterwards – significant for Ron, because like many goalkeepers he was regularly damaged, either diving onto the kicking feet of centre forwards or breaking his ankle (against Plymouth Argyle, Michael Foot's team) or ending his career in 1963 because of a dislocated shoulder. He was also one of the first professional footballers to wear contact lenses, as I did. He was something of a revolutionary (which I'm sure Jack Robertson wasn't): one of the earliest agitators for a fair deal, he outspokenly represented the Professional Footballers' Association, a natural champion of employees' rights and a plotter of insurrections, together with his more famous soul-mate Danny Blanchflower.

For all these reasons, though a radio comedy addict, I disliked as too disrespectful the regular "Ron and Eth Glum" section of *Take It From Here* on the radio (despite the virtuosity of Dick Bentley and June Whitfield) strictly on the basis of the "Ron", since no one could be less gormless than Ron Glum's heroic goalkeeping namesake, busy dignifying the Christian name at White Hart Lane. This, my real Ron and fellow-Gemini, passed away on June 2nd 1999, on his 71st birthday and just short of my 56th: my diary says I was at the dentist, having just buried my favourite aunt, out of work and off to Bruges for a curative weekend; otherwise the news of Ron might have been the last straw. He had spent his thirty years of retirement as an insurance broker, who perhaps at another time could have got Jack Robertson private medical treatment. But being Robertson, the latter was doubtless an NHS loyalist.

And guess what – another great sportsman, Everton de Courcy Weekes, whose brother I so nearly had caught in the slips by Nicol Williamson in 1969, has died today, 1st July 2020. Together with Clyde Walcott and Frank Worrell, he was one of the legendary Three Ws, who all made their Test debut in 1948 against England. I saw them at Lord's in 1950. Three Barbadians, they had been born within seventeen months of each other, within a mile of Kensington Oval in Barbados, and possibly delivered by the same midwife. They were, all three, superlative batsmen.

A Justice of the Peace once his cricket career was done, Weekes suffered a heart attack in Barbados a month ago. He was 95.

***

Now I sit with my beloved Prue weathering the Coronavirus crisis, thus far unscathed. Boris Johnson has just announced on a Friday that open-air theatres "will open" on the Tuesday of next week, without considering (or knowing) how the scripts would appear, or what actors would rehearse, learn and perform what plays, or how the tickets would be sold.

Among many other things, Prue is the Chair of Cardboard Citizens – a great Company specialising in live theatre for and by the homeless – and always has work to do, for them and for the Clore Leadership and the Nureyev Foundation, to which she's also attached, though in this time of Plague much of it depends on Zoom. For the first time since the Lockdown began, and ignoring Johnson's ignorant announcement, BBC News has mentioned tonight, as a curiosity *en passant*, that theatres are going to have to wait a very long time indeed before they can re-open – unlike really important things such as restaurants, hair salons and sports arenas. At which point I thought I detected a little cynical chuckle in the reporter's voice, a little familiar touch of The Luvvies Had It Coming. These announcements were made on the anniversary of my father's death-day, May 14th: he would have been furious, as furious as the day when as a young barrister he found that physiotherapists were not to be accepted into the BMA, and so represented them (successfully) in court.

I've also noted that everyone in the BBC TV's ten o'clock news studio these days seems to be dressed in quietly rhapsodic blue suits, like Donald Trump on a diet. It's like a right-wing prerogative used to introduce specialist reporters – Fergus Walsh (Medical, lots to say), Hugh Pym (Health, lots to say), who, you could swear, don't move from their chairs until they're there the same time the next evening to confront Anchor Man Huw Edwards (Welsh valley accent like – sometimes – mine), or to introduce the latest selection of ravaged faces who talk for half an hour about the end of the known world. I don't mind any of these royal blue witnesses to the national crisis, but I greatly prefer Fergal Keane, any day. And it is startling to note that these lawmakers always describe their activities as "ramping", or "rolling out" one thing or another – Test and Trace, The Vaccine – you'd think they were pastrycooks.

Talking of which, indifferent to most of it, we cook. We talk. We eat in the garden, the weather having been so ironically good all summer – as good as it was in 2018, when I was battling with my ocular problems, utterly cured in the end by Prue as well as by the ophthalmologists; now, and marvellously, my sight has never been better. We sympathise with the bereaved, and profoundly, passionately despise the Tory Cabinet and its leader. This deathly time has reminded us to super-enjoy: the sun pours through the trees, and, as you see, we feel at home among our Memories – for the time being, all the work I have slated to do is a *Star Wars* Convention.

And tonight Diana Quick has been on TV giving a really wonderful online solo performance, shot in her own house, of Adam Brace's *Midnight Your Time*, directed by Michael Longhurst as a Donmar production. What a labour of love that must have been. Then Andrew Scott, who is a better actor than I was at his age, excelled in Simon Stephens's *Sea Wall*.

Meanwhile the fuchsias are out and a climbing rose is in full bloom, not fragrant but extravagantly beautiful. We walk in the woods. Then we watch the astounding filmed performances of Waltraud Meier and Ian Storey in *Tristan und Isolde* in Patrice Chéreau's historic La Scala production. Or, last week, James Corden in his triumph in *One Man Two Guvnors*, in which my friend Tom Edden from *Arturo Ui* (the voice of sense in the boys' ribald dressing room) gives an astonishingly funny performance worthy of a great mime. A couple of bummers from the NT, but on the other hand Jonathan Miller's *Così Fan Tutte*; and I write to Trevor Nunn congratulating his daughter Ellie on the Shakespeare sonnet (No 33 – "Full many a glorious morning have I seen") – that she's recorded online. This was part of an initiative by Jermyn Street Theatre in lieu of our *Tempest* – Shakespeare's 154 sonnets, each done by a different actor.

I rounded up David Suchet and Penelope Wilton for them and did No 110 myself:

> Alas 'tis true I have gone here and there
> And made myself a motley to the view

— a wonderfully funny poetic apology, I'm convinced, by an unfaithful touring actor to his partner at home.

***

Every morning during the first Lockdown I've been reading Prue a Chekhov short story, re-meeting the characters that I absorbed from my researches into the man in the 1980s – official busybodies, defaulting doctors, drunken peasants, desperate spinsters, disappointed idealists, bullies, cobblers, the Devil himself. Gorki is the next genius in line, and Tolstoy awaits, in deference to the fact that I once planned a three-man show for them rather than just a solo Chekhov. And then Dostoyevsky as well, who was kind enough to write *Crime and Punishment* so that I could emaciate myself into Raskolnikov, a man like a wolf without calories. I've even for the first time read *Gusev,* written as Chekhov sailed back from Sakhalin Island after his gruelling survey of prison conditions there in 1890 and witnessed a dying man being pitched overboard into the Indian Ocean. It made more impression on him, I sometimes think, than Sakhalin itself. Then there's a Moscow waiter's return to his roots in *Peasants,* and also the story called *Into Exile*, inspired by the forced migration to Siberia of the Decembrist Rebels of the mid-1820s which led to the founding of Irkutsk. And *The Bet.* And *Easter.* And *The Kiss.* And *Romance with a Double Bass.* There are hundreds of marvels there. True masterpieces. It's now thirty-six years since I first climbed into Anton Pavlovich's suit and stiff collar and I hope skin, his pince-nez and National Theatre wig and beard, and offered you his company for two hours. I miss it, badly, and mean to return to it. The last time I played the generally soft-spoken Chekhov in his own right, Eileen Atkins sat in the back row of the Hampstead Theatre and said later it was as if I was sitting next to her speaking in her ear, for her only – as nice a compliment as one actor could pay to another.

And in between the Chekhovs, I plan to read aloud some sixty nearly-as-good stories by Vladimir Nabokov, also a master of the form, if a bit more remote. And Gorki's fantastic autobiographical trilogy. Also today I'm seventy-seven, whatever that means; I feel in a few low moments as if I'd been forcibly retired by common consent, and so am, not for the first time, thinking of old times and old parts. Of Leontes in *The Winter's Tale,* whom you must above all make the audience understand and perhaps forgive. Of Coriolanus, and the particular stress of that great role, largely due to the fact that all the climactic hand-to-hand fights happen in the first Act, not the last. Of the rhapsody of Macbeth, the "bellicose ecstasy" Kenneth Tynan attributed to Paul Rogers in the part, and would perhaps have done to me, were he not dead by then. And of Archie Rice. And perhaps of Strider, my other all-time treat. And Antony to Kim Cattrall's Cleopatra.

It strikes me that I'm thinking about Chekhov just for the pleasure of it, as Gorki recommended – Gorki, who also said that seeing *Uncle Vanya* had made him feel like "a garden from childhood being dug up by a great pig", that everything else was written with a log, not a pen, and that he felt he was being sawn in half by a "dull saw, whose teeth go straight to the heart." I wouldn't go quite so far, but *Vanya* is certainly a life-changer. The most startling version I ever witnessed was the Vakhtangov Company's, directed by the Lithuanian Rimas Tuminas, which I saw first at their theatre in the Arbat in Moscow and then in London in 2012, each time thinking of Chekhov's joy, of which I am convinced, at its eccentricities: he, whose roots were in the mocking comedy of vaudeville, I know would have loved it – he used happily to say that all he wanted to do was to show audiences how stupidly they lived. And much as I love Chekhov, at the same time I'm a heretic, and here Rimas blatantly set the Chekhovian cat among the pigeons. Gestural, playful, nervy, but full of indelible images, the interventions in his *Vanya* offended many orthodox Chekhovians by largely abandoning the detailed realism of Stanislavski for another great Russian manner – the expressionism of Stanislavski's disciples Meyerhold, Vakhtangov, and, later, Yuri Lyubimov, with their taste both for absolute truthfulness but also sport, acrobatics, music, mime, symbolism, all kinds of grotesqueries. Rimas preserved every word of his text, but nothing looked or sounded as we expected. A stage free of clutter, but the distant prospect upstage centre of a stone lion, a known symbol for Petersburg. The Professor and his young wife, Yeliena, whose rural visit causes so much havoc, are normally seen as tragically mismatched; here they clearly still enjoy an actively rumbustious sex-life and, when Vanya tries to shoot the Prof, Yeliena is the first to interpose her body. And for all his ecological fervour, the visiting Dr Astrov is a drunken buffoon who, in his cups, engages in a disastrous bit of DIY carpentry with the Chaplinesque Waffles, while glugging from an enormous many-gallon Vrac hung from his waist with a plastic pipe to siphon the alcohol briskly into him. This (the brilliant Vladimir Vdovichenkov) must also be the first Astrov to assist Vanya to take his morphine in the final scene rather than demanding it back from him. Vanya's niece, Sonya, is no spinster but a young girl whose passion for the doctor verges on hysteria; Yeliena, stunning in white silk, bowls a circus hoop. Marina, the family nurse, is played by 97-year-old Galina Konovalova, and she occupies a make-up station upstage left and spends much of her time with a giant powder puff, creating great ballooning clouds of complexion powder like a Hollywood vamp, from *Sunset Boulevard* perhaps. Astrov shows Yeliena his images of deforestation on a projector with an unmistakably phallic funnel that emits puffs of steam. And in an extraordinary moment at the end, Sonya ministers to Vanya, beautifully played by Sergey Makovetsky, as if he were a run-down machine that she now has lovingly to reassemble. When she's done with him and he looks presentable, he gradually, gradually starts moving in small steps backwards towards the great Petersburg lion as the lights dim. He is in every way retreating into history. In all, it is an evening of unforgettable audacity: and the author would have been in seventh heaven. The Vakhtangov at its best shows Russian acting also at its best, simultaneously precise and dangerous, reckless and delicate.

***

As for my blood-family, Mark is teaching his students in this country online – quite a few of the rest have returned to their families in Russia and China – and grows wonderful vegetables in his garden in Witney. Louis is gardening (and being paid) near St Albans and making his own *musique concrète*. Evie is doing her final exams at the Royal College of Fashion, and unlike a relative of hers two generations back does not bluff her way through poets she hasn't read. I'm hoping the same euphoria will apply to my losses, and indeed my own departure.

And now ... Zoom!

Out with Skype, useful as it was when, sitting in New York playing King Lear, I had a regular need to speak to and see Mark, Louis and Eve as well as to hear their voices. But I never worked out how to finish the conversation except by lowering my eyes as if in shame – in fact it was an attempt to find the disconnect button.

Zoom is taking its time installing in me, but has suited well lately for readings from *The Odyssey*, an address (rather than a lecture) I gave the other week to support the Rose Theatre Trust, who have managed to preserve that first of Shakespeare's London theatres, from which Shakespeare learned so much how to write on Civil War (*Henry V*). Next week the outside world comes Zooming in on me for a Conversation with Gregory Doran, the boss of the RSC, who wants, as a promotional tool, to have a public celebration with me about my history with the RSC: it's planned to be a hopeful look towards the day they can plan and re-open. I feel I must be robustly helpful.

Prue speaks to her family, some dozen of them; but more often we both seek out our dear Robin Ellis and his wife Meredith Wheeler, when we can laugh yet again that when he played Claudius at Cambridge to my Hamlet, a stage hand was one night late completing a scene change in a blackout: the new lighting state came up to reveal him moving furniture around, so that Robin's Claudius, thinking of Hamlet, started the new scene – correctly but hilariously – with:

"How dangerous is it that this man goes loose…!"

We also Zoom often with the dearest of Norwegian acting friends, Ola B Johannessen and his wife Marit Østbye. I first met Ola when he emailed to invite me to do my Shakespeare show *Sweet Wllliam* in a theatre in Oslo – one of several he's run and directed in as well as acting for: in replying by email I'd forgotten that a first name ending in "a" is not female as in England but male as in Japan and Scandinavia. We met to discuss, and seeing a fine six-foot man approaching the café rendezvous to meet me certainly broke the ice. Ola (born on St Patrick's Day, like my cousin Martin), has a distinct resemblance to Max von Sydow and I would say a talent as great, and when we're all allowed to travel again we shall see him and Marit every couple of months when they arrive to catch up on all the new shows in London. They're brilliant friends, as passionate about friendship as their work; Marit has scored bull's-eyes over the years with all the Ibsen heroines, particularly, as you might expect, with Hedda Gabler. That was before we met, and hence the thrill of seeing her in a new and searching Norwegian play about Alzheimer's called *Absence* by Peter M. Floyd came as a revelation, a harrowingly great demonstration of absence indeed. Ola meanwhile has become the Norwegian equivalent of our Knight of the Realm – not only because he's acted in all the mediums all over Scandinavia (including the wonderful TV projects that we get in the UK), but because he's directed, taught, produced and run municipal theatres such as the Trøndelag Teater in Trondheim and Rogaland Teater in Stavanger.

He and I also have a number of the parts in common – especially those who have the same lean passion, the same knife-edged intentness. It's a hidden drive he certainly does share with von Sydow – the tension within his stillnesses is irresistible; his success in his favourite part – Leontes in *The Winter's Tale* – was spectacular because of it. Among homegrown parts he was especially fond of Old Mikkel Borgen in *The Word* (by Kaj Munk) and also Maximus in *Emperor and Galilean* and Bishop Nikolas in *Pretenders*, both by Ibsen.

It's always wonderful to take a visit to Oslo to see them and to have lunches on a bluff overlooking the harbour – we never got to their sauna chalet in the woods, lacking their self-refrigerating skills. But to have them round a lunch table with Robin and Meredith in the Languedoc or London was also one of the regular joys of our life until the Plague began – how we long to survive and resume. When I told Ola today I was writing about him and Marit, he expressed his surprise (little me!) and only asked me to be sure to use his initial B in all correspondence; he insisted that nobody would know who he was without it (which I doubt – his standing in Norway is not unlike Caramitru's in Romania!).

Meanwhile my dear John Shrapnel is suddenly two months lost, after fifteen years of prostate cancer and a few days after perhaps our most hilarious half-hour on the phone, even after our thousands of hours of such talks. A few days later, when I called again, he was raging against the dying of the light because he couldn't do up a button on his jacket, like Falstaff on his deathbed. And then he was gone. But can Caesar die? Can Oedipus? Can Agamemnon? Can Willy Loman? Can a friend who once travelled from Glasgow to Stratford in the middle of a production week of his own to see a preview of my *Timon of Athens*? Can the King of the Voice Overs step down? For ever?

Now Richard Eyre has sent me a beautiful poem he's written about John – which, oddly, also reminds me vividly of the side of Richard which played Happy in our *Death of a Salesman* at Cambridge, and indeed the lead, Cliff Richard's part, in Wolf Mankowitz's *Expresso Bongo*. A couple of weeks after reading it, and then seeing John's latest TV performance in the movie *The Duchess,* he now seemed to me, though he had barely a word to say, to be emphatically back with us. For some reason, when we last spoke, I had reminded him of a moment in Newcastle when we were on tour from Cambridge in 1962 (our undergraduate *Macbeth* was the last show at the Empire Music Hall and the resident pianist played Scottish airs like 'Loch Lomond' in the interval): as Gillian and I came into the coffee bar that he (Macduff) was patronising one day – together with Richard (Seyton) and Trevor Nunn (director) – John called fortissimo: "here come Gilly [Goodman] and Michael, wearing each other" (some affectionate trading of jackets, I assume). Needless to say, this is the least significant of my memories of a man who for more than half a century was lodged as my best friend and colleague.

Only now does it fatuously occur to me that perhaps my relationship with Gillian was doomed mainly because I didn't like her initial being G: I would have preferred my girlfriend to be the gentler Jilly, not Gilly. Perhaps this was because I had a cousin called Jilly – the very cousin who patiently tolerated my early performances every Christmas Day. But on the day of John's Suffolk funeral – the day of final rehearsals before my first preview of *The Tempest* in London, so with the best will in the world I couldn't attend – Cousin Jilly has also died, suddenly struck by a cancer.

In the event, *The Tempest* opened extremely well but was cut short by government edict a week later – so we made a good quality sound recording and also a two-camera filming of the show as a sort of collateral, as we hope to revive the production in the autumn or next spring. Out of the blue today meanwhile comes an email from Ronald Harwood. I'm very glad he's alive, after a rather long pause in our long friendship since his beloved wife Natasha died. Among other good cheer I'd now told him that I was writing my memoirs:

Dearest Michael,
How lovely to hear from you. I am delighted you are putting pen to paper and hope that all you say about me is favourable. I am in West Sussex, just north of Chichester in a beautiful village two minutes' walk from my daughter.
 I do hope that when this horror is over you will come and visit.
Love to Prue.
Ever,
Ronnie

Dear dear Ronnie, who wanted his knighthood so badly – almost as badly as did Donald Sinden. And both suffered: when Donald was notified that he was to be regaled, and after he'd replied with whatever kind of letter you have to do to accept, he telephoned the Palace to make absolutely sure that they had received his letter safely. Ronnie's symptom was slightly different; as soon as he got his, he started worrying in restaurants in case the waiters didn't realise he was a Knight of the Realm. He's adorable, though sometimes resembling Mr Toad in his new car.

And as I revise this chapter, Ronnie too has passed, as the saying goes, and now I have to indulge more memories. The scene is my dressing room at the Gielgud Theatre in 1994, where I'm playing Claudius and the Ghost of Hamlet's father in Peter Hall's latest *Hamlet* with Stephen Dillane under commercial management. After one show I've been on the phone with Marianne Faithfull, who was Ophelia to Nicol's Hamlet (and my Laertes) at the Roundhouse in 1969 (I recommend the movie – Tony Richardson directed). Since then she's become something less like a pretty young pop star and a bit like Lotte Lenya, but we'd always liked each other and now she was inviting me to a house party for the weekend – without my girlfriend of the time. Hanging up, I recovered from the exchange by the door bursting open, to reveal – bunched, beaming and overflowing with a kindly energy – unmistakably, Ronnie Harwood. We'd never met but I'd had an inkling that he was interested in my doing his next play, *Taking Sides*. He now declares that I was, with this Claudius, "at the peak of my powers" (!) and that Harold Pinter, his dear friend, had heartily recommended me to him since I was "a Colossus". This flattering view may have had something to do with the fact that I had taken part in the first Pinter Festival earlier that year at the Gate Theatre in Dublin, when I'd played in *Old Times* and *One for the Road*. Now Ronnie has another prosecutor for me, the American Major Arnold in his new play investigating Wilhelm Furtwängler's ambiguous wartime relationship with the Reich.

This sort of unexpected thing is lovely of course, and Ronnie and I parted in a welter of goodwill. It wouldn't be long before I wrote a book about *Hamlet*, and Ronnie would compare me on the cover to Harley Granville-Barker. The scene changes: Fulham Road, and a lunch table for four early in 1995. I'm a bit late, so Ronnie, Daniel Massey and Harold are in full flow. Dan appears to be singing the orchestral effect of Furtwängler's conducting of Beethoven's Fifth. Not many people could do this. Harold and Ronnie are delighted.

Harold is to direct *Taking Sides* and I had heard that they'd tried to get John Neville to play Furtwängler: he would have been very good, but Dan turned out to be surpassing, a definitive performance which was tragically his last before Hodgkin's lymphoma got him (he'd had it a bit since 1992). And shook him for three years, before laying him down in Putney Vale. The passage of my life with Ronnie, Dan and to an extent Harold was utterly precious, rich beyond measure. Dan was angelic except when he was disturbed – as he once was at the Criterion Theatre in Piccadilly Circus as Furtwängler because of the noise coming through the ceiling of his dressing room from the restaurant upstairs, Marco Pierre White's Criterion. In the interval therefore, Sally Greene, who owned the theatre, was summoned. Dan stood fully clothed before her as Furtwängler – linen jacket, tie etc, but no trousers for some reason. And she pulled off a very fast deal with Marco Pierre, in which he improbably promised to persuade his clientele to stand up and sit down silently, without scraping their chairs on the floor. Or there was the night when Dan decided I was being too hostile towards him on stage and – daftly – took it personally instead of via the character. We spoke no word to each other backstage for the next six nights, before tossing the quarrel away like a used newspaper. Dan was a big baby, even more so than me.

Imagine also, if you will, a round table at the Ivy Restaurant after *Taking Sides* another night. In its throne sits Virginia Bottomley, recently appointed Secretary of State for National Heritage (with no apparent qualifications) but nevertheless perceiving it as her duty to attend a performance of our highly recommended show at the Criterion. On her right, in full grovel mode, sat Ronnie. On his right were Sally Greene and her husband Robert, looking hopefully about. On Robert's right Dan, who had already downed a glass or two of wine to recover from his bravura performance as Furtwängler. On Dan's right and my left was Natasha Harwood, and on her right, to complete the circle, was myself, and on mine Virginia.

I was all fired up because this could be a chance for me to challenge the awful government initiative planned at that moment to put all actors onto PAYE (the result would be the inevitable collapse of the newest generation of young performers, afflicted by debt). Virginia's posture throughout the meal was to sit upright, silently swinging her head this way and that through 180 degrees as evidence of interest, but with her hands clasped together in front of her on the table as if she was in prayer – as perhaps she was. Dan started by raving at her about the importance of non-star-led commercial theatre doing the kind of ensemble work in the West End which "Larry" *(sic)* and "Johnnie" (even more *sic*) had pioneered. He addressed Virginia throughout this as "darling" – whenever he drew breath in fact. At least he felt obliged in a muddled way to promote the idea of public subsidy. Sally and Robert had little to offer, but Ronnie immediately insisted that public subsidy was unimportant to him, since all his plays had been successfully done in the commercial theatre, and never once at the National.

So far so hopeless, a lost opportunity, and it struck me as the baton moved on to me on Virginia's other side that I should emphasise the necessity of subsidy: however, just as I drew breath, Natasha plucked me by the left sleeve and asked me if she'd ever told me about how Ronnie and she used to make love when they were in weekly rep on whatever onstage sofa had been used for the evening's show – and had never been apprehended (she had told me this over the years, perhaps a dozen times, and so, separately, had Ronnie).

In this moment Virginia saw her chance and began to make her excuses. Everyone got to their feet to say farewell, Ronnie executing a deep bow from the waist, bidding her goodnight. He looked a little like a Japanese concierge ushering you into the hotel lift. I admired him for this physio-therapeutically if not artistically: for a man of his stockiness and lack of verticals, the pressure on his lower back muscles would have been considerable. However, his core stability was impeccable. As Virginia rose, I saw in a flash the meaning of her recently clasped hands on the table: they had put her wristwatch directly in her eyeline whenever she looked down at her place for comfort. Seeing the advantage, and having not quite finished with her, Ronnie broke in again to marvel at what an extraordinary thing it was that the National Theatre had never done his work at all. As everyone else was saying their goodbyes Ronnie, again executing his deep bow, bade her goodnight as "Minister".

I don't think anyone had had more than one course.

And that was that, though I did get quite a nice note from Virginia a few days later, with plenty between the lines. She was already half out of her post as Minister for Heritage. Perhaps the thought of endless theatre folk around a table had done for her.

***

I like having a record of everything, whether it does me credit or not. For instance, I so much enjoyed being in *Romeo and Juliet* at the RSC in 1976, having just arrived on the Trans-Siberian from Vladivostok, that I decided one night of its Aldwych run to record a section of it – once my Mercutio was dead. I had time then to plant my cassette recorder in a dark corner of the wings (with something covering its red light, I hope) very near the stage, for the big scenes that followed between David Waller as Friar Laurence and Ian McKellen as Romeo after he's banished for killing Tybalt. The Friar's sympathetic advice is also palpably infuriated:

> O monstrous sin! O rude unthankfulness!
> Thy fault our law calls death, but the mild prince
> Hath... turned that black word death to banishment;
> This is mere mercy, and thou seest it not...

– but this night it was suddenly accompanied by a similar series of wounded fortissimi, my recorder having flipped from Record to Play, where the great Billie Holiday was singing *Don't Explain*. "You mixed with some dame" sings Billie, and so did Friar Laurence too, you might say, annoyed by Romeo's obsession with Juliet. So what I thought was a blank side of tape which could be filled up with Waller and McKellen turned out to be full of 'Lady Day', beginning a few minutes after I'd planted the machine, but before it was presumably leapt upon and silenced by an ASM. Hiding away ashamed in the loo and in need of thinking time after my rather flamboyant

Mercutian gesture, I realised that though I could shortly sneak out of the Stage Door and go home and no suspicion would necessarily fall on me (unless from my absence at the curtain call – Mercutio dies early and traditionally it's pretty much allowed), as, surely, the ASM who found the recorder would have disarmed or destroyed it. Nevertheless I realised that I would have some form of explaining to do the next day.

Here's the kind of man Trevor Nunn, then the RSC's chief, is. I was going out a bit with his PA at the time, Diana Spencer Russell: I confided in her that night, and we agreed that she should speak to Trevor, who would have read his nightly performance report tomorrow by mid-morning and know that somebody had done this something, but not who, because nobody else knew either – until I then called him and ate the humblest, most apologetic of pies. His first reaction was how awful it must have been for me, and he laughed (or perhaps smiled loudly); and then asked me for form's sake to write an apologetic round robin to the Company, individually. That way we'd both be seen to have done our job. Which I did, then went in the next evening in trepidation, to be greeted with affection and warmth all round. Honour satisfied.

This tells you something about the nature of our generous profession, or guild, or team, or family, or whatever it is, and it makes me very proud. And of a boss who had been the soul of kindliness, even as he explained that he should formally tick me off. My future at the RSC remained intact, with its prospect of playing Hamlet *et al*, but Trevor understood exactly how such a thing could have come about: mine was the same kind of misdirected ingenuity that had no doubt seen him through various scrapes in his own job. But then I had known him since his artistic infancy some fifteen years before, when despite being a star undergraduate director, his heart was touchingly broken by a particularly ambitious but in the end very Housewifey girlfriend. Now, to conclude our disciplinary interview, he reminded me that at Newcastle for the RSC residency a few weeks previously we had been having a drink in the hotel bar when the barman observed that this hotel was exactly on the site of the old Empire Theatre – where we had played our 1962 undergraduate *Macbeth*.

***

There's something missing here.

John Barton, Trevor's most trusted directorial influence with the RSC, lent himself so readily to and I think enjoyed the legendary comedy that attended him: his accidental destruction of mugs of coffee, his falling off empty stages, his hapless romances and so on. He wouldn't have tape-recorded a performance over a Billie Holiday track, but he might spill Nescafé all over the stage.

All of which coexisted sweetly with his undisputed genius; if you see any of his filmed Playing Shakespeare workshops from 1984 you meet them, representing the impact on him of "the form and pressure of the time". But I would rather recommend the two previous, semi-improvised workshops of 1979 that we did for Melvyn Bragg's *South Bank Show* that I mentioned earlier and which evolved into the longer, masterly but sometimes slightly over-formatted series that they gave rise to and which are still remembered.

For in that first foray, *Word of Mouth*, you see John as we truly remember him in his glory: passionate, dazzlingly articulate, animated to the point of self-harm, spotting every possible hint in the blank verse – hint, that is, that might help the actors, not reassure or confound the scholars: throughout, he was magnificently on fire and infectious.

In the same programme you also see Trevor Nunn and Terry Hands at the top of their game, and Alan Howard, in case you never saw his greatest work – subtle, flexible, revelatory; David Suchet on the rise, Patrick Stewart, Ian McKellen and myself having a good laugh. As for me, I remind myself in it of nobody so much as my grandson – very slightly standing if not aloof, then only gradually, gradually joining in with even some distinction. The last time I watched it, it reduced me to tears, not simply because of the loss of collegiate friends but at my astounding good luck at having been a part of this enormous benefit: the RSC was an astonishingly powerful force in those days, vibrant, progressive and inspired, with the most imaginable respect for their material, and nobody who came after should feel resentful or denied if I say nobody could have brought it about better than John: he completely exemplifies the time. No wonder we all overran in our tributes and recitatives at his funeral in 2018, then drank away an ocean of tears, so that the whole service threatened to force a reschedule of the next burial. As had happened with Richard Griffiths and Norman Rodway in Holy Trinity Church in Stratford (*qqv*); John affirmed everything that is, or could be, best about us all.

As chance would have it, while writing this account, I have had – quite out of the blue, text messages being what they are – three from Trevor's PA Diana, with pieces of her news and enquiries about mine. Let me tell you some more. She's eighty-two and in a care home, and it's many years since I've seen or spoken with her, not for any particular reason. Her text duly reminds me of the old days, though not of Billie Holiday. Maybe I'll go and see her in the northwest before it's too late, it's probably the least I can do. I recall first meeting her at a cast-welcoming reception given by the RSC staff to the newly assembled Company in Stratford in April 1976, a few years before the above events. There was much good cheer and some speeches and a good deal of milling around, much of it female; and when Diana made herself known to me as Trevor's PA and what good things she'd heard about Mercutio, she emerged as by far the stillest and most polite of the staff – modest and pleasant, not Stratfordish or actressy, not hanging out her colours, the perfect PA quite obviously for an Artistic Director; and, it began to dawn on me, maybe a perfect Mercutio companion as well. Diana was limitlessly kind and affectionate for several years, come what may and despite certain turnings of the head on my part, until we moved back to London where, as I say, she saved my bacon regarding Billie Holiday's Shakespearean debut. She then worked for Edwin Shirley's Trucking Company and for Ginni Gillam, who had helped design my book *Rossya* about my Trans-Siberian journey that I was self-publishing, with beautiful line drawings by Roger Rees.

But in my own defence I too have saved some bacon, as she did. In Southampton in 1989, with my own ESC, I remember rescuing an actor who once nearly wrecked his own evening by not turning up. We were on the road in Southampton with *The Wars of the Roses,* and Barry Stanton (the Chorus in *Henry V*) missed his necessary teatime ferry from the Isle of Wight, where he was staying, and had to miss the show; however, the understudy, in breach of his contract, had never bothered to learn the lines, and so couldn't go on, and I, who was having a contractual night off, strode on instead to do all five of the Chorus's Act Prologues. (This came about because after three years of playing King Henry, I'd passed the part on to John Dougall, who deserved the break, while I spent the evening going over budgets and other ESC business in my dressing room.) Now I was flying by the seat of my pants – Acts One and Four have rightly famous speeches of introduction by the Chorus; those for Acts Two, Three and Five are much more difficult to remember or do, but I flung myself at them and fortunately remembered the lot – they were obviously in my bones – and got away with it. Trevor Nunn, another boss, would have recognised all this – Barry's mistake, the contract breach by the understudy, the need to cover it up kindly, and, in me, a daredevilry in the cause and certainly a better tongue-in-cheek gesture than a misjudged celebration of Lady Day. It would have rung a bell: he would know that artistic directors always have to step into the breach once more, dear friends, once more.

***

Today, some thirty years later, I've had to give a sort of interview to some New York drama teachers about my memories of Peter Shaffer, *The Gift of the Gorgon* in particular. It has been my first international Zoom interview and I've been lining up my jokes about this delightful genius for several days. Not only jokes, but, as in Maxim Gorki's remark about Chekhov's death, sometimes it's delightful to wake and simply spend the entire morning thinking about him. The interview had been set up with infinite care; but then, five minutes in, we lost the synchronisation between sound and vision – the interviewer's face in New York froze paralytically, though he continued to rattle loquaciously along.

Here really is the best story I could and still can tell the world about *Gorgon*. It features my cousin Martin, reluctant colleague with his sister in my seminal Christmas Day shows circa 1952, who owned for many years an almost ruined but still just roadworthy bus, which he would leave parked in a camp-site in Brittany with invisible frontiers. I'd never seen it before, but then I'd always avoided camping in general; however, I accepted his offer that I could go with my then friend Jenny Quayle to stay a week or two in the parked bus after we'd finished *Macbeth* with the ESC – the last show I would be doing with my own Company, as I was eager by then to see if I could break back into the industry as it stood. Halfway through, I had a call from Peter Hall, urging me to come post-haste back to England to meet Peter Shaffer, who had a new play that they were both interested in me for. Rather grumpily (why couldn't they just OFFER it...?) I got the train to the airport and came back to London for just twenty-four hours, in which time I met this man of enormous playwriting gifts, success and myriad all-round talent, grinning boyishly from behind his thickish lenses, wearing his fame lightly, and realised that what with his interest and Hall's determination, I had no choice but to do the play. Then I went back to continue my holiday, completely understanding why I had felt impelled to go so far as to cross the Channel and keep the appointment. Peter Shaffer's charming later conviction that he'd written my part specifically for me because of my Welsh-Russian-ness has since been fully accepted by my other PS, my Prue Skene, who is insistent that such a surprising thing is possible.

Many years later, I celebrated Shaffer, by now very frail, to a full house on a Sunday in Chichester with Albert Finney, Derek Jacobi, Michael Billington and Jamie Glover (who'd just directed *Black Comedy* there); next, in 2014, we dined in New York and he came to see *King Lear*, which I was doing for Theatre for a New Audience – then back in London, soon after he died, we held a celebration of him at the National Theatre in which I impersonated him throughout, answering questions from Simon Callow and reminiscing in Peter's own voice (a tricky one to catch). I had also listened in full detail to his appearance on *Desert Island Discs* (which surprisingly revealed him as being as much moved by Mendelssohn and Stravinsky as by Mozart and Handel), and continued to prepare by listening to a lecture he gave once in the US, a wonderful assessment of Shakespeare by a fellow-playwright:

> William Shakespeare is a magus, a conjuror, a universal public statue covered with the droppings of other people's special pigeons…

According to Peter, Shakespeare wrote two kinds of play only: about Love, as in *Romeo and Juliet,* and another kind of love, for *Macbeth.* He seems less keen on *Hamlet* and recounts taking a young American graduate to see it; during the show the delighted student grabbed his arm with "Oh my God, does anyone *know* about this play?" Shakespeare, according to Peter, wrote plays within plays, as in *A Midsummer Night's Dream* and *Love's Labour's Lost,* because a play within a play was what he felt life was – and on *Love's Labour*'s final and underrated song, 'The Owl and the Cuckoo', he speaks superbly, just as elsewhere he points out that Shakespeare more or less invented the state of sleepwalking for Lady Macbeth – no one in his audience would have known what it was.

And thus off I went to the NT Celebration, where it transpired there was no time for a rehearsal proper, just a quick general placement before the audience came in. I continued to attempt that cadence in Peter's voice – that hesitation, that mix of shyness and campness, sheer brainpower and an accent hanging between New York and Liverpool – reminding myself of his history as a short-sighted Bevin Boy and librarian, of the research he once did on holiday in Marrakesh into the storytellers on the Djamalfna, when he realised that they instinctively knew more about what holds an audience than most theatre practitioners; of the magnificent stage direction in *The Royal Hunt of the Sun* – "They cross the Andes"; of the best joke of my theatre lifetime – the darkness for light and light for darkness of *Black Comedy,* based on something serious he'd seen at the Peking Opera; the genius of basing the horse-blinding scene in *Equus* on the account of just such a real-life crime given him by his Norfolk friend James Mossman (*qv*). The dazzling creation of Salieri ("the voice of God") and Mozart ("the voice of some obscene child") in *Amadeus*. All this makes me forever proud to have known him and still more delighted to have pleased him.

And now he's gone, and no doubt is flirting with John Gielgud in heaven – a heaven to his own liking I hope, which strikes an astute balance between the influence of Apollo and that of Dionysus. Gielgud, whose classic Richard II Peter saw at the age of eleven at Golders Green Hippodrome, thanks to his marvellous Liverpudlian mother's determination (opposed by his unhelpful father) that he should above all have culture – just the same age as I was when transfixed by *Macbeth* at the Old Vic, and clearly with an identical long-term effect. Peter couldn't have guessed that he would more or less enter the world of West End fame with his *Five Finger Exercise*, directed by none other than Gielgud himself, who by then terrified him. Peter afterwards commented:

> In the sunburst of the play's success, I felt my last inhibitions dissolve. I knew then that it would be my task in life to make elaborate pieces of theatre, to create things seen to be done, like justice; yet also to invoke the substance of things unseen, like faith.

Thus Peter, sweet but blisteringly intelligent, gave himself to the muse of imagination. Theatre and music had, he believed, saved his life – though he nearly lost it the morning after the premiere of *Gorgon,* not so much because he had to have overdue heart surgery while we were performing, but because, waking in the morning, he saw beside his bed a kindly nurse leaning solicitously over him with the words "Oh Mr Shaffer, I'm so VERY sorry about your play," because she'd read one of the very few negative reviews we had garnered.

And just as Gorki said of Chekhov's curative powers, so I think of "Ruby" Shaffer (as the director John Dexter used to call him) as a sort of genius. Which helps, in my first Zoom interview ever, to be so agreeable about him. And looking back, I see that *Gift of the*

Gorgon is where several rivers cross. It dealt graphically with the question of forgiveness or retribution for sin – as it, astonishingly, turned out, the Press Night coincided with the IRA bombing of Warrington. The play was a huge turning-point for me which prevented me disappearing up my own backside in trying to re-champion the now alchemically declining ESC. My character was called Edward Damson, and Judi Dench was Helen Damson, my wife. This was our second major outing together, and as I had played Mirabell in the first, the 1977 RSC production of *The Way of the World,* it gave me on a plate my first-morning-of-rehearsal joke, that I got all the plum parts when I was with Judi. Hall and Shaffer seemed delighted, and Judi and I have addressed each other as Mr and Mrs Plum ever since: indeed for a long time we kept up a record that birthday presents in either direction were plum-inflected: plum brandy, a plum tree, plumber's wrench, a plumb line, and so on. This year, for my seventy-seventh, I get a lovely plum jam and a bag of prunes.

***

For my online accounts, VAT particularly, I have an Excel layout, and it keeps giving me a fright. If I turn it on after a few days, all my columns of figures, so carefully constructed, have switched, every one of them, into looking-glass mode: they're upside down, back to front, right to left, near enough illegible and, you would think, altogether lost to man. I have now happened upon the cure, though not before cursing my most recent computer technician, and I hereby share it: if it happens, just scroll down vertically twenty or thirty cells as yet unfilled in any column; stop, move across a bit, and then calmly scroll back again – again on any column. Every single time I've remembered to do this, the offending cells have instantly righted themselves, as if snapping to attention, and are perfect. You gasp with relief and get on with it, now making them whatever size you want.

I suppose I've reached an age when I'm only too likely to interpret the above cyber-fright as an indistinct metaphor for a working life.

If it looks upside down one day, the next day it will have effortlessly righted itself. The required laugh is in place, the scene it's in is also in place, and the situation entirely clear to see; the invented lives have adhered, dead-letter perfect. Or not. And when I forget my lines, as we all do, when a word slips, I grab it with my claws, suddenly sharpened for the purpose, an animal pouncing at great speed on his own mistake...

A slightly different but related question crops up now – "Michael, why do you like playing such awful men"; by which is meant Ibsen's dread Master Builder Solness, Rubek in *When We Dead Awaken*, John Gabriel Borkman; all uneasy companions, hard to learn and hard to like, but they do have the devil's best tunes. To some extent I seem increasingly to have specialised this way as I've grown older: I'm also reminded of the well-named Sir John Brute in Vanbrugh's *The Provok'd Wife*, the hair-raising quiet torturer Nicolas in Pinter's *One for the Road*, Deeley in *Old Times*, and both Major Arnold and Wilhelm Furtwängler in Ronnie Harwood's great *Taking Sides*.

Or – more extremities – there was Posthumus in *Cymbeline* on TV, one of that great trilogy of jealous husbands in Shakespeare but the least familiar. In this I was much praised, I must say by Elijah Moshinsky, and, just as good, by the great, I must say, Helen Mirren (Imogen), who said that if a director just lined up a close-up on me and kept pushing closer and closer and closer in, he or she would get only more and more truth, nothing but the truth. It was Helen and I who, amusing ourselves during shooting breaks, plotted an imaginary future for ourselves as Parisian hairdressers for female and male stars – *Les Coiffeurs aux Vedettes*. Somehow we never got round to it: no, Missus, nor to *that*, either.

***

I was also able to survive (with delight) playing other handfuls such as Molière's *Misanthrope*. After the first preview of this at the Old Vic, Peter Hall gave me an unforgettable note: although Alceste's first speech is a lengthy expository tirade, he felt that the one thing the audience all knew of me (flatterer!) was that I could indeed think and speak very quickly, and they would like me better in this speech if I consciously tried almost to Dry Myself. In other words, to hesitate, to become uncertain, to stop dead, and re-gather strength, let matters lurch about a bit, find a new idea for the next bit. Above all, forget the virtuosity. It was a brilliant note, and the absence of Peter from my life, and with him his creative mischief, is dreadfully hard to bear; he is, like Fulvia in *Antony and Cleopatra,* a great spirit gone.

Actually the combination of Eduardo and Anton Pavlovich and Peter Reginald Frederick Hall were among the best of my working life. I passionately respected Peter but he was also sometimes my slave: on some things I was quite the know-all. When we rehearsed *The Seagull,* Peter would from time to time hand over to me, particularly on the subject of characteristic behaviour among middle-class Russians of the 1880s, about which I knew a bit because of my Chekhovian pursuits. I told the Company that as all Russians know, it was a superstitious habit when such people, once they'd spent their summer sojourn in the country and were returning either to Moscow (the intelligentsia) or Siberia (the army) – when finally every bag is packed and they're waiting for the carriage, to sit in a complete and apparently meaningless silence, concentrating speechlessly on their feelings at the very last moment of acquaintance. Very Chekhovian in fact, this can be a piercing moment if played well, and very theatrical in the best sense. However, I did wonder about the etiquette of the director turning to his Trigorin for guidance at this point. It was akin to a moment when we did *Hamlet* with Stephen Dillane (I was Claudius), and if ever Stephen seemed to Peter to be struggling, Peter would ask me what I had done with that particular moment when I played the part in 1980, which didn't do a lot for my relationship with Stephen.

Then along came Eduardo. I had been urging Peter for some years to do *Filumena* as a terrific vehicle for him, myself and Judi: he eventually accepted and the show was planned. On the first morning he announced to the assembled cast that he had resolved to do the play in order to work again with his dear friend (I slightly stiffened in expectation) – Judi Dench. It was a genuine moment – but Peter, don't take TOO MUCH credit. I retaliated in this silly but quite funny game a little later that day, by offering the production a number of extremely atmospheric photos of the seamy side of Naples I'd taken during a research trip I had just returned from; they would end up helpfully dominating John Napier's set. Around this time in rehearsals, I also reminded him of a film that he didn't seem to know at all – Visconti's great *Rocco and His Brothers* – which definitely reflects something about all Southern Italian families migrating (or hoping to) to the industrial north – the Sorianos in *Filumena* aren't about to do that, but the self-improvement implied must have occurred to them. And of course everything in Naples is diametrically opposite to its counterpart in Milan or Rome.

So I gave Peter my tape of *Rocco* but it outlived him, having I'm sure stayed in its box.

And then again there was Coriolanus, whom I played as a scarfaced thug albeit with a good poetic education. And the bisexual Jaffier in Otway's extraordinary *Venice Preserv'd*, and Henry in Tom Stoppard's virtuosic *The Real Thing*, and the nightmares of Raskolnikov in *Crime and Punishment*. And ran the ESC, if not the RSC. And (perhaps proudest boast of all), I got on top of Archie Rice in John Osborne's *The Entertainer*. I've already commented that most actors have shied away from even courting any comparisons by trying to follow Olivier in this great virtuoso role. At the time, needless to say, I immediately felt that Sheridan Morley was one of the truly great visionary critics of our time: as indeed I did the anonymous one who came along to see a play by Ian Curteis in which I played Robert Maxwell enacting his unexpected meeting and subsequent friendship with Mother Teresa (the mighty Anna Calder-Marshall). According to this witness:

> It was an awesome physical transformation – Pennington has all of Maxwell's light-footed vastness, both physically and emotionally…

But Lyn Gardner, standing in for Michael Billington in *The Guardian* (as she was allowed to do far more often than she should have been) declared:

But what finally scuppers this play is Michael Pennington's eyebrows, which give him the lurid appearance of a pantomime villain. The makeup artist should be sacked immediately.

Ms Gardner was ever the definition of a second-stringer – here she doesn't even know that in the theatre actors plan and execute their own make-up, so it would have had to have been me that was sacked. It was also she who rubbished my 2016 Lear because I had allowed the character to get "sidelined" in the production.

Of course to play Robert Maxwell I had to have a supernatural inkling of Trump, but also to reconnect with Leach in *The Connection* in Cambridge. But then, to be able to be Charles Dickens I had to remember Rudkin's Johnnie Hobnails juggling with his pears. In this regard I am impossible to typecast, rather the opposite.

What I do know for sure is that all performers live for transformation: they listen to audio tapes, they watch filmed evidence, then they imagine the rest at full tilt, everything. I've passed myself off as Oscar Wilde, as Michael Foot, Anton Chekhov, Anthony Blunt, Degas quarrelling with Pissarro (with Henry Goodman and Alison Steadman), and the great scientist/philosopher Werner Heisenberg, who among other extraordinary experiences was one of ten prominent German scientists incarcerated in England under Operation Epsilon in 1945 at Farm Hall in Cambridgeshire, so that MI6 could bug them to see how advanced the German nuclear programme might have got. However, on 6 August 1945, the scientists at Farm Hall learned (from the newspapers) that the USA had dropped an atomic bomb on Hiroshima. At first, there was disbelief – in the weeks that followed, the German scientists discussed how the Americans might have built the bomb. Heisenberg, along with other physicists including Otto Hahn and Niels Bohr, was glad the Allies had won World War II: Heisenberg told other scientists that he himself had never contemplated creating a bomb, only an atomic pile to produce energy. Only a few of the detainees expressed genuine horror at the prospect of nuclear weapons, and Heisenberg, obeying his Uncertainty Principle perhaps, kept his counsel. The failure of the German nuclear weapons programme to get there first is of course the territory of Michael Frayn's *Copenhagen,* and as I write this I have been offered a revival of the play, in which I would have played Nils Bohr; but much as I love Michael Frayn as well as the idea of going back to work, this is one territory I decided I don't need to revisit.

Going back in order to move forward – there was also George III in Alan Bennett's sensational play, and – a degree more fictionally – Sherlock Holmes, cryogenically preserved in a rather good CBS pilot, and Dr Prentice in Joe Orton's *What the Butler Saw.* And Strindberg's Captain in *The Dance of Death,* of which Michael Coveney declared (forgive me) in *The Independent*:

> Michael Pennington provides a monstrous portrait of smiling, vengeful malignity, executing that famous dance with all the panache of Olivier and the heel-clicking decisiveness of Ian McKellen in the role ten years ago. But he adds something more, a sort of gloating, vulpine glee in the havoc he wreaks.

***

All of these adventures – and other less extravagant ones – have brought me joy to various degrees, the greatest perhaps having been the anguish of Tolstoy's poor horse Strider, tied to the end of a rope which was itself tied to a central post, high-stepping a recklessly wild circuit of the stage (at some risk – the rope had to be tested every night, and so did my knees and ankles, twice over). And Edgar, that warm-up for Hamlet. I've felt at times of late that I was passing on the lessons of the great Japanese teacher-performer Zeami Motokiyo, who more or less invented Noh Theatre in the 1400s – as arcane a theatre form as exists – while at other times saying things that sound like those of a professional next-door neighbour: that when you play anger you must remember to "have a tender heart", because it creates a "sense of novelty"; that sometimes an actor is at his best when he is "doing nothing". For what it's worth, I have passed this and much else by Zeami on to young actors if they've asked, and have been rewarded as Zeami predicted by being thought of as being "an old tree which has fewer branches and leaves but still bears some flowers … he has truly mastered the secrets and the flower has remained to him." Zeami also beautifully describes an old man dancing – purposely just missing the beat, remembering to "stretch your arm forward and put it back a little after the emphasis."

And if a performance should always lead to a drink, I remember Pinero's Ferdy Gadd in *Trelawny of the Wells*, too proud to be the Demon King in the panto straight after playing Romeo, even though he's married to the Principal Boy; in support of the insulted Ferdy, the whole acting company goes off to the pub. I remember also those wonderful Greek tragedians whose friezes you can see in the ruins of the arena of Aphrodisias in Turkey, so off-duty that they look exactly like friends of mine – a company of actors after the show, having a smoke, having a drink, gossiping, throwing their tatty linen masks into a corner. They've probably just been doing the entire *Oresteia*.

***

And now, in the middle of Lockdown, Crackdown, or whatever it is, Ronnie Harwood has gone to meet his dearly beloved Natasha. He's thus joined an extraordinary batch: John Barton. Roger Rees. Richard Pasco. Alan Howard. Ian Richardson. For a moment I thought I might be in for Obituary duty: years ago I did Harold Pinter's obit for the *Independent* (see Appendices). Ronnie, in a fit of modesty, had passed the job onto me, and it took a year or two to get it as I wanted; the much awaited and dread Point of Use finally fell on Christmas Day 2008, when I was biting into a roast turkey with my son, his kids, his ex-partner and a new boyfriend of hers. I had to leave the table and take refuge in the bathroom to finish, update and email it to the editor, who had suddenly called to give me the bad news. Where's Grandpa? In the loo, finalising Harold Pinter's obit.

It was fitting enough: when I was still at Cambridge I did a piece for Granta about whether Harold had sold out by doing too much

TV and radio after his initial theatrical success. Years later Harold read it and laughed like a drain; and as you see, he didn't boycott me, proud and jealous of his reputation as he was. The latter *angst* he kept for Ronnie it seems: there was once an evening in a restaurant (probably the Wolseley) when the two of them compared how many of their respective plays were running in London at that moment. Ronnie said "three" with some delight. Harold said "four", and then, inexplicably, got up as if very offended, left the table and went home, as if he had been somehow bested rather than the conqueror in the argument.

***

I've been busy writing to politicians at every opportunity to urge them to support our industry in getting back on its feet after Coronavirus, and have had no acknowledgement, let alone a letter, from any of them. This is contemptible: apart from the pleasant letter from Virginia Bottomley, the last time I wrote to a politician was to Tony Blair about the dilemma for young actors confronting the punishment of PAYE – nothing much happened, but he replied warmly and encouragingly a couple of days later.

I've helped to rescue the Rose Theatre on Bankside, probably the site of Shakespeare's earliest work on his arrival in London, from developers. I remind myself sometimes of Bottom in the *Dream*, who wants to play the Lion as well as Pyramus. And I still know the Chorus in *Henry V*. And all of Hamlet. And I'm available. And what's more important than all this – I told my mother not to worry, I can survive the slings and arrows of this profession.

So. Once upon a time (in the spring of 1964), two eager student actors, Caramitru and Pennington, chanced to play Hamlet before leaving their colleges. Later, they did the parts again as professionals. Likewise, in 2020, they both played Prospero at the same moment.

And what's more, I've just read that Bob Dylan has achieved his unprecedented ninth Number One in the LP (not to be confused with the Singles) Charts, all of course with entirely original material. Looking back for his most recently released single, I notice that it's a beautiful song now covered by Tom Jones, titled 'What Good Am I?' And it could have been written by Tim Hardin, whom Dylan allegedly once declared he admired as the best singer/songwriter in America. And Bob Dylan is seventy-nine, and still on the road, stepping onstage into his own footsteps every night somewhere and never singing an old song the same way twice. He just finds his way to its heart by a different route at each performance.

Just listen to it, it barely ever changes – a musical statement of intent in the first bars, followed by the modulation into the relative minor – C minor from E or A minor from C (this is folk music) – where the flame starts roaring every time.

Tim Hardin did this too, and Billie Holiday, and Charlie Parker. All of them in their own footsteps. I rest my case.

Acknowledgements

I have visible and invisible debts. To Richard Eyre and to Antonia Fraser for alerting me to the possibilities of self-publishing, now that I've written eleven books. For a year now, old publisher colleagues have been crouched beneath various versions of Lockdown: one asked me for a full-scale breakdown of the project and then couldn't find the courtesy to acknowledge it, not with a single word. Only my dear Dinah Wood, Head of Drama at Faber, has remained professional, stalwart and loyal; and she was the third deity, after Richard and Antonia, to introduce me to Sam and Alice Carter.

Then I have a debt for all the permissions-to-print I've happily accepted from interested writers who have, sight unseen, agreed to be quoted – Christopher Hampton, author of *Savages*; Michael Smith of *Captain Jack's Revenge*. To the Arvon Foundation and to Gordon Dickerson on behalf of John Osborne (*Look Back in Anger*), whose agent he remains even beyond the grave.

And to all the photographers who have recorded me and don't mind it being known – I've had the good luck to be illustrated by John Haynes, Catherine Ashmore, Laurence Burns, Donald Cooper, Nobby Clark, Idil Sukan, Robert Workman and Marilyn Kingwill; also to my son Mark, and my dearest Prue, who took the lovely final photograph of my dear John Shrapnel that accompanies Richard Eyre's poem; my ex-wife Katharine; and to Louis and Evie and their mother Caroline, only just out of view.

To all of them and many others, my thanks, thanks, and ever thanks.

Appendices

Harold Pinter: Nobel Prize-winning playwright and poet who dominated British theatre for four decades
By Michael Pennington

How to describe such a life as Harold Pinter's, or to ask about his achievement without hearing that ringing baritone demanding (as he once did when asked how he was that day), "What kind of question is that?"

Pinter was actor and director, poet and prose writer, the author of 20 screenplays, a cricketer and an impassioned political witness to his times; above all, for over 40 years he dominated the theatre. Not to mention that he was a superb (though of his partner quite demanding) bridge player.

When *The Birthday Party* opened in London in 1958, it ran for a week following catastrophic notices. On the Thursday afternoon the young playwright crept towards the Dress Circle to observe the matinee. He was alone: when an usher came to see him off since the circle was closed, his admission that he was the author softened her attitude: "Oh, you poor chap ... in you go." If instead he had sat downstairs in the stalls, he might have noticed Harold Hobson of the *Sunday Times* cooking up a review that would decisively launch his career the morning after the production closed. It was the beginning of half a century in which, in his own words, he gave his audience not what they wanted, but what he insisted on giving them.

Behind him, at this first of many turns in the road, had been a warm but introverted boyhood in Hackney, east London, as the heartily loved only child of Jack Pinter, a ladies' tailor, and his wife Frances. After various bruising evacuations from London in the Blitz, Pinter found a place at Hackney Downs Grammar School, where he met his English teacher and great mentor Joe Brearley, with whom he would walk from Springfield Park to Bethnal Green shouting speeches from *The Duchess of Malfi* and *The Revengers' Tragedy* at the trolley buses, and under whose direction at school he played the parts of Macbeth and Romeo. Then, to Jack's and Frances's horror, he was twice arrested and fined as a conscientious objector to National Service; expecting worse than fining, he took his toothbrush along to the tribunal.

He had tried RADA but found it too class-bound and dropped out, then done a two-year stretch as an actor in Anew McMaster's touring company in Ireland, playing everything from the Greeks to Shakespeare to Wilde to Agatha Christie – the experience left him with a rhapsodic regard for barnstorming classical acting, though he subsequently had little formally to do with it. Then there was a novel, *The Dwarfs* (which he later dramatised), three years in rep, his first marriage, to the actress Vivien Merchant, and the birth of their son Daniel.

And now the fiasco of *The Birthday Party*. Anybody can flop: the manner of recovery makes the man. For two years afterwards, like its hero Stanley refusing to be told what to do, Pinter determinedly prepared for success, nursing the play back to health by means of a revival and a TV adaptation, writing three new plays and overseeing the premieres of two written earlier, *The Room* and *The Dumb Waiter*. After the runaway triumph of *The Caretaker* in 1960 he needed no more time for recovery.

Like the death of John F. Kennedy, this play's debut records a moment in many lives. Though forewarned a little by Samuel Beckett, audiences were taken aback by a play that featured a description of electric convulsive therapy and yet was riotously funny, in which language drawn directly from the street but entirely original in its crafting was used as a tactical weapon in a three-sided battle for large and small advantage. *The Caretaker* has played all over the world, in an infinite variety of ways, its three great parts attracting a host of actors and endless celebration and debate.

Over the next decade, Pinter moved on to Broadway, to many awards and the reward of a CBE. Working in tandem with Peter Hall on *The Collection* in 1962 he began a lifelong partnership as well as his own career as a London director; he also became a screenwriter by virtue of films of his own work (*The Caretaker*, 1964, and *The Birthday Party*, 1968) and his four adaptations of others' (among them *The Servant* and *Accident*, vintage collaborations with Joseph Losey, 1963 and 1967); and he created another theatre milestone, *The Homecoming*, in 1965. The story of Ruth's triumphant progress through the predatory jungle of male sexual confusion confirmed Harold's fascination with the ultimate undefeatability of women; the tribalism of the men proved that an upwardly mobile writer had forgotten nothing of his childhood.

In 1970 Pinter was immortalised by Stephen Sondheim, who wrote him into a lyric in *Company* as conclusive evidence of chic, and he was awarded the German Shakespeare Prize. Accepting guiltily, since at that moment he wasn't writing anything and wasn't about to, he wondered poignantly about the identity of "this fellow called Pinter" whom people wanted to shake hands with. In fact he was pausing, looking for the oxygen that can be as hard to find after success as after failure.

His new work with Losey, *The Go-Between*, would win the Palme d'Or at Cannes in 1971, but he was seriously reviewing how to go forward in the theatre; he knew that he couldn't travel any further with "this bunch of people who open doors and come in and go out", but it was taking some time to settle the alternative. At 40, his own landscape was changing; his marriage was beginning to disintegrate, and while some of his generation were hesitant, a new group of more evidently political playwrights – Hare, Edgar, Brenton, Griffiths – was beginning to move into the light.

Typically, Pinter negotiated all this by continuing to change on his own terms – his work becoming if anything more internal, preoccupied with time, human solitude and separation. In *Old Times* (1971) he suggested how the past could be continually reinvented: a fascination with creative memory had already been broached in *Landscape* and *Silence* in 1969. He then spent 12 months, which he described as a kind of homecoming, "swallowed up" in adapting Proust's *A la Recherche du Temps Perdu*, a period of great personal satisfaction but practical disappointment: the screenplay was never filmed, though it was published, and finally adapted for the theatre in 2000.

Pinter became a director of the National Theatre in 1973; and he adapted *The Last Tycoon* for Sam Spiegel and Elia Kazan in 1974. His awesome *No Man's Land* also arrived with great suddenness in 1974: as the play went into production the following year, Pinter started his relationship with Antonia Fraser, attracting a particularly unpleasant frenzy of press attention that slowed down his writing. Instead he directed Noël Coward (*Blithe Spirit*) and Simon Gray (*Otherwise Engaged* and *The Rear Column*), and came back with his own *Betrayal* in 1978.

Antonia and he married in 1980. Now came, for lack of a better word, the politics, which of course had always been there. Pinter's public role was never, as some thought, a coat he suddenly decided to wear. He'd been shocked into political scepticism as a teenager by the anti-Semitism and anti-Communism (under a Labour government) of the immediate post-war years, and he never forgot the way one of the judges at his military tribunal for conscientious objection had falsified his testimony, accusing him of being a man who wouldn't even defend his sister in time of war.

Harold's sense of injustice and instinctive anti-authoritarianism were deep in the bone; in the 1970s he'd already attacked American involvement in the overthrow of Allende in Chile and defended the Soviet internee Vladimir Bukovsky. However, the Eighties press, still tumid over his love life, responded to this apparent new turn with the special fury aimed at the writer who gets too big for his boots, that greatest of English sins.

Pinter's subsequent position on the US economic blockade of Cuba and intervention in Nicaragua, his contempt for US foreign policy and British compliance with it, down to the NATO bombing of Yugoslavia, Bill Clinton's attack on Iraq and the allied attacks on Afghanistan after 11 September, were uncompromising; after his tireless human-rights campaigning and scrutiny of the meretricious language of politics he might, almost, choose his epitaph.

In the early 1980s he continued to adapt (*The French Lieutenant's*

Woman, 1981; his own *Betrayal*, 1983), and to direct (*Quartermaine's Terms*, 1981; *The Common Pursuit,* 1984) – but his political work both slowed down his original writing and sharpened its aim. The tremendous triple bill *Other Places* in 1982 was followed by a two-year silence broken by the sound of a bullet – the brief *One for the Road* on the subject of state-authorised torture, written in a single enraged breath one night after the discussion of the subject at a Turkish family's birthday party.

What the press derided in Pinter the public man were often acts of exceptional courage. During a momentous fact-finding visit to Turkey in 1985 with Arthur Miller (they were Vice-Presidents of PEN, and, the more you think about it, natural partners as citizens and writers), Pinter exploded at a journalist during a dinner at the US Embassy and effectively had the two of them barred from the country. That was the headline, but the week they spent there thrust the torture in detention of hundreds of thousands of that country's "political" prisoners inescapably under English and American noses – and also engendered the first draft of the 20-minute *Mountain Language*, dealing with the brutal suppression of a minority culture. Oddly, when a group of Kurdish actors rehearsed a revival of the play in North London in 1996 the police, accompanied by helicopters and marksmen, arrested them for carrying (prop) weapons and forbade them to communicate in their own language – the very matter of the play.

By the time of the 1988 opening of *Mountain Language* a vengeful press was permanently parked outside Pinter's house as if for some squalid festival, mocking to the death his June 20th Society, a harmless discussion and debating group of liberal-to-left writers and broadcasters: such public damnation is a measure of the intolerance that sluiced through the media during the Thatcher years.

Knowing who his enemies were but also his friends, Harold entered the 1990s with a four-hour radio tribute, *Pinter at 60*, but with the press still on his back and a rare disappointment in his screenwriting career – *Remains of the Day*, an assignment which for various reasons he didn't finish. His sharp eye on what he used to call "the state of affairs" didn't miss the deportation of Iraqis at the beginning of the Gulf War, and he wrote a savage short poem, "American Football", which blew the euphemisms off the rhetoric that followed Operation Desert Storm. The broadsheets refused to publish it. *Party Time* and *A New World Order* (both 1991) expressed the same anger theatrically. There were major revivals of *The Homecoming*, *The Birthday Party* and *Betrayal* (which the critics finally approved), and Donald Pleasence, the original Davies in *The Caretaker*, appeared in the part once more. Pinter himself returned to the stage in *No Man's Land* at the Almeida in 1992: his mother Frances died, and the beautiful *Moonlight* the following year was in many ways the result.

Harold was in this full flood of writing, acting, directing and being an eloquent public nuisance when I had the good fortune to be directed by him in Ronald Harwood's *Taking Sides*. I'm only the latest to report his pride in and unfailing kindness to the fellow-actors he directed. You felt ushered towards a performance rather than shoved or cajoled. His self-effacement was that of a carpenter working on a perfect chair: he worked with the same economy that perhaps lay behind the speech in *The Dwarfs* when a nutcracker is criticised as an inefficient instrument for cracking a nut because of the unnecessary friction at its hinge. There was no carry-on in his direction, only the gentlest authority, punctuality, affection and trust.

Around this time I first encountered him in the context of bridge, which he played with passion, frequently with the director Karel Reisz and his wife Betsy Blair (model, dancer and eventually blacklisted film actress, previously married to Gene Kelly), who had directed his 1981 script of *The French Lieutenant's Woman* (in which he very nearly cast me in Jeremy Irons's part (opposite Meryl Streep — a pleasure that I had to wait another thirty years for, as Michael Foot in *The Iron Lady*, having passed the time playing Hamlet and running my ensemble, etc). Harold was certainly an expert player, but like another devotee, Nicol Williamson, could be a little outspoken about the fall of the cards — Harold the loving and sensitive director of actors then become Harold the profoundly disappointed. Fortunately his regular partner, in bridge as in life, was, as you would expect, his beloved Antonia Fraser; and I smile to think of the two of them squaring (lovingly) up to each other in the interest of ideal bidding.

It was a good time to be with him; with the greatest good humour he seemed to be doing everybody's job better than they did. He had *Old Times* playing at Wyndham's, *Taking Sides* at the Criterion, and was personally wowing them in *The Hothouse* at the Comedy. What seemed to be some extravagant late flowering was really the start of a long summing-up on all fronts.

Continuing down to the present to clean up in every department, Harold Pinter went on to direct *Twelve Angry Men* (1996), Simon Gray's *Life Support* (1997) and the underexposed *The Late Middle Classes* (1999); to play in *The Collection*, *Breaking the Code*, *Mojo*, *Mansfield Park* and *One for the Road*; to take part in two Pinter Festivals in Dublin, and to complete *Ashes to Ashes* (1996) and *Celebration* (2000).

He faced the final obstacles in his road with an appropriate truculence and a sense of business as usual. A week after announcing, in February 2002, that he had cancer of the oesophagus, while his own production of *No Man's Land* played at the Lyttelton, he premiered a new work at the NT, *Press Conference*, performing it himself as part of a programme of his sketches. Soon afterwards he released his poem "Cancer Cells".

In June 2002 he was appointed a Companion of Honour (he had rejected a knighthood in 1996), and in August appeared at the Edinburgh Festival to announce, "I am no less passionately engaged, nevertheless I think I have come out of this experience with a more detached point of view." Thus armed, he continued to attack politicians for their abuse of language, in due course declaring that George W. Bush and Tony Blair were war criminals who should be impeached: "When I hear Bush say [after the events of 11 September 2001] that ‹on behalf of all freedom-loving people we are going to continue to fight terrorism› and so on, I wonder what ‹freedom-hating people› look like: I've never met such people myself, or can't even conceive of it. In other words, he's talking rubbish."

After being celebrated across radio and television in the "Pinter at the BBC" season in the autumn, he embarked on a campaign against the British military involvement in Iraq, speaking at the mass demonstration in London in February 2003, contributing to Faber's instant book *101 Poems Against the War* (he brought out his own pamphlet, *War*, in June 2003), and campaigning in the press. "The US and the UK couldn't care less about the Iraqi people. We've been killing them for years," he said. "What is now on the cards is further mass murder. To say we will rescue the Iraqi people from their dictator by killing them is an insult to the intelligence."

In 2005, not long after directing Simon Gray's *The Old Masters* in the West End, he seemed to be announcing his retirement from the theatre to concentrate on his political work; *War* won the Wilfred Owen Award for Poetry and he also carried off the Franz Kafka Prize. His 75th birthday in October was celebrated by the broadcast of *Voices*, a collaboration with the composer James Clarke, in which he drew on plays such as *One for the Road*, *Mountain Language* and *Ashes to Ashes* to create a narrative accompanied by Clarke's radiophonic score.

A few days later came the award of the Nobel Prize for Literature – news which he seems to have received on the telephone with something closer to a Pinter silence than a Pinter pause: "I was speechless". One news channel announced that he was dead, then changed its mind and confirmed he had won the Nobel Prize. "So I've risen from the dead."

He sensed that his political activities had been "taken into consideration" in the award. No wonder: they have completed an extraordinary axis in his life of polemics, the spit and sawdust of theatre practice and literary culture. In December 2005, everything that Pinter stood for was fused in a superb speech of acceptance. "I have often been asked how my plays come about," he said. "I cannot say. Nor can I ever sum up my plays, except to say that this is what happened. That is what they said. That is what they did." But he was unusually explicit about his work and method. "The author's position is an odd one. In a sense he is not welcomed by his characters. They resist him, they are not easy to live with." He could write obliquely in fiction, he said, but uncompromisingly in politics because there were ambiguities he stood by as a writer but could not as a citizen. And with a great writer's simplicity he dealt with the justifications for the Iraq war with resounding repetitions: "We were assured that was true. It was not true."

It sounded like both a manifesto, and, poignantly, a farewell: in January 2006 he won the Europe Theatre Prize and in October he delivered himself of a great piece of acting in Beckett's *Krapp's Last Tape* – fortunately recorded for posterity, as was his radio performance the next spring as Max in *The Homecoming*. Beckett and Pinter were of course natural allies; but there is a story that these two great and parallel figures once agreed to sit in front of a microphone for an unrehearsed radio conversation about matters of common interest. It was to be a great coup – though what couldn't perhaps have been expected (or perhaps could have been) was that they would immediately start finding fault with England's batting line-up in the current Test Match, moving on to cover other current subtle aspects of the great sport, and spoke not a single word about art, themselves or the theatre etc. Not one word.

Early in 2007 came the Légion d'Honneur; and throughout the year he was with us in spades. In February *The Dumb Waiter* was in the West End, and a film version of *Celebration* was seen on television. In July *The Hothouse* was at the NT while *Betrayal* was at the Donmar. The Broadway production of *The Homecoming* opened at the end of the year, shortly before the same play's triumphant revival at the Almeida. Then earlier this year (2008) a double bill of *The Collection* and *The Lover* opened in the West End and a 50th anniversary production of *The Birthday Party* was staged at The Lyric Hammersmith.

Harold had slept next to a sheep on the road with McMaster, but as a man of letters he became part of a tradition that included Joyce and Eliot. He would have liked to have a drink with Proust and Kafka – but, as he said, he never got around to it. Reams have been written about him as a writer, not all of it relevant, and he has, of course, earned his own personalised adjective, usually seriously misapplied. His ear for the vernacular was unerring, his comic escalations riotous; his sense of personal politics included the "piss-take", that means of mocking others without their being quite sure of it. He redistributed the weight of language in the theatre; he was able to make a word or a silence travel in a way that was at once poetic and hilarious; he believed that every sentence written should pay for its keep. His originality, the breadth and depth of his gifts, the thoroughness with which he reorganised his audience, bucked his critics and embraced his citizenship, have been fabulous.

Now he's having his drink with Proust, or better still with Len Hutton. For an enormous public the silence will be felt by degrees, and for his colleagues the loss is hard to measure. Along the way, Harold immortalised many people: the soft-hearted usher on *The Birthday Party*; Anew McMaster; Joe Brearley; even the disgruntled box-office clerk at a theatre who didn't recognise him, and when reminded replied with a verbal quirk – "Why would I know *that*?" – which delighted him. For a man of such pride, his sense of self-mockery was acute.

Add to this exceptional loyalty and generosity, his brilliance as a raconteur and a high degree of personal imitability, and it is easy to see why anecdotes cluster closely around him. We already miss the Satanic grin, the bullnecked intemperance in the cause of good theatre that would make him try to stop the traffic outside a rehearsal room for *Taking Sides,* or kill a buzzing fly, and which once enabled him to halt the sale of Smarties during a performance; his undeflectable kindness to his colleagues; his half-serious fury at half-imagined slights.

Harold Pinter was thought to be frightening, and he was certainly a cutter of crap; but really, like Chekhov, an encounter with him made you want to be simpler, more yourself. For all his fabled belligerence, this was a man of enormous warmth, who made you feel that we were, after all, about something. To have known him was a joy and enrichment; to have been a colleague in the same profession has been the greatest privilege.

Harold Pinter, actor, playwright and director: born London 10 October 1930; CBE 1966; FRSL 1967; Associate Director, National Theatre 1973-83; CLit 1998; CH 2002; Nobel Prize for Literature 2005; married 1956 Vivien Merchant (died 1982; one son; marriage dissolved 1980), 1980 Lady Antonia Fraser (née Pakenham); died 24 December 2008.

The Independent, 26th December 2008

*John Shrapnel (b.27/04/1942, d.14/02/2020).
Photograph by Prue Skene.*

SHRAP

Richard Eyre

Nearly sixty years ago
On a Cambridge student stage

A phosphorescent shell burst
And pierced my skin and eyes,
My adolescent brain, my unformed heart:
Thin Shrapnel splinters were dispersed

And lodged themselves within me until
Now – though we live in one another still
And death is, in William Penn's decree,
But a crossing of the world as friends do the sea –
I'm adding to his testament a codicil.

On that cool October night
He bore his gifts with innocent allure
Like a well-worn leather jacket,
And for me, the student neophyte
He became mononymous, joined the one-name list,
Was heretically seen to co-exist
With the god-like Brando, whose taxi scene
Chanted like an alexandrine,
Became liturgy for our eucharist.

John was the fox who knew many things;
I was the hedgehog who knew one thing:
That I knew nothing but country ways.
When he knew Beethoven's quartets,
And the quartets of T. S. Eliot,
The tragedies of Euripides,
And cycling as a sport.

In My Own Footsteps

Until his father, I had never met
A journalist;
Until his mother, I had never met
An artist;
Until him, I had never met
An actor.

We shared a mutual love of high silliness:
Scrutinised Mort's drawings in Mad Magazine,
Catalogued the films of Elvis Presley,
Swapped bad jokes like stamp collectors,
Queued all night for the Beatles,
Drew a map of Eddie Cochran's
Cut Across Shorty to prove Miss Lucy's plan,
In half-satirical hipsterdom, called each other "man".

Your guileless spontaneity became
In time a watchful virtuosity –
Noble, true, tenacious, quirky –
And the percussive clatter of the Shrapnel name,
Modified into a soft-shoe slap:
The loving sobriquet of Shrap.

In life's periodic table, grief
Does not have the same half-life as joy;
It's a porous, unpredictable alloy
And time passing is its sole relief.

But love decays in glacial steps like granite rocks,
And you'll forgive me for the painful paradox
That you had to die to hear your friend unlock
Such awkward, tender, words as "Goodbye…man",
To a friendship that began

On a Cambridge student stage
Nearly 60 years ago.

INDEX

Acton, Harold 215, 221
Airplane, Jefferson 19, 21, 23
Albee, Edward 23, 48
Albery, Donald 135, 136
Alexander, Bill 210
Alexander, Bob 190–91, 192–95, 200–201
Amyes, Isabelle 92
Amyes, Julian 92
Annis, Francesca 18–19, 21, 102, 103, 107, 203
Apted, Michael 43
Arbuzov, Alexei 106
Artaud, Antonin 43
Ashcroft, Peggy 46, 56, 57, 61–3, 71, 76–8, 122, 202
Askey, Arthur 35
Atkins, Eileen 249–50
Attenborough, Michael 196
Attenborough, Richard 36, 103

Baddeley, Angela 216
Banzie, Brenda de 88
Barker, Katharine ("Kate") 19, 47–48, 72–73, 78, 80, 83–84, 86–88, 90, 94–95, 97–98, 239, 277
Barkworth, Peter 97
Baron, Alexander 88
Barrington, Ken 76
Barton, John 46, 71–2, 76, 78, 80, 116–20, 123–26, 140, 195, 203, 210, 261–62, 273
Bates, Alan 156
Baylis, Lilian 179
Beale, Simon Russell 273–74, 192, 234
Beauman, Sally 131
Beckett, Samuel 15, 37, 90, 134, 280, 286, 287

Beevers, Geoffrey 85
Bening, Annette 234
Bennett, Alan 46, 54, 173, 272
Benthall, Michael 179
Bentley, Dick 246
Beresford, Stephen 181
Bergman, Ingmar 180–81
Berry, Cis 186
Betjeman, John 35
Billington, Kevin 77, 78
Billington, Michael 138, 234, 264, 270
Blair, Betsy 284
Blair, Cherie 60
Blair, Tony 60, 274, 285
Blake, William 13, 78
Blakely, Colin 218
Blakiston, Caroline 87
Blanchflower, Danny 246
Blunt, Anthony 38, 45, 54, 271
Bogart, Humphrey 15
Bogdanov, Michael xi, 62, 119, 133, 156, 159–160, 190, 200
Boggis, Caroline 273, 277
Bond, Edward 137
Bond, Gary 97
Bottomley, Virginia 257–59, 274
Bourne, Robert 257–58
Boyd, Michael 189, 192, 210, 211
Bragg, Melvyn 124, 140, 261
Branagh, Ken 197
Braz, Osip 213
Brearley, Joe 279, 288
Brecht, Bertolt 43, 48, 135, 142, 167
Bree, James 87
Brenton, Howard 13, 117, 133, 281
Brindley, Madge 85
Britton, Tony 95–96
Brook, Peter 59, 72, 166, 167, 174,

293

185, 220, 244
Brown, Dee 10
Brown, Murray 86, 87
Brown, Sid 2
Büchner, Georg 132
Buckle, Richard 68, 192
Buckley, Lord Richard 121, 145, 174
Buckley, Tim 172
Bukovsky, Vladimir 282
Bulgakov, Mikhail 122, 138
Burge, Stuart 90, 93
Burke, Alfred 105
Burn, Jonathan 85
Burns, Nica 135
Bush, George W. 285
Bushell, Kirsty xvi
Butcher, Michael 41–42
Butterworth, Jez 208

Cadell, John 84, 90, 95
Caird, John 192
Calder, Gilchrist 21
Calder, John 37
Calder-Marshall, Anna 270
Callow, Simon 264
Calvert, Phyllis 95–97
Cameron, David 230
Campion, Sean 136
Canby. General Edward 11, 12, 22, 23
Canning, Heather 85
Čapek, Karel 37
Caracas, Micaela 171
Caragiale, I. L. 227
Caramitru, Ion 108, 109–113, 165–66, 168–71, 173–74, 227, 254, 274
Carey, P.A. xviii
Cattrall, Kim 250
Ceaușescu, Elena 109
Ceaușescu, Nicolae 109–111, 165, 171, 233
Charleson, Ian 115, 116, 173, 230
Chaucer, Geoffrey 41, 126
Chekhov, Anton 5, 44, 59, 128, 133, 171, 172–73, 196–7, 213–16, 219, 223–25, 228, 239, 263, 266, 288
   MP playing Chekhov 92, 156, 216–18, 245, 249–50, 269, 271
Chereau, Patrice 248
Christie, John 13
Ciulei, Liviu 112
Clapton, Eric 23, 102
Clare, John 211
Clarke, James 286
Clarke, Tom 104
Cleese, John 43, 47
Clinton, Bill 282
Clinton, Hillary 169
Cocteau, Jean 43, 44, 48
Codron, Michael 90
Collier, Patience 70, 90, 97
Cook, Jill 5–6, 33, 255, 264
Cook, Martin 5–6, 33, 171, 229, 253, 264
Congreve, William 157
Constantine, Emperor 52
Conti, Tom 24, 25
Corden, James 248
Cordery, Richard 197
Corner, Jill 40, 41
Cosby, Bill 92
Cotton, Oliver 239
Cottrell, Richard 106, 216
Coveney, Michael 272
Cowan, Eliot 172
Coward, Noël 43, 96, 97, 193, 282
Crowley, Aleister 38–39
Crutchley, Rosalie 93
Curteis, Ian 270
Cusack, Sinéad 105, 201, 210

Dale, Charles 160
Dalton, Timothy 92
Daniels, Maurice 46
Daniels, Ron 117, 120, 138, 210
Darren, James 44, 55
Davies, Howard 209

Dean, Robert 98
Degas, Edgar 237, 271
Dench, Judi 53, 62, 117, 156–59, 191, 200, 203, 218–220, 267, 269
Desert, Wilfred 86
Dexter, John 266
Dickens, Charles 86, 271
Dickenson, Emily 100
Dickerson, Gordon 277
Dillane, Stephen 256, 269
Dobie, Alan 161, 226
Dodin, Lev 166, 167
Doggart, James Hamilton 177–78
Donne, John 72
Donnellan, Declan 166
Doran, Greg 119, 189, 192, 196, 210, 211, 252
Dostoyevsky, Fyodor 249
Dotrice, Karen 73
Dotrice, Michele 85, 101
Dotrice, Roy 70, 71, 73, 75–76, 78, 122
Dougall, John 263
Douglas-Home, Alec 73
Dunne, J. W. 52
Dürrenmatt, Friedrich 106
Dylan, Bob x, 67, 144, 172, 274–75

Edden, Tom 248
Eddington, Paul 77
Edgar, David 117, 120, 137, 208, 244, 281
Edwards, Huw 247–48
Einstein, Albert 227
Eliot, George 53, 100
Eliot, T. S. 63, 287, 291
Elizabeth I 110, 161
Elliott, Marianne 208
Ellis, Robin 39, 43, 47, 53, 63, 69, 73, 94, 95, 98, 252, 254
Elwyn, Michael 37–38
Eminescu, Mihai 169
Euripides 60, 117, 137, 138, 291
Evans, Edith 45, 57, 60

Evans, Graham 88
Evans, Kim 191, 201
Ewing, Maria 155
Eyre, Richard 42, 43, 49, 60–61, 110, 201, 209, 218, 254, 277, 291
Eyre, Ronald 93

Faithfull, Marianne 19, 102, 256
Farage, Nigel 230
Farquhar, Malcolm 95, 268
Featherstone, Vicky 208
Finch, Jon 19
Filippo, Eduardo de 46, 156, 213–16, 218, 220–22, 224–25, 228, 239, 245, 269
Finnerty, Warren 49
Finney, Albert 239, 264
Firbank, Annie 196–97
Fletcher, David 192, 199, 200
Floyd, Peter M. 253
Fo, Dario 219, 221
Foot, Michael 246, 271, 284
Ford, Harrison 144
Foreman, Carl 103
Forsyth, Bruce 141
Fowler, Gavin 238–39
Foy, Chris 192, 193, 197–98
Francis, Raymond 91
Franks, Philip 184–85
Fraser, Antonia 277, 282, 284–85, 289
Fraser, Ronald 17
Frayn, Michael 239, 271
Frears, Stephen 43, 44
Frei, Nicola 162
Freud, Clement 13

Galsworthy, John 83
Gambon, Michael 173
Gardner, Lyn 270–71
Garrick, David 68
Geeson, Judy 105
Gelber, Jack 43, 48, 232
George, Susan 105
Gielgud, John xvi, 15, 37, 45, 57,

59–62, 97, 244, 266
Gilkes, Denne 72–73
Gill, Peter 105–107, 115, 156, 162, 174
Gillam, Ginni 262
Ginsberg, Allen 48
Glass, Philip 13
Glen, Iain 136, 172
Glover, Jamie 264
Goddard, Jim 92–93
Gold, Jack 104
Goldoni, Carlo 43, 156, 220
Gooch, Anthony 73
Goodman, Gillian 42, 43, 55, 72, 231, 240, 254–55
Goodman, Henry 271
Gordon, Noele 84
Gorki, Maxim 249, 250, 263, 266
Gorrie, John 84, 85, 88
Graham, Clive 17, 100, 101
Graham-Dixon, Andrew 170
Grandage, Michael 135
Grant, President Ulysses S 11, 14
Granville-Barker, Harley 156, 226, 228, 256
Graves, Robert 104
Gray, Simon 63, 132, 282, 285, 286
Greenaway, Peter xvi, 22
Greene, Sally 257–58
Greer, Germaine 86
Gregson, John 106
Greig, David 135, 136
Griffith, Hugh 70
Griffiths, Richard 107, 115, 120–122, 131, 145, 160, 174, 203, 262
Griffiths, Trevor 281
Grillo, John 43
Groban, Josh 31
Guinness, Alec 57, 63–64, 94, 158

Hack, Keith 106, 117
Haddon, Mark 171
Hall, Edward 161, 162
Hall, Peter 46, 47, 62, 71, 79–80, 84–86, 117, 122, 155–63, 179, 189, 202–203, 207, 216, 218–19, 226, 256, 264, 267–70, 280–81
Halliwell, Ken 86
Hamilton, Patrick 37
Hammershøi, Vilhelm 237
Hampton, Christopher 24, 25, 277
Hands, Terry 119, 123–25 189, 190, 203, 210, 261
Hardin, Tim 14, 19, 20, 172, 275
Hare, David 13, 208, 281
Harris, Richard 77
Harris, Zinnie 208
Harrison, Carey 43, 53–54
Harrison, George 23
Harwood, Natasha 255, 257, 258, 273
Harwood, Ronald ("Ronnie") 46, 184, 228, 255–59, 268, 273–74, 284
Havel, Václav 113
Hayter, James 95
Heath, Edward 18
Hegel, Georg Wilhelm Friedrich x, 45, 46
Heisenberg, Werner 271
Hendrix, Jimi 20
Hendry, Ian 15, 104, 105
Henry, Lenny 143
Higgins, Anthony 22
Higgins, Paul 136
Hill, George Roy 17
Hill, Jimmy 245
Hiller, Wendy 50
Hilton, Andrew 208
Hitler, Adolf 228
Hobson, Harold 45, 279
Hoffman, Michael 201
Holiday, Billie 259, 261, 262, 275
Holm, Ian 46, 70–76, 78, 122, 202
Homer xi, 125–28, 130
Hopkins, John 105, 239
Hopkins, Tony 102
Hordern, Michael 116
Howard, Alan 118, 120, 122–25, 131–32, 134, 139, 141, 165, 174,

296

202, 203, 211, 218, 261, 273
Howerd, Frankie ix
Hurst, Geoff 83
Hurt, John 97
Hutton, Len 3, 4, 288
Hytner, Nick 121, 173, 174

Ibsen, Henrik 44, 193, 224, 228, 253, 268
Ingham, Barrie 88
Ionesco, Eugene 44, 112
Irving, Henry 57

Jack, Captain 10–11, 23
Jackley, Nat 35
Jackson, Glenda 86
Jacobi, Derek 264
Jagger, Mick 101, 102
James VI 161
James, Henry 100
Jameson, Pauline 95
Jarvis, Martin 83
Jayston, Michael 104
Jewesbury, Edward 22
Joffé, Rowan 116
Johannessen, Ola B 253–54
Johnson, Boris xiv, xvi, 230, 247
Jones, James Earl 145
Jongh, Nicholas de 23, 219
Jonic, Bettina 186
Jourdain, Eleanor 50–52, 101
Joyce, James 132, 134, 143, 287
Justice, Barry 97

Kafka, Franz 286, 287
Kaufman, Gerald 207
Kay, Charlie 70, 75, 88
Kean, Edmund 14, 138
Keane, Fergal 238, 248
Keast, Kenneth 37
Keith, Penelope 87
Kendal, Felicity 226, 229
Kennedy, Bobby 11
Kennedy, John F. 280

Kenwright, Bill 84, 157–58
Key, Janet 159
Kidman, Nicole 136
Kientpoos, Chief *see* Jack, Captain
King, Martin Luther 11
Kinnock, Neil 133, 143
Kissinger, Henry 14
Konovalova, Galina 251
Kosminsky, Peter 104
Kundera, Milan 185
Kyle, Barry 133, 138, 210

Langridge, Philip 155
Lapotaire, Jane 105, 116, 122, 141
Laughlan, Agnes 95
Laurenson, Jimmy 78, 160–61
Lavery, Bryony 208
Lawrence, D. H. 91, 105
Leavis, F. R. 41, 53, 100, 231
Leigh, Mike 92
Leigh, Vivien 68
Leigh-Hunt, Barbara 190, 211
Lennon, John x
Leonard, Hugh 87
Leonardo da Vinci 78, 162
Lesser, Anton 125
Lindwall, Ray 3
Lipman, Maureen 77
Littlewood, Joan 54
Livesey, Roger 15
Livingstone, Quentin 77
Lloyd, Marie 145
Loach, Ken 85, 89
Lockhart, Calvin 92
Longhurst, Michael 135, 248
Loren, Sophia 218
Losey, Joseph 281
Lucas, George 144
Lynn, Jonathan 44, 77
Lyubimov, Yuri 171–72, 251

McBain, Kenny 106
McCartney, Paul x
McCullin, Don 39

McCullough, Sir Charles 191
McDiarmid, Ian 107, 137, 144, 203
McDowell, Malcolm 92
McGough, Roger 92
Mackay, Angus 47
McKellen, Ian 53, 57–58, 106, 203, 210, 218, 222, 239, 244, 259, 261, 272
McKenna, Kilian 132
McMaster, Anew 280, 287, 288
Macpherson, Conor 144
McQueen, Steve 159
McShane, Ian 106
Mailer, Norman 48
Makovetsky, Sergey 251
Malcolmson, Carol 200
Malory, Thomas 125
Manson, Charles 11–12
Margolyes, Miriam 40, 43, 44
Marie Antoinette, Queen 50–52
Marquand, Richard 144
Marx Brothers 44
Marx, Karl x, 45
Mason, Brewster 70, 75
Mason, Portland 95–96
Massey, Daniel 256–58
Mastroianni, Marcello 218
Mathias, Sean 222
Maugham, Somerset 21
Maxwell, Robert 270, 271
May, Bunny 17
Meier, Waltraud 248
Mendes, Sam 135, 196
Merchant, Vivien 280, 289
Merrick, David 18
Meyerhold, Vsevolod 251
Miller, Arthur 44, 283
Miller, Henry 44, 48
Miller, Jonathan 248
Miller, Max 33, 35
Minciotti, Maria Teresa Biondi 149–153
Mirren, Helen xvi, 122, 203, 268
Mitchell, Justine 142

Moberly, Charlotte Anne 50–52, 101
Molière, 221, 229, 268
Molina, Alfred 131
Molloy, Dearbhla 132–33, 211
Monet, Claude 177
Montesquieu, Charles 51
Morgan, Abi 208
Morgan, Jane 134
Morley, Sheridan 229, 270
Mortimer, John 60, 90
Moshinsky, Elijah 268
Mossman, James 106, 266
Motokiyo, Zeami 272–73
Murolo, Roberto 218
Murphy, Cillian 172
Murphy, Gerard 157

Nabokov, Vladimir 39, 250
Napier, John 270
Neville, John 47, 91, 257
Neville, Richard 37
Newell, Michael 43, 92
Newman, Sydney 85
Nichols, Mike 25, 26
Nietzsche, Friedrich 100
Nixon, President Richard 13, 14, 15
Noble, Adrian 189, 196, 198, 203–204, 207, 216
Normington, John 70
Norris, Rufus 208
Northam, Jeremy 159
Nunn, Ellie 248
Nunn, Trevor 43, 44, 47, 63, 106, 117, 119, 122–24, 136, 140–41, 162, 189, 203, 210, 231, 248, 254, 260–63
Nykvist, Sven 180

Obianyo, Gloria 140
O'Brien, Maureen 125
O'Casey, Eileen 133
O'Casey, Sean 117, 132, 133
O'Keefe, John 132
Olivier, Laurence 31, 45, 57, 61, 62,

68, 73, 88, 197, 209, 218, 229, 235, 258, 270, 272
Olivo, Robert ("Ondine") 13
Orton, Joe 86, 272
Osborne, John 14, 23, 40, 63, 229, 270, 277
Østbye, Marit 253–54
O'Toole, Peter 17, 68
Otway, Thomas 229, 244, 270

Pacino, Al 25, 26, 234
Paddick, Hugh 89
Palmer, Tony 20, 44
Pankhurst, Emmeline 184
Parker, Charlie 48–49, 275
Parry, Natasha 59, 137, 139
Pasco, Richard 131, 190, 211, 273
Pearce, Jacqueline 98
Pearson, Richard 88
Peck, Bob 53
Pennell, Nicholas 83
Pennington, Dorothy 213
Pennington, Eve ("Evie") x, 159, 225–26, 252, 277
Pennington, Fyfe xiii–xiv, 4, 9, 33, 35-6, 38, 40, 55, 67–8, 72, 91, 98, 102, 156, 158, 180, 194, 243–45, 274
Pennington, Louis x, 1, 3–5, 159, 226–27, 252, 277
Pennington, Mark x, xiv, 1, 3, 153, 159, 200, 252, 277
  childhood 9, 16, 19, 73, 80, 83, 84, 87–88, 94, 98, 131, 150–51
Pennington, Vivian 5, 9, 33–6, 38–40, 54, 55, 67–9, 72, 91, 98, 120, 132, 194, 214, 217, 243–45, 247
Perry, Simon 43
Peter, John 173
Phelan, Brian 54
Phillips, Robin 86, 87
Pinero, Arthur Wing 121, 273
Pinter, Daniel 280
Pinter, Frances 279–80, 284
Pinter, Harold 38, 228, 256–57, 268, 273–74, 279–289
Pinter, Jack 279–80
Pintilie, Lucian 112
Pirandello, Luigi 49, 215, 219
Piscator, Erwin 43
Pleasance, Donald 284
Plowright, Joan 62, 218
Poitier, Sidney 92
Polanski, Roman 19
Poliakoff, Stephen 106
Pope, Jonathan 192, 193, 197–200, 214
Porter, Eric 67, 78, 79, 84, 145, 202–203
Powell, Enoch 120, 244
Pratt, Mike 17
Priestley, J. B. 99
Proust, Marcel 281, 287, 288
Prowse, Dave 144–45
Pryce, Jonathan 122
Pym, Hugh 247–48
Pyne, Frederick ("Ricky") 239–40

Quant, Mary 226
Quayle, Anthony 197
Quayle, Jenny 264
Quick, Diana 248
Quinn, Patricia 21

Rattle, Simon 155
Rawlinson, Brian 88
Redgrave, Michael 39, 45, 53, 57
Redgrave, Vanessa 73, 142
Rees, Roger 131, 203, 262, 273
Reisz, Karel 284
Reynolds, Dorothy 47
Reynolds, Ron 245–46
Richardson, Ian 73, 273
Richardson, Ralph 47, 57
Richardson, Tony 14, 102, 256
Rickman, Alan 116
Rigg, Diana 73
Ringham, John 85
Robertson, Jack xviii, 2–4, 33, 77–78,

194, 243, 245–46
Rodway, Bianca 134
Rodway, Norman 132–34, 139, 140, 142, 143, 262
Rogers, Paul 79, 91, 250
Roose-Evans, James 86
Root, Joe 1
Rose, Clifford 70
Rourke, Josie 135
Rudkin, David 117, 120, 137–38, 271
Rylance, Mark 57
Rylands, Professor George "Dadie" 45

Sainsbury, David 194, 197
Sainsbury, Susie 193–95, 197, 200–201, 210
Saint-Denis, Michel 72
Santayana, George x
Sartre, Jean-Paul 43
Sassoon, Siegfried 104
Savident, John 85
Scales, Prunella 92
Scofield, Paul 24–28, 30, 53, 57–59, 61, 73, 74, 78, 79, 93, 97, 123, 202, 234, 244
Scott, Andrew 248
Selby, Nicholas 69–70
Serban, Andrei 112
Seyton, Richard 254
Shaffer, Peter 106, 125, 156–58, 263–67
Shakespeare xiv, 67, 68, 73, 76, 110, 126, 161–62, 201–202, 205, 252, 265, 274
Shaw, George Bernard 78, 193
Shepard, Sam 12, 13, 106, 115
Sher, Tony 211, 236
Shirley, Edwin 262
Shrapnel, John x, 39, 42–43, 47, 49, 53, 69, 196, 230, 254–55, 277, 291–292
Sim, Sheila 36
Simenon, Georges 84–85
Sinden, Donald 46, 73, 75, 76, 78,

117, 131, 203, 238, 255
Skene, Prue x, xv–xvi, 159, 163, 169–71, 182–84, 186, 247–49, 252, 264, 277
Slater, Guy 43, 105, 230–31
Smith, C. Aubrey 15
Smith, Maggie 19,
Smith, Michael 9, 11–13, 22, 277
Smith, Ray 85
Sondheim, Stephen 135, 281
Sophocles 38
Spencer, Colin 86–87
Spencer Russell, Diana 260, 262
Spinetti, Victor 54
Squire, William 78
Stallybrass, Anne 88, 91
Stanislavski, Konstantin 5, 43, 76, 250–51
Stanton, Barry 263
Steadman, Alison 271
Stein, Peter 172, 216
Steiner, George 45
Stephens, Robert 17, 19, 21–22, 125
Stephens, Simon 248
Stevenson, Juliet 138–39
Stewart, Patrick 122, 137, 138, 139, 140, 261
Stock, Nigel 88
Stokes, Ben 1
Stoppard, Tom 52, 229, 270
Storey, Ian 248
Streep, Meryl 284
Strindberg, August 209, 228, 272
Suchet, David 116, 125, 203, 229, 249, 261
Sutton, Dudley 17
Suzman, Janet 70, 75, 88, 100, 122, 155
Sydow, Max von 253

Tate, Sharon 17
Taylor, C. P. 123–24
Taylor, Don 99
Taylor, John Russell 87

Taymor, Julie xvi
Tennyson, Alfred Lord 41, 63, 232
Terera, Giles 143
Teresa, Mother 270
Terry, Nigel 93
Thatcher, Margaret 18, 283
Thomas, Charlie 80
Thomas, Madoline 72
Thorndike, Sybil 57
Timothy, Chris 93
Titmus, Fred 76, 77
Tolstoy, Leo 156, 183–84, 244, 249, 272
Townson, Nigel 167
Trump, Donald 247, 271
Tuminas, Rimas 250–51
Tynan, Kenneth 15, 48, 250

Unwin, Stephen 190

Vakhtangov, Yevgeny 251
Vaughan, Michael 54
Vdovichenkov, Vladimir 251
Vegas, Johnny ix
Vlad the Impaler 170

Waites, Zoe 195
Walcott, Clyde 246
Waller, David 259
Walsh, Fergus 247–48
Warhol, Andy 13, 21
Warner, David 46, 67, 72, 79
Warner, Deborah 111
Washbrook, Cyril 3
Waterman, Dennis 105
Watson, June 88
Waugh, Evelyn 132
Wax, Ruby 116
Webb, Alan 93, 94
Webster, John 43
Webster, Max 184
Weekes, Everton de Courcy 15, 246–47
Weiss, Peter 72

Wells, Stanley 201, 210, 211
Wertenbaker, Timberlake 218
Wesker, Arnold 135
West, Sam 190
West, Tim 72
Whatham, Claude 99
Wheeler, Meredith 252, 254
Wheldon, Sir Huw 86
White, Marco Pierre 257
Whitemore, Hugh 78
Whitfield, June 246
Whyman, Erica 208
Wilde, Oscar 36, 89, 95, 98, 228, 271, 280
Wildeblood, Peter 89, 105
Wilder, Thornton 213
Wilkins, Mark 182–83, 184, 186
Williams, Kenneth 89
Williams, Michael 137
Williams, Raymond 53
Williams, Roy 208
Williamson, Nicol 14–19, 24, 61, 101–102, 104, 105, 107, 135, 246, 256, 284
Wilson, Harold 18, 73, 106
Wilson, Lanford 12
Wilson, Robert 166
Wilton, Penelope 75, 106, 136, 181, 249
Wittgenstein, Ludwig 38–39
Wolfit, Donald 119
Wood, Charles 59, 137
Wood, Dinah 185, 277
Woodward, Edward 105
Woolf, Virginia 100
Woolfenden, Guy 70
Worrell, Frank 246
Wright, Nicholas 13, 14, 23, 24
Wymark, Patrick 90, 102–103

Yeats, W. B. 41